GREAT LAKES
SALMON AND TROUT FISHING

THE COMPLETE TROLLER'S GUIDE
Captain Dan Keating and Captain Chip Porter

KP BOOKS

© 2004 Dan Keating and Chip Porter. All rights reserved. No part of this book may be reproduced, stored or transmitted in any form or by any means—mechanical, electronic, recording, photocopy or other means—without the written permission of the authors.

Manufactured in the United States of America

ISBN 0-9748549-0-5

Cover design by Josh Visser
Interior design by Angie Barnes
Diagrams by Maureen Kimmell

To our Dads

Contents

Acknowledgments vii
Foreword 1
Preface 3
Introduction 5
A Brief History of The Great Lakes 11

Chapter 1—Species Analysis
Success begins with understanding the behavior of your target! .. 17
    King (Chinook) Salmon 18
    Coho Salmon 23
    Steelhead (Rainbow) Trout 26
    Lake Trout 30
    Brown Trout 34
    Other Species 37

Chapter 2—Great Lakes Tackle
*Everything you wanted to know about today's
salmon and trout tackle and more!* 39
    Boat Set Up: Setting Up the Perfect Fishing Platform 41
    Rods, Reels and Other Necessities 51
    Electronics: Do You Really Need a Degree in Technology? 70

Chapter 3—Great Lakes Lure Selection
*How to enter a tackle store in the twenty-first
century without losing your mind!* 85
    Spoons 88
    Crankbaits 95
    Attractors: Do You Really Need Them? 100

Dodgers, Flashers and Flies: Everything You Ever
Wanted to Know and More! 103
The Group Dynamic: How to Build an Irresistible Lure Spread . . 118

Chapter 4—Down And Out on The Great Lakes
Reaching the strike zone! 125
Fishing with Downriggers 128
Everything You Can Imagine About Using Dipsy Divers 136
Wire Line—The Least Understood Delivery Device 142
Get the Lead Out: Fishing Lead Core 148
Reaching Out With Planer Boards 150

Chapter 5—Putting It All Together
How to find and catch fish all season long! 157
Spring Fishing 159
Shallow Water Techniques 160
Offshore Action—Deepwater, It's Better Than You Think! . . 170
Go Long for Great Mixed Bag Action! 185
The Summer Transition 189
Summer Fishing on The Great Lakes—Big Fish Time! 190
Locating Summer Salmon and Trout 192
Summer Techniques 206
Here They Come! The Offshore Staging Process 225
Fall Fishing Techniques for The Great Lakes 229
Locating and Catching Autumn Salmon in Shallow Water . . 229
Deepwater Fall Action 239

Recipes 245
Order Page 247

Dan would like to thank:

My parents, Tom and Joann Keating: Dad, thank you for all those Saturday mornings on the Lake. Mom, thank you for all your support and encouragement—from sitting out on the ice with me while ice fishing, to helping run the charter business and now editing this book. Thank you both so much!

My wife Mary: My best friend, soul mate and life partner! Without your help and patience, this book would not be here. To our children Rebecca, Ethan Daniel and Katherine Elizabeth: Our three precious gifts from God. I can't wait for all the fishing adventures that lie ahead!

My ol' fishing buddies: Jim Flickinger and "Doc" Rupprecht—Team America!

Chip would like to thank:

The list of people I could thank for being able to reach the point where I could even logically consider writing a book, is nearly endless. I have so many friends in the fishing business that have shown me such unconditional kindness, support, and help, that if I started to name them all, I'm sure I would miss one, and that would devastate me. For that reason, those people know who they are and know that my door is always open for whatever they need, as theirs has been for me.

My parents are obviously the first. You know they did something right with us, as my brother, Matt, is a world champion goose caller, while I have spent most of my formative years fishing. There was almost always an open seat in Dad's boat or blind and for that, I am grateful.

My wife, Sherry, and my boys, Kirk and Erik, are the true sources of joy in my life. They probably had more to do with any success I've had than anyone. Simply wonderful as people, they make me want to be a better person every day. They are my inspiration and my greatest source of enjoyment.

Foreword

Anyone who has seen Dan Keating and Chip Porter at a Salmon Master Seminar has come away with information overload. I know of what I speak as I accompanied these two professional Captains around the Midwest as a fellow speaker for two winters. I have to admit, I learned more than I taught, sitting with the rest of the attendees and listening to their presentations designed to help the average angler-as well as the expert-catch more of our Great Lakes fish. These guys know a lot-way more than they can communicate within one day of seminars.

That's why it's great that these two guys wrote this book. Dan, who has chartered for more than 20 years and fished the Lake for more than 30, wrote Chapters 1, 3 and 5. Chip, who has produced two videos, chartered for more than 10 years and is Field Editor for Great Lakes Angler, wrote Chapters 2 and 4. Not that what's in these pages encompasses everything these guys know-we'll just have to wait for future books to get the rest.

What you'll find here is a logical, no-nonsense approach to the gear and tactics that are unique to our vast freshwater seas. Dan and Chip reveal lots of the "little things" that they've learned from decades of chasing our Big Water salmon and trout, both as recreational anglers and as professional charter Captains. I think that anyone—beginner or seasoned veteran—who enjoys the sight of downrigger rods popping, planer boards sweeping back and the sounds of drags singing will be glad to have this book. You'll want to keep it handy for reference throughout the upcoming seasons.

        Dave Mull
        Editor
        Great Lakes Angler Magazine

Preface

Since salmon were first introduced into the Great Lakes in 1966, there have only been a handful of books written on catching salmon and trout in open water. The last major printing was well over a decade ago!

We feel a book on catching salmon and trout in the Great Lakes is long overdue, as much has changed within the fishery. Fish migration patterns, tackle, technology, rigging, fish catching techniques and subtle nuances in the ecosystem are different today than 10 or even 5 years ago. Patterns and tactics that once ruled the day are now obsolete in favor of new presentational methods.

This book is designed to help you become the fisherman you are capable of being. It is filled with a wealth of knowledge and experience, previously unavailable in any single source. We strategically developed this book to be the stepping stone fishermen need to take their angling to the next level.

> Captain Dan Keating
> Captain Chip Porter

Introduction

In the world of fishing, salmon and trout are some of the most highly treasured catches. They are a fish that some only dream of while others pursue fanatically. At no other time in the history of sport fishing have so many salmon and trout been accessible and catchable for so many people. Today, the Great Lakes are a premier fishing destination for landlocked anglers who want a taste of Big Water and Big Fish!

Capitalizing on this incredible fish catching opportunity requires anglers to think differently than in the past, as today's fishery is very different than it was in the past. The key to consistent success involves much more than, "where, what, when and how." In the following pages, we take you beneath the surface and explain the "why" of salmon and trout fishing. Whether you are an experienced salmon and trout angler or just thinking of making your first foray after salmon and trout, *Great Lakes Salmon And Trout Fishing* has something for you! Those of you who pursue salmon and trout on the ocean or other bodies of Still Water will also profit from the practical and theoretical information.

Our goal is to help you become a complete and intelligent salmon and trout angler. We do this by giving you the most comprehensive and current snapshot of how to locate and catch salmon and trout on the Great Lakes. After a careful reading of *Great Lakes Salmon And Trout Fishing*, you should be able to read the waters, formulate a plan, locate fish, choose the proper delivery tools, select the optimum combination of baits, react to the conditions and deliver a complete and irresistible trolling (group) dynamic to the fish! While this book is full of highly useful information and techniques, more importantly, it will teach you to think like a fish.

What you can expect to find in the following pages.

In *Great Lakes Salmon and Trout Fishing* you will find a wealth of technical information, tactical advice, theoretical teaching, equipment suggestions, common sense observations, behavioral patterns, history and seasonal guidance. After a brief look at the history of the fishery the book is divided into five chapters. The first three chapters focus on the technical aspects of the game. The final two chapters are application oriented. Most anglers are at different levels. *Great Lakes Salmon and Trout Fishing* is structured to give you easy access to the areas you want to explore. If you approach *Great Lakes Salmon And Trout Fishing* as a manual, you will catch more fish!

Chapter 1

You can't hit the bull's eye if you don't know where to aim! Knowing whom your target is and how they behave is vital to success. In Chapter 1 we define our targets. We provide you with background information and a brief biological sketch of the five dominant target species; coho and king (chinook) salmon, steelhead (rainbow trout), brown and lake trout. Understanding the behavioral tendencies of your targets will help you locate them spring, summer and fall.

Chapter 2

When you build a house you need a variety of tools to complete the job. Fishing is no different . . . with the right tools you will achieve a greater level of success! Chapter 2 is the nuts and bolts of Great Lakes salmon and trout angling. Buying equipment today can be a bit overwhelming as anglers are faced with a myriad of tackle choices. This section will direct you to the equipment you need to successfully catch salmon and trout. We begin by taking a critical look at boat set-up; how to make your boat a complete, well organized fishing platform. Next, we'll tell you about the latest rods, reels, components, lines and rigging tips used by today's top fisherman. We will also explore the ever-expanding world of electronics!

Chapter 3

If you've been in a Wal-Mart or a Bass Pro Shop lately, you know selecting lures can be a bit overwhelming. Where does one even begin? In Chapter 3 we expose the truth about salmon and trout lure selection. Choosing hot baits is part art, part science, part experience and a little bit of luck. We won't leave you in the tackle store; however, as we go beneath the surface and look at the underlying mechanics of how lures function and impact one another.

We will equip you with the skills on how to pick the right individual lures for a variety of conditions. Picking lures is a lot like coaching a football team. If you want to win the game, do you put 11 quarterbacks on the field? No, a coach skillfully selects a combination of running backs, linemen, quarterbacks and wide receivers to move the ball down the field. Along with educating you about lure selection, we will teach you how to integrate the individual baits into a complete *trolling dynamic*. We include several handy reference charts to help you choose baits.

Chapter 4

Down and out on the Great Lakes! This is where we roll up our sleeves and get down to the actual business of catching fish! How do we attack the strike zone! In Chapter 4 we describe in simple terms the various methods anglers utilize to place their baits in the strike zone. We walk you through the mechanics of how to use downriggers, side planers, Dipsy Divers, super lines, wire line and lead core line. Remember, a fisherman is only as good as the individual 'parts' that make up the whole. As we go through tackle deployment, we will keep the trolling dynamic in mind.

Chapter 5

This is where we put all the pieces together. We walk you through a typical Great Lakes season and explain productive techniques for specific conditions and seasons. We systematically unpack the individual elements that today's top anglers use day in and day out. We discuss how to react and adjust your trolling dynamic to the multitude of variables and transitions facing Great Lakes anglers today.

We also address the theoretical aspect of how to locate fish spring, summer and fall. The Great Lakes encompass a broad expanse of water. An element of *hunting* is involved in every fishing trip. In Chapter 5 we give you clues that will aid you in your search for salmon and trout. Lets face it, the ability to consistently find fish is half the battle!

Big Water salmon and trout fishing is exciting and challenging. Success requires one to learn a variety of individual techniques and to understand a host of variables. The individual parts, however, must transcend themselves. One must learn to weave the individual parts into a complete and fully integrated system. Anglers need to think creatively and react to the ever-changing moods and conditions of the Lakes.

Captain Dan Keating holding one of his favorite fish, a king salmon. Dan has over 30 years of Big Water experience that he shares with you in the following pages.

Introduction

Great Lakes Salmon And Trout Fishing will help you become a successful and versatile angler spring, summer and fall. Those who can grasp the many parts and fit them together will catch more fish! The Great Lakes are full of trophy fish . . . it is quite likely that a few of these trophies have your name on them!

If any of you have any questions or comments, we would love to hear from you. You can e-mail Chip at chipporter@chipporter.com. You can e-mail Dan at captaindan@mindspring.com. We hope you enjoy the book!

A Brief History of The Great Lakes

Over the past 100 years, the Great Lakes have been swept over by a sea of change. The Lakes, their ecosystems and the fisheries within have been through a series of transformations. The salmon and trout fishery has not been immune to this process. Throughout this ebb and flow of nature and humanity's footprint, the salmon and trout fishery has thrived!

When looking back at the history of this relatively young salmon and trout fishery, we can see how change has impacted the Lakes. During the past 30 years anglers have faced many ups and downs, disappointments, thrills and surprises. Foreign "invaders" have entered the playing field, baitfish populations have fluctuated, stocking numbers have risen and fallen, weather patterns have changed and some years were just better than others. Yet, throughout all the ups and downs, the Great Lakes continue to produce trophy size fish and countless hours of enjoyment for a large cross-section of society.

Let's take a brief tour of the history of the salmon and trout fishery in the Great Lakes. Did you know that coho salmon, king salmon, steelhead and brown trout are not native to the Great Lakes? That's right. Lake trout are the only salmonoid native to these Inland Seas.

European immigrants initiated experimental stockings of several salmon and trout species in the 1800's. These early salmonoid stocking efforts failed to bear any lasting fruit. A lesser known early stocking, however, did take hold. Smelt were introduced to the Great Lakes via White Lake, Michigan. The Europeans initially stocked smelt as a forage base for the atlantic salmon they stocked. The modern day salmon and trout program was launched in 1966.

Prior to the 1950's, the Lakes supported a thriving lake trout fishery. The collapse of the lake trout fishery in the 1940's and 1950's was the result of a combination of factors including commercial over fishing, sea lampreys and pollution. The final factor in the decline of the lake trout was the invasion of the sea lampreys. These tremendous predators migrated up the Welland Canal and quickly took root throughout the Great Lakes. The indigenous lake trout population had been so depleted by this time that the remaining trout could not withstand the lamprey invasion. Finally, in the 1960's the lampreys were brought under control through an aggressive eradication process that involved poisoning the larvae in the streams hosting the spawning lampreys.

Following the collapse of the lake trout fishery and the demise of the sea lamprey, the Great Lakes were overcome by the second foreign invader to migrate out of the Atlantic Ocean: The alewife. Alewives migrated through the Welland Canal and quickly spread throughout all five Great Lakes. On the surface, this second invader appeared to be much less threatening than the lamprey. Looks can be deceiving as these small salt water fish that resemble a shad adapted well to the sweet water of all five Great Lakes.

Today, we consider the alewife a vital part of the Great Lakes ecosystems. In the 1950's and 1960's, many viewed the proliferation of the alewife as a disaster. Following the destruction caused by the lamprey invasion, there were no predators left to prey on the booming alewife population. With no natural predators, the alewife population exploded! Off cities like Chicago, the alewives were so prolific that huge die-offs left massive numbers of dead and stinking fish collecting along the beaches. Bulldozers were used to remove the dead fish!

The one-two punch of the lampreys and alewives started out as an ecological disaster but soon turned into one of modern day fishing's greatest success stories! Since the collapse of the lake trout population, the top end of the Great Lake's food chain was lacking a predator. A group of biologists, led by Dr. Howard Tanner in Michigan, envisioned salmon as the missing predator.

Dr. Tanner and others believed Pacific coho and king salmon could adapt to and thrive in the Great Lakes. Pacific salmon live in salt water but their lives begins and ends in fresh water. Salmon are a highly migratory species that thrive in cold, open water. Pelagic's, such as salmon, also require a great deal of food to survive. With twenty-percent of the world's fresh surface water contained in the Great Lakes, space was not an issue. With alewife populations breeding unchecked, the stage was well set for the birth of the Great Lakes salmon and trout fishery!

The dream soon became reality. Today, the Great Lakes support one of the most productive salmon and trout fisheries in the world. The coho was the first star to appear on the horizon in 1966 followed by the mighty king (chinook) salmon and the rebirth of an outstanding lake trout fishery. Add to this cast of characters the acrobatic steelhead (rainbow trout) and brown trout of world class proportions, and you can understand why Great Lakes anglers spend so much time on the water!

Fast-forward to the twenty-first century. The Great Lakes fishery is not the same today, as it was in 1982 or 1995. Feeding and migration habits of fish have changed. As we try to understand how the *changes* affect our fishery we need to remember that the Great Lakes are an open system. There are many variables external to the Lakes that influence the daily ebbs and flows of the Great Lakes ecosystems.

Yes, the Great Lakes are contained by real boundaries in the form of shorelines. They are, however, very open in the sense that a variety of external variables enter and exit the Lakes. To illustrate this scenario, think of five broken circles. Each circle represents one of the Great Lakes. The circle is the shoreline but the openings in the circle represent the many variables that infiltrate and impact the Great Lakes ecosystems.

How is this porous effect possible? The Great Lakes are an open system because of natural and human influences. First, let's examine the structure and natural setting of the Great Lakes.

The Great Lakes are viewed as one watershed. The Lakes are linked to the problems of other inland waters through the many rivers and streams that flow into the Great Lakes. Historically, pollutants and alien organisms have been introduced through these access points. If we look at a chart, we see that the five Lakes are also inter-connected. That is why, as history demonstrates, a problem in one Lake is often shared with the others.

The human influence has had a profound effect on all five Lakes over the past 75 years. Human progress has effectively opened the Great Lakes to the larger global ecosystem. With the opening of the Welland Canal, a host of foreign invaders have entered the Great Lakes through their own ability and in the ballast water of foreign freighters. Sea Lampreys and alewives were the first invaders. They quickly made their way, via their own tails, into all five Lakes and began reproducing. Their 'tail prints' are well documented.

Lampreys and alewives may have had the largest overall impact on the Lakes so far; however, a variety of other exotics entered the Lakes through the ballast waters of foreign freighters. Believe it or not, tiny creatures such as spiny water fleas, gobies and zebra mussels ride across the open oceans in the ballast water of freighters. Once these vessels

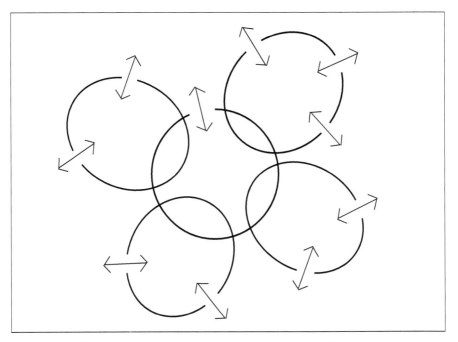

The Great Lakes are an open system. Because of natural and human influences, foreign organisms can enter and exit the system.

reach their destinations in the Great Lakes, they frequently discharge their ballast water. The result is that creatures from the other side of the world are introduced into the Great Lakes ecosystems! In effect, the Welland Canal has connected the Great Lakes to many foreign bodies of water.

Once foreign exotics enter the Lakes they have the opportunity to breed and enter the Great Lakes food chain. A number of these exotics have adapted very well to life in the Great Lakes. In fact, some have dominated native species! The reality is, these exotics are changing the dynamics of the Great Lakes food chain. The food chain, from top to bottom, is forced to adjust and live with the new organisms.

The Great Lakes region is populated by millions of people not to mention all the industry ringing the Lakes! Over the course of time, people and industry have had a positive and negative impact on the ecosystems. Yes, humans have created problems, but other people work to cleanse the negative influence left in their wake.

Today's salmon and trout program exemplifies this. Because of human pollution and the Welland Canal (built by people), the original Great Lakes food chain was damaged. Because of human clean-up efforts, lamprey eradication and stocking programs, the Lakes have a different, but healthy food chain.

The salmon and trout populations of the Lakes are controlled to a large extent by human stocking programs. There is a limited amount of natural reproduction with kings and steelhead in some regions. The majority of salmon and trout, however, are stocked. By implication, the top of the food chain can be controlled by the amount of fish stocked each season. This adds a very artificial sense to the ecosystem.

Today, thanks to zebra mussels, the super filters of the Great Lakes, our waters are clearer and bluer than most people remember. Weed growth has increased and other native species of fish are starting to flourish. Alewife populations rise and fall and rise again. In boom years, stock up on tackle as fat, trophy fish are common. Some years see great angling for salmon and other years, steelhead or brown trout save the day.

Schooling patterns of salmon and trout change from year to year. Historically most fish were caught in less than 100 feet of water. Today, the deep, offshore waters produce awesome catches of all species. What will tomorrow hold? The unpredictability of the Great Lakes is what sharpens our angling skills and keeps many anglers coming back.

As you can see, there are many factors that impact the ebb and flow of the Great Lakes ecosystems and their fisheries! These variables add an element of surprise and unpredictability to the Great Lakes fisheries. Despite all the changes that have swept over the Great Lakes, they continue to produce world-class fishing, year after year. This is evidenced through the consistently high catch rates and the number of state record fish that continue to be produced.

Chip Porter makes a new friend. Chip is a leading Great Lakes expert and one of the industries top communicators and instructors.

CHAPTER 1

Species Analysis

Success begins with understanding the behavior of your target!

We live in a society that craves knowledge. In many areas of life, success is built on knowledge and understanding. Salmon and trout fishing on the Great Lakes are no different. Believe it or not, how successful you are at fishing often depends on what you know and do before you put the first line in the water. Ultimately, how you approach the Lake will determine how many fish you catch.

When you head out on the water, what factors determine where you begin fishing? Do you play "follow the leader," looking for the greatest concentration of boats? Do you randomly pick a location because it just "feels right?" Or, do you go back to an area because last year on the same weekend you did really, really well in that spot?

All these factors can be clues, but we want to teach you how to think for yourself. Our goal in *Great Lakes Salmon and Trout Fishing* is to equip you with the tools to read the water and locate salmon and trout. Basically, there are two ways to go trolling. You can head out on the water, pick a spot, set a few lines, and randomly troll around, hoping to catch a few fish. Or, you can approach the water with a goal in mind. If you clearly understand the nature and behavior of your targets, salmon and trout, you will greatly increase your odds of finding and catching fish.

So what you're saying, Dan is that "if I know what I am looking for, I have a better chance of finding it?" Exactly! Before you catch fish, you must find the fish. Although this may sound elementary, it is amazing how many anglers do not grasp this concept. Many anglers simply head out on the water and just go fishing. Every fishing trip, however, also involves a hunting component. You can have the nicest boat and the right lures and equipment, but if you can't find the fish, you will not catch fish.

The first step to being a consistently successful salmon and trout angler is developing the skill to find fish. In this chapter we identify our targets: king salmon, coho salmon, steelhead, brown trout and lake trout. By understanding your prey, you will be able to eliminate large areas of water. You will be able to narrow down your search range and identify the key areas that hold salmon and trout. Ultimately, you will spend more time catching fish and less time looking (or hoping) for fish!

KING (CHINOOK) SALMON

The mighty chinook salmon is our favorite fish! Kings are one of the hardest fighting fish found anywhere in fresh water. Famous for making long, heart stopping runs, battles can last in excess of 20 minutes as chinooks display incredible endurance. The first reel-smoking run of a king sends everyone onboard into action as line begins melting from the reel at an alarming rate! Some people scream, others clear lines and others just hang on and enjoy the thrill, hoping the reel holds enough line! When more than one big king is hooked, pandemonium reigns!

Kings are also a fish of great beauty. After a grueling battle, anglers are treated to the near-mythical sight of a battling king slicing through the blue water—dorsal fin cutting the surface like a shark, thick shoulders and flanks flashing shades of silver and purple iridescence—and the lucky angler holding the rod praying that the fish does not make a final run!

For countless landlocked anglers, Great Lakes kings will provide a taste of 'big game fishing.' Nowhere in freshwater can you encounter a predator with the raw strength, size, speed and endurance displayed by chinooks. It is understandable why kings are the star attraction of the Great Lakes salmon and trout fishery.

Today, the Great Lakes contain some of the largest concentrations of these great predators to be found anywhere in North America. Lakes Ontario, Huron and Michigan have the most productive king fisheries. Lake Superior has fair numbers of kings, but does not receive the angling pressure of the other three Lakes. Lake Erie has minimal numbers of chinooks.

The Great Lakes offer landlocked anglers daily opportunities to catch big fish. Many anglers dream of catching a fish, any fish, over 10 pounds. If you fish in king country, you may catch a 20 pound fish at any moment! While Great Lakes kings do not grow as large as their cousins

King salmon are the feature attraction of the Great Lakes fishery!

in the Pacific Northwest, the Great Lakes record is an impressive 47 pound 13 ounce Lake Ontario fish.

Great Lakes kings come in many sizes, depending on their year class, genetics and available forage. Historically, Lake Ontario kings average heavier. Fish over 35 pounds are caught yearly on Ontario. In fact, Lake Ontario is known for producing kings over 40 pounds! The average mature Lake Ontario fish will weigh between 20-35 pounds. Many anglers feel it is just a matter of time before the first 50 pound king is pulled from Ontario!

Average weights for mature Michigan and Huron kings varies from year to year and from port to port. Kings of 15-25 pounds are average in Lakes Michigan and Huron; however, larger fish in excess of 30 pounds are caught yearly. Because of the shorter growing season, Lake Superior kings are smaller in size. Lake Superior kings will average between 10-15 pounds at maturity, but larger fish are available if one is lucky enough to catch them!

Mature fish are not the only kings caught by anglers. Immature kings are caught throughout the season. These fish may weigh between 3-20 pounds. These fish usually will not spawn at the end of the year. Like the larger kings, they are excellent targets.

Behavior

King salmon are the pinnacle of the Great Lakes aquatic food chain. Because of their large size and metabolism, they need a larger supply of alewives to survive than coho. They are an aggressive predator who prefer much deeper, colder water than coho. The peak feeding range for kings is a chilly 42-44 degrees! The broader temperature range to target kings is 42-46 degrees. During low light periods some kings will move up into the thermocline to feed. As light penetration increases, these fish will usually drop back down into colder water.

Chinooks, along with lake trout, will be the deepest salmonoids in the water column. Water temperature is one of the dominant keys to locating and catching big kings. Our results, along with many top anglers, show that kings prefer much colder water than most fishermen realize. We will look at the significance of water temperature and catching kings in Chapter 5!

Kings are a school fish. Kings will mix with other species but experienced king anglers know big numbers of kings will be caught when the schools of kings are located! Kings will frequently school with other kings based on size. When you catch one big, mature king, chances are good that there will be other big fish in the immediate area.

Kings like structure. In fact, they are the most structure sensitive of the salmon species found in the Great Lakes. Structure elements can be defined as bottom features, baitfish schools, currents and water temperature. All four structure *forms* will influence daily king locations and movements. These elements will be discussed in Chapter 5.

In our attempt to find and catch Great Lakes kings, we will classify them under two major criteria:

1. Those that relate their daily movements to bottom relief.
2. The nomadic, open water kings.

The bottom-oriented kings will be found closer to the shoreline. They will often be found where 42-46 degree water intersects bottom relief. Their movements often run parallel to the shoreline.

The open water kings will display a nomadic character. They spend much of their lives roaming deep open water. Throughout much of the year they will be found suspended from 50-150 feet down over 180 to 500 feet of water. Even though these fish will be roaming open water, structure, as defined above, is vital to locating them! How far down will kings go? On Lake Michigan we have caught kings as far down as 240 feet. Former New York State DEC Fisheries Biologist and Lake Ontario charter Captain, Ernie Lantiegne, has caught kings as deep as 270 feet!

Mature Great Lakes chinooks spawn between the months of September and November. A month or two prior to entering their spawning locations they will begin staging offshore of stocking sites. During this period some of the heaviest catches of the year will be taken. As the spawning urge overtakes kings, they enter the shoreline streams, rivers and harbors to spawn. While there is some natural reproduction of kings in the Great Lakes, the majority of the fishery is sustained through stocking programs.

King Basics

While kings are big in size, you don't need heavy tackle and line to catch them. In fact, a favorite set-up of both Chip and me for catching big kings is a clean spoon on 12-pound test mono line! This light line is run on a short, six-foot rod with a small, high quality reel. The battles are spectacular!

Why such light line? Since zebra muscles have cleared up the Great Lakes, light line consistently out-produces heavier line when spoon or plug fishing. What you do need, however, is a reel with a super-smooth drag and a line capacity of 300 plus yards. When a big king burns 100 yards of line off a reel, the drag heats up. Quality reels will last longer and lead to more boated kings.

Rods need to have a soft tip but enough backbone to beat a king. Historically, Great Lakes anglers have preferred longer rods. In the past several years, a number of experienced light line anglers have taken a cue from salt water anglers and have begun using shorter, lighter rods with light line. The results have been impressive! In Chapter 2, Chip will unpack what to look for when selecting rods, reels and components for catching kings.

Anglers utilize downriggers, Dipsy Divers, super line, wire line, lead core and side planers to catch kings. Since kings tend to be found deeper in the water column, most kings will be caught off downriggers, Dipsy Divers, wire line or lead core. When targeting spawning kings in shallow water and in some locations during the spring, side planers will be key elements for bait delivery.

Lure selection for chinooks is as varied as the people pursuing them. Kings can be caught on spoons, body baits and flies and dodgers/flashers. Under various conditions, one lure group will out-produce the others. We will examine lure selection for king fishing in Chapters 3 and 5.

Kings can be caught spring, summer and fall. The best king fishing, however, is typically found during the summer and fall periods. There are exceptions to this and some locations feature fast king action during the spring months. The biggest kings are usually taken during the later half of July and August. This is when the mature fish are packing on weight in anticipation of their fall spawning runs.

Anglers worldwide dream of catching big fish. For many people, those dreams will become reality when the line begins screaming off the reel. Encounters with Great Lake's kings will thrill thousands of people this year…don't miss your chance to catch a king!

COHO SALMON

The coho was the pacific salmon that began the fishing revolution on the Great Lakes! Coho were first introduced into Lake Michigan in 1966. They adapted rapidly to Lake Michigan's ecosystem and were soon introduced into the other Great Lakes. Today, Lakes Michigan, Ontario and Huron have the most productive coho fisheries. Lake Superior has a limited coho fishery while Lake Erie does not support a substantial coho fishery.

Who is Mr. Coho? If we were to categorize the ideal gamefish, in terms of fighting quality, abundance, catchability and table quality, Mr. Coho would be a finalist. You don't have to be an expert, nor do you need to invest in specialized tackle to catch coho. While finesse and stealth are needed to catch many great gamefish, coho are very forgiving of angler error and technique. When coho schools are in a region, fast action is the rule. Coho are a great fish to introduce children and novice anglers to, as non-stop action can be expected!

What makes the coho such a great gamefish? Coho are aggressive feeders and are relatively easy to fool into striking. They are a highly 'social' fish, if you find one coho, chances are they will have company. Once coho cross the seven-pound threshold, they become a very strong opponent on the end of a fishing line. Adult coho are rather sneaky opponents known for their twisting, boat charging antics. When large coho (7-15 pounds) are in the area, tackle losses and fifty percent catch ratios are typical!

In the kitchen, it is hard to beat fresh coho fillets grilled, baked or deep-fried. After 20 years of chartering, coho were the hands-down favorite take-home guest of my customers!

Behavior

Coho seek out 48-54 degree water. If conditions permit, coho will gravitate toward the upper layers of the water column. Coho will usually be found in warmer water than kings. Spring coho tend to favor the surface layers and are usually found in the top 20 feet of water. During the summer months, coho will move offshore and descend with the thermocline. Typically, you will find summer coho feeding in and just below the thermocline. During the summer months, if cold water is nearby, they will move into warmer water to chase down schools of alewives.

Coho are an open water fish that will suspend during the summer months. It is not unusual for coho to be found suspended 40-80 feet down over deep water (100 feet plus) many miles offshore. Having said

It was the coho salmon that started the modern day fishing revolution on the Great Lakes. When schools of coho are located, fast action is the norm!

that, some coho schools will move parallel along the shoreline seeking to stay in the bottom layers where cold water intersects the bottom. This scenario will set up if large schools of alewives are along the shoreline.

Between stocking and spawning, coho will roam the open waters of the Lakes. They are highly migratory and will move around within the individual lakes following baitfish, water temperature and currents. During their time in the Lakes their one goal in life is eating. Coho have a huge appetite and will feed throughout the day.

Coho mature toward the end of their second year of life. As they prepare for the fall spawn, adult fish will begin to stage off their original stocking or birth location. Once they enter the spawning mode, coho cease feeding. It is physiologically impossible for spawning coho to ingest food. When mature coho return to spawn in the fall, adult fish are stripped of their eggs. The eggs are fertilized by the milt of male fish and hatched in fish hatcheries. The young fish are raised in the hatchery then stocked in select streams, rivers and harbors.

For all practical purposes, Great Lakes coho are the same fish one finds in the Pacific Northwest. They have a two to three year life cycle. Spawning occurs between September and November. Typically, young coho (smolts) are held in the hatchery for 12-18 months before stocking. The young fish are approximately six inches in length when stocked. The majority of Great Lakes coho do not naturally reproduce. In effect, Great Lakes coho are maintained as a put-and-take fishery.

Depending on available forage, Great Lakes coho will grow from 6-18 pounds. Larger fish are possible and years with a strong forage base will feature large numbers of trophy coho. How big do Great Lakes coho grow? The all tackle world record coho is a Great Lakes fish! The record coho weighted 33.45 pounds and was caught in Lake Ontario.

Coho Basics

Coho are the most predictable of the five major species of Great Lakes salmon and trout. Year after year they follow similar patterns. In terms of catchability, they are the easiest of the salmon species to catch. Smaller spring coho (2-5 pounds) are very easy to locate and catch. They can be boated on very light tackle including much of the equipment used for inland angling.

As coho grow in size, you will need to use quality line in the 8-20 pound range. A reel with a smooth drag and a rod with a light tip section will improve your odds of boating larger summer and fall coho. Large coho are known for making short, quick runs at the boat and spinning in the line. For this reason, one needs to check the final four feet of line after hooking a coho.

Coho are an aggressive fish. They are highly stimulated visually as well as through their lateral line. For this reason, lures that have a lot of flash, zip and bang tend to draw the most strikes. Historically, flies and dodgers/flashers are the top coho producers. Under certain conditions, which we will address in the following chapters, body baits and spoons will be equally productive and may even out-produce the fly and dodger set ups.

During the spring and early summer coho are often found feeding heavily in the top 20 feet of water. These fish are easy to catch on flat lines, side planers and Dipsy Divers. As the waters warm up during the summer, coho prefer to stay in the higher layers of the water column. For this reason, they often move offshore, suspending from 40-80 feet down in pursuit of 48 to 54 degree water and forage. During periods of very warm water coho will be found deeper than 80 feet. We have caught coho as far down as 140 feet. Summer coho fishing requires the use of downriggers, Dipsy Divers, super line, wire line and lead core line.

STEELHEAD (RAINBOW TROUT)

If we had to classify fish as athletes, steelhead would definitely receive gold medals in high-jumping and sprinting. Great Lakes steelheads strike a lure with the force of thunder and zeal unlike any other freshwater fish! The shear impact behind the strike has left many anglers straining to pull the rod out of the rod holder as the hooked steelhead heads toward the horizon. Many of us have excitedly tried to scream "fish on" but the hooked steelie was airborne before we could get the words out! And we've all seen our favorite spoon flying through the air as Mr. Steelhead goes in the opposite direction. Welcome to steelhead fishing!

What exactly is a steelhead? In layman's terms, a steelhead is an overgrown rainbow trout on a high protein diet. Overgrown 'bug eaters' as Chip refers to them. For all practical purposes, the large silvery Great Lakes steelhead are the same fish as the colorful rainbow trout one finds in smaller lakes and streams. What sets them apart is diet and environment.

Great Lakes rainbows live in large lakes with miles of open water to roam. While our Great Lakes steelhead will often be seen feeding on

Great Lakes steelheads are one of the hardest fighting fish found in freshwater. Steelheads slam lures with reckless abandon and are known for their lightning runs and spell-binding leaps!

insects along the surface, their primary forage is minnow type fish including alewives, lake shiners and sticklebacks. It is the protein in the baitfish that allows the steelhead to grow so large.

Just how large do Great Lakes steelhead grow? The Great Lakes record is an impressive 31 pound 8 ounce trophy taken in Lake Michigan off the port of Waukegan, Illinois. All five Great Lakes contain steelhead: However, the most productive steelhead fisheries are found in Lakes Michigan, Ontario and Huron. Lakes Superior and Erie support lesser numbers of these great gamefish.

Behavior

Of all the fish in the Great Lakes, steelheads are the most nomadic and unpredictable. They have a reputation of showing up off a port and providing spectacular action for several days and then disappearing overnight. General migration patterns and timetables can be applied when targeting steelhead, but experienced anglers realize that of all fish, steelhead will determine when and where they dance.

Those of us who have spent any amount of time chasing steelhead have learned to accept their unpredictable nature. Because of the steelhead's highly nomadic lifestyle good hunting skills are the key to catching steelhead. Anglers who target steelhead know that part of the day may be spent hunting. They also know that while they may leave the dock with preconceived ideas of where to find steelhead and what to use to catch them, the rules of the game may change at any minute.

Great Lakes steelheads exhibit a wide range of temperature preferences. Their preferred range is quite broad at 42-61 degrees. During the spring months 42-44 degree water is the hot zone. During the summer months they can often be caught in the upper portion of the thermocline in 56-62 degree water. What does this tell us about locating steelhead? Steelheads are not as easy to pin down as the other species. They also appear to be more opportunistic in their feeding habits and they have a higher tolerance to a broad range of water temperatures.

Great Lakes steelheads come in a variety of shapes and sizes. A variety of different steelhead (rainbow) strains including Chambers Creek, Arleen, Kamloops, Skamania, Domestic rainbows and Shasta have been stocked in the Lakes. Because of the variety, one can encounter short, plump rainbows as well as the long, torpedo shaped fish and everything in between. The majority of steelhead are stocked fish although some biologists estimate natural reproduction in some regions is as high as 20 percent. Spawning time varies with strain. Some strains spawn in the spring while other fish are fall or winter spawners. Skamanias return to spawning rivers in the summer but don't actually spawn until later in the year.

Steelhead Basics

Steelheads are a tremendous fish to hunt and catch. They can be taken throughout the fishing season across the Great Lakes. Activity varies between regions and some locations will have periods of hot steelhead fishing and slow periods. Those who want to target steelhead may apply general schooling and migration habits to help them determine when and where to target steelhead. One must remember, however, that within the patterns and history, there may be a wide range of seasonal variation. Steelhead activity is cyclical and some years produce more steelhead than others.

Because of the steelheads ferocious fighting ability, quality equipment is a must. More hooks will be ripped off the backs of spoons and more split rings and swivels will be broken by steelhead than any other Great Lakes gamefish. This is all due to the shear force in which a steelhead smashes a trolled lure. Quality swivels and split rings are a must! Reels with smooth drags and fresh line are mandatory. Rods with soft tips will be more forgiving.

Steelhead can be found almost anywhere in the water column. During the spring and fall months, they will most commonly be caught in the top 10 feet of water. As the waters warm, some steelhead will migrate offshore with bands of cold, surface oriented water. Other steelhead populations will follow the cold water and thermocline down.

Summer fish will often hold from just below the thermocline to 10 or 15 feet above the thermocline. Yes, Mr. Steelhead is a highly unpredictable creature.

A variety of trolling techniques and lures will catch steelhead. Steelheads have great vision, and at times, a great deal of stealth will be needed to catch them. At other times, they will behave much like a coho and the more flash and commotion you can create, the more steelhead you will catch.

During the spring and fall most steelhead will be caught off side planers and on shallow set Dipsy Divers. During the summer months they will be caught via a variety of presentations including downriggers, Dipsy Divers, side planers, lead core, wire line and super line. Body baits, spoons, and flies with dodgers/flashers will all produce steelhead. Experimentation plays a large role in catching steelhead as their preferences change from day to day. We will look at specific steelhead techniques in Chapter 5.

Steelheads are one of the great American gamefish! They have been captivating anglers hearts around North America for many years. Because of their unpredictable nature and their tenacious fighting ability, they can be a frustrating fish at times. However, if you spend any amount of time pursuing them, you will understand why they receive such attention and have a cult-like following. The steelhead is a worthy opponent.

LAKE TROUT

For many anglers, lake trout have an almost mythical background. Many of us were raised on stories about mysterious fishing trips to the northern reaches of Canada where the lake trout resembled the oars on a sixteen-foot Lund. We attended sport shows where we saw pictures of huge lakers some lucky angler on a walleye trip managed to capture. For many of us, the lake trout remained in the realm of the imagination. For many anglers, the lake trout lived a quiet, fictional existence, rarely seeing the light of day.

Since the re-birth of the Great Lakes, however, the lake trout's mythical existence has been shattered on a near-daily basis. No longer do anglers need to travel to the remote woods of Canada to tangle with lake trout. All five Great Lakes contain schools of these colorful gamefish. Lake trout thrive in clean, deep, cold water and with twenty percent of the world's fresh surface water locked up in the Great Lakes, we have plenty of habitats to grow fat and happy lake trout.

Behavior

Lake trout have something in common with native Floridians. Unlike the other species of salmon and trout found in the Great Lakes, Mr. Lake Trout is the only true native. Before the opening of the Welland Canal and the increased productivity of commercial fishing, the Great Lakes supported a thriving lake trout fishery. Once the Welland Canal opened, the insidious sea lamprey invaded the Great Lakes and slowly decimated the lake trout populations. Between the lampreys and the commercial fishing, the lake trout were wiped out in all but Lake Superior.

Once the sea lampreys were brought under control and commercial fishing was regulated, stocking programs began to restore lake trout populations in Lakes Superior, Michigan, Huron and Ontario. Today all four Lakes support thriving populations of lake trout. Erie supports minimal numbers of lakers. Despite the re-population of lake trout to the Lakes, much of the fishery is still dependent on stocking. Biologists are troubled by the lack of natural reproduction. As of this printing, biologists feel that most of the lake trout in the Great Lakes are stocked fish.

Lake trout grow to massive sizes. The modern day Great Lakes lake trout record is a massive 61 pound, 8 ounce fish caught from Lake Superior in 1997! Lake trout grow slower than the other species but their life span is longer. Lakers have been known to live for up to 25 years.

Lake trout prefer cold water and their ideal feeding range is 44-48 degrees. When the water is cold from top to bottom during the spring and fall, one can find lake trout anywhere from the surface to the bottom. Once the lakes begin to warm, lakers will usually be one of the deepest gamefish in the water column.

Lake trout are a structure-oriented fish. Bottom structure, such as drop-offs, humps, rocky reefs and hills, will often dictate the location of both suspended and bottom hugging fish. At times, lakers will hold so tight to the bottom that they may not show up on fish finders. The only way to catch these bottom-hugging fish is to literally drag your lures across the bottom. At other times, lake trout will relate to the bottom but they will suspend just above the bottom.

Lakers are fall spawners. There are several different strains of lake trout being stocked in the Great Lakes today. Some lake trout spawn over deep water reefs and structure well offshore. These deep water spawning sites are rocky in composition. In some locations, lake trout prefer to spawn over rocky, shallow water shoals. These fish will move into breakwall areas, riprap, river and harbor mouths and some will even move into rivers. These shallow water trout are excellent targets for small boat anglers during the fall months!

Lake Trout Basics

People either love lake trout or hate them. They are one of the prettiest fish in the Lakes and they grow big. They are not aggressive fighters like kings and steelhead; however, if you tangle with them on light tackle, they will lead you to some sore arms!

Lake trout are one of those species that if they are actively feeding, they are very easy to catch. It is when lake trout are dormant or in a non-feeding mode that they become a very difficult and challenging target. Non-feeding lake trout are one of the toughest trout to catch and truly great anglers will stand out on their abilities to catch these 'off' fish. They succeed by fine tuning their presentation and paying close attention to a myriad of details.

During the spring months lake trout can be caught on six to eight pound test line and clean spoons and body baits such as jointed Rapalas run along the surface on flat lines and side planers. Some of the biggest lake trout of the year will be caught from the surface during May. Once the water heats up, the lakers will retreat to the deep, cold waters below the thermocline. Lake trout are known to suspend over deep, open water as well as orient themselves tightly to the bottom.

Historically, the most productive Great Lakes lake trout action took place by bouncing the bottom. Today, post zebra mussels, it seems as if lake trout are just as likely to be found suspended over deep, open water. This often depends on local features and can vary from season to season. In other words, each port and Lake is different so you will need to adapt your presentations depending on where you are fishing. Consistent lake trout anglers will be able to catch them off the bottom or suspended.

Suspended and bottom oriented lake trout can be caught on downriggers, wire line, sinker drops, super line and by deep vertical jigging. While dodgers and flies are probably the most popular lake trout baits; spoons, body baits and odd little lures such as Spin N' Glows will catch lake trout.

Lake trout are a classic American gamefish. They are a fish most

Lake trout are the only salmonoid species native to the Great Lakes. Lakers grow big and favor deep, cold waters.

anglers across the country dream about, but seldom, if ever catch. They are a beautiful fish, which grow big. If you enjoy eating smoked fish, lake trout are excellent for the smoker. Our Great Lakes are home to schools of these deepwater denizens. Lakers are reliable targets that are often available when other species are scarce. Learn how to catch lake trout and they might just turn a slow fishing trip into a great success!

Brown Trout

Brown trout are a fish of legends. They are preceded by a mystique that transcends the very waters in which they swim. Browns are highly efficient predators that grow to very large sizes. Despite their legendary history, Great Lakes browns receive less fishing pressure than any of the other target species. In spite of the apparent lack of intentional angling interest, browns can be found in all five Great Lakes. Lakes Ontario and Michigan have the strongest brown trout fisheries.

Some of the biggest brown trout in the world come from the Great Lakes. Each year, the Great Lakes produce large numbers of browns in the 8-15 pound range. This brown weighed 18 pounds.

Brown trout are the ideal game fish for small boat and shore anglers. Browns are a shallow water fish that spend the majority of their time in close proximity to the shoreline. This puts them within reach of small boat anglers and shore fishermen throughout much of the fishing season.

Another reason more people may want to take an interest in brown trout is their size. Great Lakes brown trout grow to mammoth proportions. If you look at the individual state records for Great Lakes collar states, they all have trophy records! The Great Lakes record is a whopping 36¾ pounds! This monster was taken off the Illinois shoreline of Lake Michigan. What angling destination has had more 30 pound browns caught than the Great Lakes? If that isn't enough, browns in the 8-15 pound range are a fairly common catch. Wow! Where else in North America can you go and find 8-15 pound brown trout on a regular basis?

Are these huge Great Lakes browns related to their debonair cousins who reside in clear mountain meadow streams? Yes, they are the same fish! Big Water browns are set apart by their high-protein based forage and the open water environment. Currently there are several strains of browns being stocked in the Great Lakes.

Behavior

Great Lakes browns are a very different fish than the other species. Their nature and behavior sets them apart. They have a higher temperature tolerance and will aggressively feed in water much too warm for coho, kings and lake trout to even bathe. They tend to be homebodies and are less migratory than the other species. Locations that produce browns will usually be productive year after year. One of their most attractive characteristics is that they are found in shallower water, much closer to the shoreline than the other four species.

Browns are a very efficient predator. Like their cousin the steelhead, browns can tolerate a broad range of temperatures. On the Great Lakes, studies suggest that browns prefer 47-65 degree water. From an angler's perspective, their peak feeding range is 54-62 degrees. Similar to steelhead, browns are opportunistic feeders and will venture out of temperature to feed.

Brown trout are a very structure oriented fish. While coho, kings and steelhead will often be found roaming deep open water, successful brown trout anglers know that you must fish near bottom structure to consistently locate browns. Key structure includes sharp, near shore drop-offs, humps and dips, rock riprap, river mouths, piers, jetties and breakwalls.

Brown Trout Basics

We said 8-15 pound browns are common. Most anglers catch very few brown trout because browns are not commonly found in the same waters as the other species. If you want to catch lots of big brown trout, you must fish for them! This may require you to ignore the other species for a day or two.

Brown trout can be caught by a variety of methods. During the spring months trolling with side planers in 10-30 feet of water is very productive. A variety of body baits and clean spoons produce during the spring months. One of the keys to success during this period is to use 6-12 pound test line for clean baits. This will lead you to more browns. In the spring months when the Lakes are icy cold, locating pockets of warmer water will lead you to browns. As the Lakes warm during the summer months, browns will move down and look for 54-62 degree water where it intersects the bottom.

During the summer months browns are typically found in 30-75 feet of water. They will suspend or hold close to bottom structure. Downriggers, Dipsy Divers, super line and lead core are the most productive tools for placing baits in the strike zone. During the summer months, spoons, body baits and flies/dodgers will all produce. Light line will lead to greater success during the summer. Captain Ernie Lantiegne, one of the top brown trout fishermen on the Great Lakes, is a believer in 8-pound test line for summer spoon and plug fishing.

Browns begin staging for their spawning runs earlier than the other species. During the pre-spawn period they will move in and hold in the vicinity of their spawning destinations. As mentioned, browns tend to be homebodies. For this reason, areas that receive heavy stockings of brown trout will often have good fishing all season long. During the staging period anglers catch some of the biggest browns of the year. A combination of spring and summer techniques will produce during this period depending on local weather and Lake conditions.

Brown trout are within reach of many small boat anglers. I remember one particular New Year's Day when a small boat, a couple of teenagers and a whole lot of brown trout got together. My teenage fishing partner, Paul Jaros and I launched a canoe off the shoreline of the now-shuttered Zion nuclear plant. We didn't have time to be cold because we caught brown trout one after the other! Brown trout are a world class species. The Great Lakes are full of big browns and they deserve more attention from anglers!

OTHER SALMONOID SPECIES

King and coho salmon, steelhead, browns and lake trout are our primary targets on the Great Lakes. Today, the Lakes host limited numbers of atlantic salmon, pink salmon, brook trout, splake and tiger trout. Most of these fish were stocked experimentally at one point or another. Atlantic salmon were first stocked in the 1800's. Today, occasional stockings of atlantics are made. The Great Lakes atlantic salmon record, 32.2 pounds,

Peak Water Temperatures for Catching Great Lakes Salmon and Trout		
	Peak temperature	Active range
King salmon	42-44 degrees	42-46 degrees
Coho salmon	48-54 degrees	45-58 degrees
Steelhead	42-56 degrees	42-61 degrees
Lake trout	44-48 degrees	42-48 degrees
Brown trout	54-62 degrees	47-65 degrees

was caught in Lake Michigan. Limited numbers of atlantics are caught with Lakes Ontario and Huron seeing the majority of these fish.

Pink salmon have adapted well to the Great Lakes and in some regions natural reproduction has established pinks. Lake Superior has the largest numbers of naturally reproducing pink salmon.

Wisconsin stocks brook trout to enhance the shoreline fishery. There are not large, system-wide populations of any of these species in the Great Lakes. Select regions support fisheries for each of these species. Great Lakes brookies grow big. The Wisconsin state record came from Lake Michigan and weighed over 10 pounds!

CHAPTER 2

Great Lakes Tackle

Everything you wanted to know about today's salmon and trout tackle and more!

I love my work! Today, I get to fish out of some of the finest and nicest crafts available. My work allows me to use some of the best tackle, accessories and high-end electronics on the market. I am blessed to have a job that I can't wait to do! But it wasn't always this way. Believe me when I tell you it all started from very humble beginnings.

Growing up only blocks from Lake Michigan, I never fished the Lake for salmon until my early 20's. I spent my youth chasing musky, walleye and bass during the summers in Northern Wisconsin. My school days were used up in sports. My first forays onto the Big Pond were out of a 14 foot Shell Lake (predecessor to Tuffy), with a 20 horse outboard. The boat became appropriately named, "The Hail Mary," after the prayers my buddy Harv and I were saying trying to get back into shore on a cold, windy, April day when we shouldn't have gone fishing.

In spite of all our handicaps, including the loose nuts behind the tiller, that boat came home with many a full cooler. Just weeks after the April incident, I purchased my first boat (the Hail Mary was a gift from my father), a used 19 foot Grady White Marlin. I was sure this boat would take me to fish—anytime, anywhere. That thought, in and of itself, is testimony to the ignorance of youth!

Tackle was everything from musky rods to bass rods. Lures were anything we could scrounge up. My rod holders were PVC pipe screwed into a wooden crate, set in the center of the boat and held in place by weights from my barbell set in the crate. When a big fish would hit, it would bend the PVC pipe and the rod would come shooting out. We'd have to grab the rod in midair as it was flying out of the rod holder to keep it from swimming away with the fish.

Chip Porter is an authority on Great Lakes tackle. What many people don't realize is that you can catch big salmon on light tackle, such as this king.

Although somewhat humorous and perhaps enlightening, this story is meant to illustrate one single point. Given the right conditions, anyone can catch salmon on the Great Lakes with any form of craft and tackle. Most people don't run out and buy a 35-foot boat as their starter, and rarely do they have the funding to outfit it with premium components and tackle. Rigging a Great Lakes craft is a growing and building process.

This Chapter of the book is dedicated to this process. Here we will educate you about boat set up, tackle, electronics and other gizmos needed to catch fish. In today's market place you have an incredible amount of variety from which to choose. Before you shop, we want you to know what you need, whether you choose to buy top shelf equipment or bargain basement. Our objective is to give you the properties that make for a good trolling reel or a good rod. A good example of this is reels. You can spend ten dollars at a swap meet for a used trolling reel or upwards of a couple hundred for the latest top of the line reel. Before looking at tackle, we must briefly look at boat set up.

BOAT SET UP: SETTING UP THE PERFECT SALMON AND TROUT FISHING PLATFORM

This is where it all begins! Over the course of a typical Great Lakes fishing season, you will encounter a variety of different weather and fishing conditions. In the spring you will be fishing the surface, maybe in 35 feet of water or in 140 feet. Summer time finds you trolling at depths in excess of 50, 70 or maybe 100 feet. Fall action finds you fishing on the beach in 20 feet of water one day and in 200 feet of water the next day. Can you fish all these different scenarios from the same boat? Or do you need two or three boats?

The good news is, if you set up your boat properly, you can fish all scenarios from one craft. To consistently catch fish, Great Lakes anglers have to consider their craft as the primary source of presentation. How successful you are is often determined, to a large extent, on how well your boat is set up. Set up properly, your boat is a fish catching machine.

Improperly, it becomes a nightmare of tangles, screw ups and wasted time on the water.

I wouldn't let Dan write this section of the book. Not because he doesn't know about setting up a boat; he's done quite a few, but because he is the essence of a 'fly by the seat of your pants' fisherman. The best illustration of this was the summer Dan had only 40 feet of cable left on his starboard boom downrigger. Rather than re-spool the cable, Dan figured that he'd just fish with it that way for the entire season. When the water warmed during the summer and the fish went deep, we all pretty much figured that Dan was down to fishing with three good riggers and one dead one. I'd call Dan on the radio and ask how the action was where he was, and wouldn't ya' know it, he's catching fish on that stinkin' 40 foot rigger when I can't mark a fish above 95 feet!

> Before you drill the first hole, good planning will lead to a more efficient use of deck space, reduce tangles when fishing and lead to more enjoyment!

From that summer, we learned a bit about other fish following a fighting fish up to the boat, but still, I wouldn't recommend to anyone that they just 'fly by the seat of their pants,' like Dan does. That is, unless Dan pulls out the horseshoe and lends it to you, which I don't see happening anytime soon.

Over the years I've had the opportunity to work with a number of different boat manufacturers. Part of my sponsorship included receiving two new boats every year—a small boat and a big boat. Each year I had to rig the boats. This gave me first hand experience at boat rigging that translated into my boat rigging company, RigMasters.

This section of the book is dedicated to how to set up and equip your floating fish arsenal. We look at applications for smaller as well as larger crafts. If you set up your boat properly from the beginning, every other aspect of Great Lakes salmon and trout fishing will be more orderly and efficient. Remember, your goal is to have a boat that allows you to adapt to changing conditions and to offer presentations in tune with the fish and the Lakes.

Regardless of your budget or size of your craft, there are certain principles that apply across the board. When setting up a boat you need to ask yourself, "What are the functions I want my boat and working space to perform?" From a logical perspective, the primary function will be presenting baits, avoiding tangling, clearing other lines when fish are on, and netting and boating fish. If you lack even one of these principles, the whole scheme suffers from either lack of bites or lost fish.

This section of the book is going to look at the placement of equipment, and how to make it functional for your environment. We will address the theoretical aspects of boat set up and examine application do's and don'ts. Along the way, we will look at large (25 plus feet) and small craft (16-24 feet) specifics. We are not going to deal with prop size, backing plates behind downriggers or where you should mount your transducers. That information is readily available from other sources.

Let's begin where it hurts, punching holes in a shiny new boat! This is the one area that really slows down the boat set-up process. Before you drill the first hole, have a complete plan for your boat. Even if you plan to set up your boat in stages, two downriggers this year, two more next year, and more rod holders in the future, have that plan for the complete set up before you drill your first hole. By planning the complete craft first, and then implementing the plan in stages, you'll have much less apprehension about altering the appearance of your craft. Well, you gotta crack some eggs to make an omelet, so do your planning and then plug in the drill.

Keep the Center Open!

You need somewhere to bring fish up to the net, and creating a wide opening in the center of the stern will facilitate this. If you think about pulling something behind a moving object, to what point does it migrate? It moves directly behind the object pulling it. Therefore, all fish will gravitate toward the center when being pulled forward.

But, Capt. Chip, you say, I have big kings run all over the place and try to race and circle the boat! True, grasshopper, but in those instances you are no longer *pulling* the fish, the fish is in control. If you sped up the boat to the point of pulling, the fish would gravitate toward the center. Many times, that's exactly what you should do; speed up to try to keep that king from tangling in your Dipsies or planer boards out to the side. Another tactic is to turn the boat slightly to keep the fighting fish dead to center. That's not to say that I haven't netted hundreds of fish off the sides, but tens of thousands more have come right up the gut, in the center of the boat.

Downriggers

Since controlled depth fishing is what salmon trolling is all about, let's start right at the transom and work our way toward the bow. Of all the various apparatus, downriggers will be the furthest item astern. Ideally, you'd like all your downriggers as far aft as possible.

The second consideration for positioning downriggers applies if you intend to mount more than 2 riggers. Place them in as straight a line as possible across the transom. By placing the downriggers on a closely parallel plane, you will greatly reduce tangles. The parallel set-up will position your downrigger weights evenly across the water as you troll. If some weights are more forward than others, they can have a tendency to swing up under the rearward weights in cross currents or on turns, creating tangles. Riggers don't have to be exactly in line, but keeping them as close to a parallel line as possible is the ideal. If your boom riggers are mounted 18 inches or more forward of the corners, you will have more issues with tangles.

Most Great Lakes anglers use two to four downriggers. To be quite honest, you can catch loads of fish with only two riggers. Dan and I both fish out of larger boats but we prefer to run only four riggers. Don't feel like you need to cover the back of your boat with downriggers.

Downriggers that point out to the sides are known as 'booms,' or 'side-riggers.' Downriggers that point straight back are referred to as 'corners.' All downriggers have a boom arm on them, however the term boom rigger means the ones pointed outwards at a 90-degree angle from the side of the boat.

Downriggers are an essential tool for deepwater fishing.

Whether you mount a swivel base underneath your rigger depends on brand and personal preference. Cannons and Walkers have fixed booms that do not move and therefore require swivel bases, at least on the boom riggers. Vectors and Big Jons have tilting booms that can be raised by swinging the boom up vertically and don't require swivel bases. Personally, I am a big fan of swivel bases as there are times when you want to swivel something out of the way, and that time is usually when some behemoth of a fish is doing its best to try and force you into another trip to the tackle store to replace lost tackle!

To minimize tangles, we want to use corner downriggers, with a short boom, to keep our weights as close to a straight line as feasibly possible with the side riggers. Our boom riggers however, should have as long a boom as possible to spread out our lines. This also broadens our trolling path and minimizes tangles. Most anglers use four-foot booms on the sides.

In step with theory number one, mount your corner riggers as close to the stern corner as possible. This will free up the center of your craft for netting fish and dropping wire lines.

Rod Holders

First, understand that you can never have too many rod holders. Salmon and Trout can wreak havoc on tackle when close to the boat. Many times, things happen so quickly, that you simply don't have time to pull lines from the spread. Moving rods to open rod holders is your best option. Multiple rod holders that are not in use, allow you to move rods out of the way quickly without having to pull lines from the spread. For example, it you are netting a fish off the stern starboard corner, move the starboard corner rigger rod (which is still set on the rigger) over to a center or port corner rigger. This will open up space on the surface and possibly avoid a last minute tangle from a struggling fish.

Let's look at rod holders for downriggers first. Ideally, you want the downrigger rod placed in a rod holder close to the downrigger. This minimizes tangles and increases downrigger efficiency. The easiest way to achieve this is to use the rod holders that come with most downriggers. These holders are mounted into the gunnels with the downrigger, as the rod holder and rigger are attached. The angle of many of these holders can be adjusted. We recommend angling these rod holders slightly above a parallel perspective to the water.

The second sets of rod holders to mount are for your Dipsies. Notice I said "sets," because there are many times when you may want to run more than one Dipsy per side. Dipsy holders are mounted on the gunnels or rail mounted just forward of your boom riggers. These rod holders are mounted to run perpendicular to the boat, sticking out at 90-degree angles. Many rod holders are adjustable and can swivel from straight up in the air, down to parallel or nearly that, with the water. We'll discuss how to run Dipsies in Chapters 4 and 5.

When mounting the Dipsy rod holders, the rearward Dipsy holder needs to be far enough forward from the boom rigger so that the Dipsy rod doesn't rub on the rigger cable. On most boats this will be from two to five feet. The forward Dipsy holder really doesn't need much separation from the aft Dipsy holder, only about 12 to 16 inches. The forward Dipsy rod holder can also double as a rod holder for planer boards, lead cores, suspended wire lines, or as that ever valuable open rod holder.

Next in line are the planer board rod holders. These are mounted forward of the Dipsy Diver rod holders. On smaller boats, mount the rod holders up the gunnels, in line. On larger boats, it may be preferable to run the rod holders up the side of the cabin or up a rail mounted between the hard top and the gunnels. Depending on the size of your boat and the amount of planer lines you will run, two to six planer board

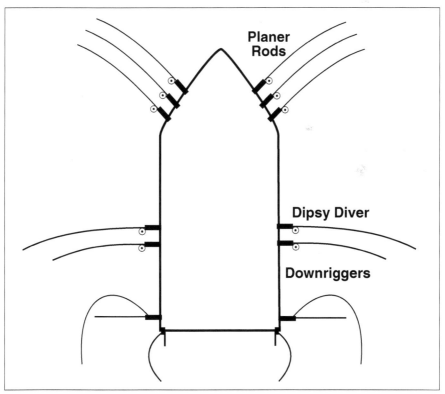

Where you place rod holders and downriggers are vitally important for tangle-free success. This diagram illustrates small boat rod holder and downrigger placement. Notice how the downriggers are placed as close to the corners as possible.

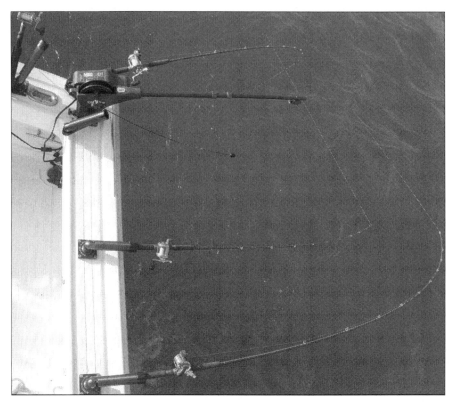

This photo shows the proper position to mount Dipsy rod holders. Notice the tip separation created by using Dipsy rods of different lengths.

rod holders per side is standard. When planers are not in use during the summer, these rod holders can hold spare deepwater rods.

One of the options that allow total flexibility with regard to Dipsy and planer board rod holders is the track mounting system. By mounting a single track along each gunnel, you can add a multitude of rod holders in a variety of positions depending on your application. Not only does it afford us tremendous flexibility, but also allows us to purchase rod holders in increments and add them at our convenience or when our budget allows. In small boat applications, where the boat may also be used for family inland adventures, it allows one to remove the rod holders quickly. A rubber step pad can then be slid into the track to make the gunnels functional and keep the clean lines and appearance of the boat.

Following the adage about rod holders, that more is better, lets start placing a few more rod holders strategically around our craft. The easiest way to add rod holders is to purchase downriggers that have multiple rod holders as part of the standard equipment. Some come with the downriggers and some, like the rod holders made by Vector, are aftermarket products you can purchase separately. If they are fully adjustable then it is even better.

The next set of accessory rod holders "fill the gaps" across our transom. Mount one rod holder in the center and one rod holder in each corner between the boom and corner riggers. Boom downriggers equipped with multiple rod holders will serve the function of the corner rod

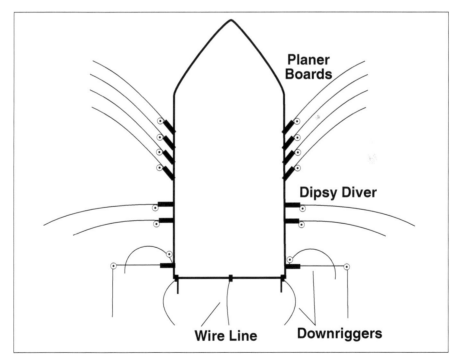

This diagram illustrates ideal rod holder and downrigger mounting locations on larger boats. The planer board holders can be mounted forward of the Dipsy holders, in the gunnels, along a hardtop, half tower or on a rail mounted system. Notice how the middle is kept open. This is where most fish are netted.

holders. These extra holders can be used for flatlines, suspended wires, lead core, or simply open spots where you can move the rods. This basic arrangement of rod holders and downriggers will enable you to fish and present a well-crafted group dynamic in most situations.

Rigger Boards

One of the items we haven't covered is the use of rigger boards. These boards stretch gunnel to gunnel across the back of the boat. Primarily used in small boat situations, I would advise against using them, unless they are the only option that makes sense. The main drawback to rigger boards is their placement on the boat. A rigger board has to be high enough to clear outboard motors when trimmed up to put the boat on the trailer. On some boats they take away valuable back-deck space because of mounting restrictions. At times rigger boards will make it more difficult to net fish off the stern or corners.

I have seen circumstances where they have been used effectively, but in most cases, they are ill thought out and the boat layout could have been much more efficient without them. If it makes sense for your boat, your best option is to keep the rigger board as low as functionally possible and as close to the transom as you can muster.

One last word about boat set up. The main consideration small boat anglers have to make over large boat anglers is how to make the most efficient use of space. There is no reason that a small boat can't run the maximum allowable number of rods with respect to the passengers on board. In areas with a three rod law, 4 fishermen on a small boat should easily and efficiently be able to run 12 rods with nary a tangle or headache if the boat is laid out properly.

In terms of fish catching ability, small boat anglers should not feel outgunned by larger vessels. Even when we fish on large boats, we don't cram every rod we can fit into the water. There are many, many days in the summer where we will only run six or seven lines. Could we run 12 or 15 lines on those days? Absolutely! The question is, will we catch more fish with seven lines or 12 lines in the water? I think you get the picture. Make the most with what you have available. Learn to use your equipment and set up to your full advantage. When that trophy king or steelhead slams a bait, it makes no difference to the fish what size boat you are fishing on!

Rods, Reels and Other Necessities

Anglers today have a huge selection of rods, reels and components to choose from. At times, the selection process is a bit overwhelming because of all the choices available. We want to simplify the rigging process. The major components needed to catch Great Lakes salmon and trout includes rods, reels, line, terminal tackle and electronics. The following pages give you an overview of what equipment you need and what properties to look for in your equipment.

If you begin with a well thought out boat rigging and the right equipment, you can greatly reduce your stress on the water. Not only will you catch more fish but you will also have less aggravation and ultimately, find more enjoyment on the water.

Great Lakes Trolling Rods

How do you choose rods for salmon and trout fishing? A number of variables including rod length, action, line test, and working space will set the guidelines for rod choices. But, before you look at these criteria, you must first determine the delivery application for the rod. Will you be using the rod to run light line on a downrigger or will you be using it with a Dipsy Diver? Delivery application is the key factor guiding you in rod selection.

Does one rod fit all needs for today's Great Lake's anglers? This would be nice, but the reality and nature of Great Lakes fishing dictates otherwise. We fish with a number of different apparatuses: downriggers, Dipsies, side planers, wire line, super line and lead core. Each of these delivery applications requires a rod with specific properties. Some rods may be able to perform double duty, like a planer board rod used on a downrigger. Other rods, like Dipsy or wire line rods, are very specific to their application. If you tried using a light line downrigger rig with a Dipsy Diver you might as well throw your wallet in the Lake. Likewise, you can't use a wire line rod with a downrigger. All said, you need several different types of rods to fish all the different applications available to today's Great Lakes salmon and trout angler.

Before breaking our rod discussion down by application, we need to say a brief word about rod action. Many of you may have heard the term, 'parabolic bend' when referring to trolling rods. Simply put, this means a rod that bends in a perfect 'C,' when flexed from tip to butt. This style is purported to have the best fish fighting properties because the rod offers so much flex and forgiveness. Because we are not setting the hooks on these fish, the boat does that, we really don't have a need for stiff graphite backbones and fast taper tips like you'd need for slinging baits or setting hooks into bony mouthed fish on the strike. A rod with a nearly pure parabolic bend has little in the way of backbone or 'beef.'

Okay, Chip, are you saying we should look for a rod with a "pure parabolic bend?" Not really. When fighting fish, we do need some degree of backbone to muscle or *gently* encourage big fish. This is especially helpful in the precarious situation of netting a big fish at the back of the boat where other lines are waiting to become tangled.

From the fish fighting perspective, the parabolic bend that essentially creates a 'buggy whip' style of rod, is not our ideal. We want a rod with a soft tip but we need some backbone. Dipsy, wire line and lead core rods require more backbone than downrigger or planer board rods.

When choosing a trolling rod the first factor to consider is length. This applies to rods of all applications. Do you prefer a long or short rod? Great Lakes anglers have battled over the merits of long versus short for years. You will find great anglers in both camps. Dan and I are both short rod guys, as we believe it offers us more control of the rod and fish. Long rod guys swear by the attribute that the longer stick has better fighting properties and they can hold a fish out away from the boat and other lines if needed. As we move through the various application processes, you will find suitable rods that cover a variety of lengths.

Downrigger rods are the most basic of our rods. Downrigger rods can be divided into two categories; spoon/crankbait rods, and dodger/flasher rods. You can run a spoon on the heavier dodger rod; however, trying to run heavy dodgers on light line spoon rods is not a good use of tackle.

Light line rigger rods range anywhere from short, six foot spoon rods up to 11 foot noodle rods. Both the short rod and the noodle rod are designed for light line but with inherently different properties. The noodle rod is whip like in action and offers little backbone. This style of rod is very forgiving of angler error. The short spoon rod often resembles a mini 'stand-up' fighting rod used by saltwater anglers. It has a soft tip but transitions nicely into a stiffer backbone. The soft tip allows you to use light line and the backbone allows you to tame even the largest of Great Lakes salmonoids in a reasonable time.

For dodger/flasher fishing you will be using slightly heavier line than

Light line spoon fishing is a dynamite technique for catching trophy Great Lakes kings. This big king was taken on 12 lb. test line, a 6 ft. rod and a light baitcasting reel. You will catch more big kings if you learn how to use light line!

with the spoons and cranks. A dodger rod should be able to handle 17-30 pound test and offers a little more beef than the spoon rods. A good dodger rod has the properties of a very soft tip that gradually transitions into the backbone section one half to two thirds the way down the rod.

Line test is a key variable when selecting downrigger rods. Lighter lines require softer tips and less backbone, while heavier lines can afford more backbone with a faster taper. Today, a number of excellent rods are available that can handle big kings on 8-12 pound test line. Dan and I both use six to six and a half foot rods with 12-pound test for spoon feeding kings.

A typical short rod setup on a well-equipped boat might include two six-foot spoon rods, and three or four seven-foot dodger rods. If you are a fan of longer rods, simply add a foot to the above specs. Today, there are many companies that make quality rods that can be used on downriggers.

Dipsy rods are the next animals on our shopping list. These rods require different properties than rigger rods. If you only run one Dipsy per side, your only consideration would be to clear the cable of your boom downrigger with your rod tip. If you are going to run multiple Dipsies per side, you'll want to consider two different rod lengths to gain tip separation. Typical separations are from 12 to 30 inches in length. A short rod guy might choose a seven foot and an eight and half or nine foot as his two Dipsy lengths, while a long rod guy would prefer an eight foot and a ten or ten foot six inch rod for his two lengths.

The actions on the Dipsy rods are designed to have a fairly stiff backbone, especially on the longer rod, yet a soft tip under load of the Dipsy. Dipsies create quite a bit of torque under load and if you choose too soft a rod, you'll have used up all the softness of the rod under load and not have anything left for shock absorption when a big fish strikes.

Planer board rods really are the easiest of all our rods to choose. Many fishermen use multiple lengths in the same set, with the shorter rods towards the aft of the boat, gradually increasing length as they move forward towards the bow or up the side of the cabin. Typical lengths are anywhere from seven to ten and a half feet. They are generally light rods, something like a downrigger dodger rod, but may have a bit more backbone because of the changing load properties they can be under due to the planer board digging in the water and then skipping over the tops of waves. Again, there are a number of rod makers who make good Dipsy and planer rods.

Specialty rods on our craft would include wire line and lead core rods. Lead core rods can really run the gamut because they can be used in a multitude of applications. Many fishermen just run lead core straight off the back of the boat, while others may fish six lead cores simultaneously with four on larger inline planer boards and two off outriggers. Planer board rods are too light and Dipsy rods, although closer to what we want to achieve, frequently don't have the soft tip.

Lead core in and of itself is a heavy line to drag through the water. A good lead core rod must be heavy enough to handle the weight of the lead line. The typical lead core rod will generally run about seven to nine feet in length.

Over the years, we have used a number of different wire line rods. They have been in a variety of lengths between seven and nine feet. Both shorter and longer models have worked well for us. Since there is no stretch in wire line, you want a rod with a forgiving tip and a soft taper. This will act as shock absorber when a big king or lake trout try to rip the rod off your boat. The rod also has to be heavy enough to stand up to pulling the wire line through the water. Pulling 300-400 feet of wire and a one-pound ball through the water takes a toll on a rod.

Wire line rods come in two basic styles, roller guide rods and hard guide rods. The braided wire that we use, (we'll discuss wire applications in detail in Chapter 4), is highly abrasive and normal ceramic or metal guides will get chewed to bits by wire. Roller guide rods are the elite rods in the class, as the guides have rollers in them. This allows for the absolute smoothest transition of wire from the reel and back into the reel. Specialized hard metal guides, like Carballoy or Hardalloy (brand names of guides), will hold up well to the rigors of wire. When using wire line, the rod tip is very important. Some outfit their rods with a specialized tip of either a roller tip guide or a Twilli tip.

Great Lakes Trolling Reels

Reels are fairly straightforward from the standpoint of what qualities the reel needs to possess. Unlike inland fishing, salmon and trout can spill hundreds of feet of line off a reel in seconds on one screaming run. This simple fact dictates that the drag system of our reels needs to be the paramount consideration in our reel choice. Secondly, some rigs will be trolled at great distances from the boat, either deep or to the side. For these applications we need to have a reel with sufficient capacity. Combining these two attributes with having a levelwind on the reel narrows our choices dramatically.

Reels that run planer boards, downrigger dodgers, and mono Dipsies require capacities of a minimum of 270 yards of 20 lb. test monofilament. We'll talk more about line choices later, but 20 lb. test is a median of the monofilaments we may use.

Spoon and crankbait reels, those that run light 10 to 14 lb. test monofilaments, require less capacity (thinner diameter takes up less space) thereby broadening our choices. If you fish in a region where big fish are common, you will want to have a minimum of 270 yards of 10-14 lb. test line on your reels. This will prevent your reel from being spooled and will allow you to strip away frayed or weak line in the middle of a fishing trip. If you are fishing for smaller spring coho and trout, you can often get away with the baitcasting reels you use for inland fishing.

Super line reels are a bit of a hybrid for capacity between light and heavy mono. A 20 lb. test super line really has a diameter of 8 to 12 lb. test mono. However, if you fish with the super line reels often, you'll find yourself stripping off ten yards of line every now and then and retying. If you do this a dozen times a year with a reel with low line capacity, you may run out of line in the middle of a fishing trip. For this reason, most anglers choose to go with larger style downrigger reels for Fire Line and other super lines. The larger downrigger reels used for dodger fishing are good choices for wire line.

Lead core reels are animals unto themselves, as they require giant capacities due to the huge diameter of the lead core. Single lead cores, those with 100 yards of lead core, need reels with capacities of around 350 yards of 30 lb. test mono. Double lead cores, those with 200 yards of lead core line, require reels with 450 yards of capacity with 30 lb. test mono.

Two other important criteria need to be considered when choosing the above reels: Handle throw and retrieve ratio. Handle throw is the measurement of the length of the reel handle from the arbor, or nut that

When choosing reels for Great Lakes fishing, line application is one of the dominant selection criteria. Different line applications will require different size reels, as demonstrated in this photo. The Calcutta 500 is spooled with wire, the Calcutta 600 with mono and the Calcutta 700 with lead core.

sticks out the side of the reel that the handle attaches to, all the way to the actual paddle where your hand contacts the reel handle. The longer the handle throw, the slower the spool will turn because it will take more time to make a revolution of the handle. This property is important because it keeps your reeling smooth and allows the drag to function better without being jumpy. Salmon and trout have soft mouths and if your reel is jumpy, you stand a much greater risk of ripping hooks out and introducing momentary slack into the line.

Gear ratio is how many revolutions of the spool occur for each revolution of the reel handle. A 4.2/1 ratio means that the spool turns 4.2 times for each revolution of the handle. Low ratios are generally ideal for fish fighting properties; again, because the slower the gears work while fighting a fish, the better the drag will function. There is a wild card in the mix though and that's called line pickup. That is simply how many inches of line come back on the spool for each revolution of the handle. A low, wide spool is going to take up less line per revolution than a narrower tall spool.

An ideal reel has both these qualities. A good example of this is the Shimano Tekota series. The Tekota's retrieve ratio is a low 4.2/1, yet the reel actually picks up 25 inches of line per handle revolution. This gives it the properties of a high speed reel for line take up, with the smooth drag properties of a low ratio reel: Essentially, the best of both worlds.

You might have noticed we haven't mentioned spinning reels. Although many people have used spinning reels for many years, they are not ideal to our application for one simple reason. As a fish is pulling out line from the drag, if you turn the handle of the spinning reel, you create line twist. Line twist can, and will, weaken your line resulting in lost fish. Because of this very serious problem, we recommend using level-wind reels and rods designed to hold those reels.

Before moving on, you need to understand reel marketing and reality. More ball bearings in a reel, does not make a better or smoother reel. Don't go shopping thinking that a 5 ball bearing reel is better than a 1 ball bearing reel, simply based on the number of ball bearings. Although manufacturers do tend to put more ball bearings in their higher end reels, there are reels out there that work marvelously with just a couple and some that are sitting in a garbage dump somewhere with six ball bearings. Roller bearings are superior to ball bearings and ball bearings are superior to bushings.

Secondly, reel frame construction is hugely important to the durability and functional smoothness of how a reel will perform over time. Frames that are bolted together flex and will wear out. Forged frames have no flex and tend to be more durable. Cold forged frames are built to higher tolerances than hot forged frames, although any forged frame is superior to bolted frames. Again, there have been some really great bolted frame reels and some fairly poor forged frame reels made.

When you go to purchase a reel, consider brand, the reputation that it maintains, frame type, bearings or bushings, retrieve ratio, line pickup and capacity, and you'll probably arrive at a decision you'll be happy with. One short note here is that spending more on a reel is usually worth the investment if you fish often. I know people that have bought lesser priced reels and have had them rebuilt or replaced several times over, while anglers who invested in more quality oriented equipment are still using it flawlessly. In the end, the purchasers of the high-end tackle actually have less of a total investment in their reels.

Terminal Tackle

Terminal tackle makes up the last phase of our basic equipping list. For salmon trolling there really are only two forms of terminal tackle: swivels and weights. Terminating dodgers or flashers requires the use of swivels, and we can't recommend more strenuously the use of high quality ball bearing swivels to accomplish this task. Swivels with a pound test rating of 20 lb. or higher are adequate, although for dodgers, most opt for 40 lb. or higher.

Stealth is not really a property of dodger/flasher fishing so smaller is not necessarily better. Spoons, however, are a stealth presentation and since we use light trolling spoons, the use of too heavy a swivel will impact our spoon action negatively. Also, larger swivels require more dragged weight to make them rotate and light spoons don't carry the mass to make them work. We recommend 20-30 lbs. high quality ball bearing swivels for spoons. Crane swivels can also perform nicely for light spoons.

Weights fall into three categories: inline, clip-on and balls. The first two weight groups are used for targeting the upper layers of the water column. In line weights are normally either bead chain or rubber core sinkers. These should range from $1/4$ ounce to 1 ounce. Some come with a keel to keep the sinker from spinning. Clipped weights usually range from 1 ounce to 6 ounces. You need to have a variety of different weights available for different circumstances.

The third category of weights, balls, are for reaching depths of 30 feet or greater. Ball weights can be used suspended or for bottom bouncing with wire line or superline. They range from 8 to 24 ounces and are round shaped. They can be attached with a clip release or via a three-way swivel rig.

Fishing Lines

Great Lakes anglers use four different types of lines throughout the season: monofilament, specialty lines (super lines), wire and lead core line. Each line type has specific properties that enhance their ability to target different species and different layers of the water column. Each individual line type will deliver a bait to the strike zone in a different and unique way.

Specific types of lines have very specific uses. For example, monofilament can be used with downriggers, flat lines, Dipsy Divers and side planers. Dipsy Divers can be run on monofilament, super lines, or wire lines. It should be noted that specific line applications will not catch fish at the same rate, but when they work, is dependent on the attitude and depth of the fish. This section will help you decipher the attributes of each line so you can make educated purchasing decisions. Use of the lines in specific circumstances and applications will be discussed in Chapters 3, 4 and 5.

Monofilament line must posses several qualities to make it ideal for salmon trolling. When fishing with multiple lines we can assume that our lines are going to contact many things, including atmosphere, water, gills, teeth, and other lines. The first line quality to consider is durability, which is really a macro category containing other qualities.

The micro qualities of durability are abrasion resistance, which is a use quality, UV light resistance and water absorption, which are storage qualities. Abrasion resistance is simply the ability of the line to withstand rubbing against something, like another line or a downrigger cable, without breaking. UV light resistance is the ability of line to resist decomposition through exposure to the sun. Water absorption is the measurement of how much water penetrates the composition of the line over time. This is usually the number one contributor to line rot. All mono lines are not created equal. So, when choosing a mono line, consider all three of these attributes.

The next quality to consider in mono is stretch. For the purposes of this discussion, we are referring to mono as all clear or translucent lines, including co-polymers, fluorocarbons, and hybrids. In a casting situation for bass, we would prefer a mono to have very little stretch so that we can achieve a good hookset. For our trolling considerations, a stretchy mono can function as the rubber band shock absorber for violent head shakes and powerful runs of a soft-mouthed fish. For that reason, we prefer a stretchy mono to other lines as it has inherently better fish fighting properties.

Dan has been catching loads of big fish for years and he credits much of his success to the use of light line. He uses Stren line because of the stretch factor. When dealing with big fish and charter clients with 'bad habits' and 'itchy thumbs,' line stretch will often help you avoid break-offs.

Typical mono line strengths for our fishing would be 10 to 14 lb. test for light spoon rods, with 12 lb. test being the median, 17 to 30 lb. test for dodger/flasher, Dipsy, and planer board applications, with 17 to 25 lb. test being the median. You never want to fish a dodger/flasher on anything less than 17 lb. test as the line will spin and twist up, even with a good ball bearing swivel. That twist will eventually break the line and you won't realize it until you go to change the bait on the rod that has been dead for a while, only to find out the dodger spun off.

Both Dan and I are firm believers that light line is the right line. It helps elicit better bait action, is less detectable to the fish, has less drag in the water and allows us to fish with lighter tackle. Our choices are 12 lb. test for spoon rods, and 17 lb. test for dodgers, planers and Dipsies, in monofilament applications. A note here is that rarely do we need a line heavier than 17 lb. test to manage even the biggest of fish when trolling the Great Lakes.

For super lines (Fire Line, Power Pro, Spiderwire, etc.) we use 20 lb. test. Dan and I both use super lines for presenting Dipsy Divers. Super lines and Dipsies go together like water and fish. Super line Dipsies are highly versatile for presenting baits to a variety of levels. If you are only going to rig four rods for trolling, we highly recommend that *at least one* of those rigs be a super line Dipsy set up.

We use 20-30 lb. test wire line. Lead core lines range from 17 to 45 lb. test with the median used being 27. Lead core is designed to achieve depth through the lead center of the line creating weight. A 27 lb. test lead core does not necessarily possess more lead than a 17 lb. test lead core. In some manufacturers, they have the same amount of lead, just

Recommended Great Lakes Line Tests by Application

Monofilament	
Spoons off downriggers	12 lb. test
Crankbaits	8-12 lb. test
Dodgers/flashers	17-20 lb. test
Inline side planers	17-20 lb. test
Direct side planers	8-17 lb. test
Super lines	20 lb. test
Wire line	20-30 lb. test
Lead core	27 lb. test

a heavier and larger diameter Dacron sheath. This can be counter productive to our efforts as the larger diameter creates more drag and therefore will not achieve the amount of depth that the lighter lead core will.

Basic Rigging Principles
Reel Spooling
Let's start with a discussion about spooling our reels. Downrigger, planer board, and mono Dipsy reels are straightforward; just wind on the monofilament of your choice and fill the spool.

Specialty lines such as super lines, wire lines and lead core are different animals. When spooling specialty lines you have the option of putting a backing line on the reel and then splicing in your specialty line, or spooling the entire reel with the specialty line. I usually elect to spool the entire reel with the super line or wire. I also choose mid capacity reels that accept somewhere around 300 to 400 yards of the specialty line when full.

Spooling the entire reel with specialty line can get expensive so many anglers opt to use a backing underneath the specialty lines. The advantage with using backing is that you use less of the expensive specialty line on large capacity reels. Using a larger diameter line as backing will help use less line and fill the spool quicker. I would advise strongly against using monofilament as a backing, due to the fact that it will rot from water absorption even when underneath your specialty line. Unfortunately, you won't figure that out until a huge king strips out enough line to get you into the backing and it breaks.

A simple trick to figure out how much backing you'll need on a reel is to have two identical reels ready to spool. Start by attaching your specialty line to the first reel and wind on the amount of yardage that you want on that reel. Splice it to your backing and wind on the backing until the reel is full, essentially creating the reverse of what you want; specialty line as backing and backing on top. Then, attach the tag end of the backing on the first reel to the second reel and start winding. Count the number of handle revolutions (or level winds) you make until you get to the specialty line. Now you know how many handle revolutions (or level winds) of backing you have to put on to create a full spool with the proper amount of specialty line on it.

As an absolute minimum, I recommend at least 250 yards of the specialty line, as trimming frays and kinks and retying will take some line away through the season. The best lines that I have used for backing for wire and super lines are 30 lb. test braided Dacron musky lines. They are

Captain Chip and Captain Ernie Lantiegne show the results of using the right tackle and proper rigging.

relatively cheap and hold up well and provide a nice cushion underneath the specialty line.

We must warn you about the dangers of spooling wire and super lines. Wind them on with EXTREME tension. Because of their narrow diameter, winding them under light or moderate tension will create a situation where, under load with a fish running out, the line running out can cut into the line on the spool and bind up, seizing the reel spool and that is never good.

Lead core, on the other hand, always requires backing, usually a super line. Because of the amount of capacity a lead core line takes up on a reel, and the fact that many times we are fishing with all our lead core in the water, we need a pretty substantial amount of backing to have enough line for a long run if a large fish hits, and they do that fairly often on lead core. Super lines allow us the capacity with a minimal amount of spool space used up.

The lead core line will have backing attached to one end and a monofilament leader attached to the business end. To attach these, pull back the Dacron sheath, exposing about 8 inches of the lead center. Pinch off the exposed lead, leaving a Dacron line without the lead in the center. This will facilitate tying a good knot that will not be bulky, and will pass through the levelwind of your reel and rod guides easily. The knot most commonly used for leaders and backing is a back-to-back uni-knot, which does well joining lines of dissimilar diameter.

The Main Knots

We will only briefly look at knots, as there are many knot-tying resources available. To catch fish on the Great Lakes you should become proficient with several knots. The most common, all purpose knot is the improved clinch knot, which we use to tie hooks on fly leaders, swivels on line, and mono line to any connector. Many people find the Palomar knot a suitable replacement for the improved clinch, although I save the Palomar for joining super lines to any connector.

The most common line-to-line knot for splicing is the back-to-back uni-knot. I'm a big fan of two knots that pull against each other, and tied correctly, it rarely fails. The last knot we use regularly is the simple overhand knot to create a loop. We use this to terminate our wire line and also on the end of fly leaders where it attaches to the dodger/flasher. To create it, simply make a loop in the line and with the line doubled over, tie an overhand knot. In wire or heavy mono, this knot never slips.

Rigging a Dipsy Rod

We've made our rod and reel choices and have our Dipsy rods, whether they are mono, super, or wire main lines. Now we have to rig the Dipsy. Unless this rod is going to do double duty in another application, which Dipsy rods rarely do, I elect not to tie swivels to the end of the line. Instead, I tie directly to the Dipsy. You may have considerations of travel and storage in which it is conducive to use a swivel, but a good rule of thumb is that less is better when it comes to terminal tackle.

Now we make our first Dipsy decision and that's which size Dipsy to buy. Buy the big one. Smaller ones can be used in early spring on lighter tackle for small fish, but unless you have an unlimited budget, buy the big ones. They will do everything the small ones do and a lot more. We use the Dipsy without the power ring for fishing above 80 feet.

This leads us to our first controversy: Whether or not to use snubbers. A snubber is simply a device meant to take up shock from the strike and offer some give while fighting a fish. Neither Dan nor I use snubbers anywhere, anytime. We allow the drag of our reels and the action of our rods to provide the necessary give. There are plenty of truly stud fishermen that would never fish without snubbers, so the debate rages on.

Whether you use a snubber or not, the basic leader rigging between the Dipsy and the bait is identical. When fishing dodgers or flashers behind the Dipsy, Dan and I both use 40 lb. test mono line. Because the dodger/flasher has so much action, we won't impede it by using such a heavy line. Tie the dodger/flasher directly to the leader line. If fishing crankbaits or spoons off Dipsies we need to down size our leader line to get better bait action. The most common down size is to 17-30 lb. test.

Some anglers will drop down to 12 lb. leader test in tough conditions. Leader length can be as short as 3 feet, but more commonly, 6 to 8 feet, or no more than the length of the rod.

Rigging a Planer Board Rod

There are two types of planer boards: mast & ski systems (direct planers) and inline planer boards. We'll discuss the positive and negative implications of both systems in Chapter 4. For now, let's just rig our rods. Rod rigging between the two systems is different.

Mast & ski system rods are rigged just like downrigger lines. The pound test line you use and how you terminate your line is determined the same way as downriggers, based on the bait you intend to pull behind it. Lighter line can be used on the mast and ski system, since the line is not supporting the board. For fishing cranks and

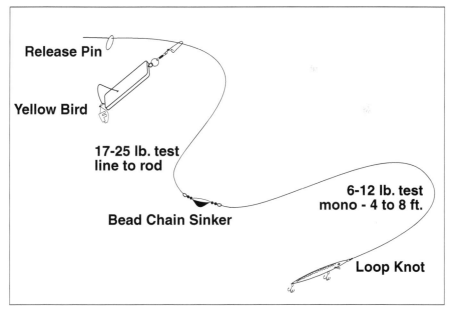

Here is typical rigging for a releasable inline planer board. Your main line comes down to a stop, in this case a bead chain sinker. Then you have a four to eight foot leader attached to your bait. Leader test is based on lure selection. The side planer in this illustration has been 'tripped' by a fish and is sliding down the line.

spoons, 8-17 lb. test is recommended. For fishing flies and dodgers, 17-20 lb. test is ideal.

For inline planer boards we recommend using at least 17 lb. test mono to handle the strain if the inline board cutting through the waves. The second major consideration for inlines is to have some form of stop so the planer board, when released, doesn't slide down and hit the fish on the nose. There are two ways to accomplish this, either with weights or with swivels, and much of this depends on what bait style you are going to fish with and what species you are going to target. (See diagram page 67)

For fishing early springtime, or anytime pulling dodgers & flies, weights are recommended. Two different style weights can be used, either bead chain sinkers that are tied into the line or rubber core sinkers that are added to the main line. Most anglers prefer bead chain sinkers, as rubber cores can sometimes fall off. Anytime the planer board hits the fish in the nose because the weight fell off is a recipe for losing the fish.

The leader running back from the sinker is generally a rod length or shorter. Leader test is determined by bait selection. If you are pulling crankbaits in calm, clear water you may want to reduce your leader down to 6-12 lb. test. If you are pulling 00 red dodgers/flashers you may want to use 20-40 lb. test to minimize spin offs.

Rigging a Wire Line Rod

Wire lines are generally used in two scenarios: either on Dipsies or with weights. Rigging a wire for a Dipsy is as simple as just tying the Dipsy to the end of the wire with a loop and overhand knot in the wire. If you want your wire line to perform double duty as a weight rig, then terminate your wire with a swivel and attach your Dipsy to the swivel.

A weight, or 'thumper' rig, can be used in a variety of applications, however the rigging for each is identical. The principle is basically a three-way rig. Now, I've never been a big proponent of allowing giant kings to drag one-pound balls and small brass three-way swivels around the Lake, so I use a 'three swivel rig.' As you can see in the diagram, one swivel is terminated at the end of the wire with a loop and overhand knot. Then we hang two swivels from that single swivel. To one swivel, we attach our leader and bait in the same way, as we would rig the trailings of a Dipsy. Many people also elect to use snubbers attached to that swivel, just the same as they would on the back of a Dipsy. On the other swivel, we attach our weight, usually 16 to 24 ounces, depending on the depth we are trying to achieve. Mostly used for presenting dodgers/flashers, the leader is 40 lb. test at a rod length.

Tackle Summary

At this point you should have a grasp of Great Lakes tackle and how to set it up. Although you may not yet understand how to apply these setups, knowing the baseline data will help you develop the application framework. In Chapter 4 we will pull the whole picture together to give you a complete understanding of Great Lakes salmon and trout rigging.

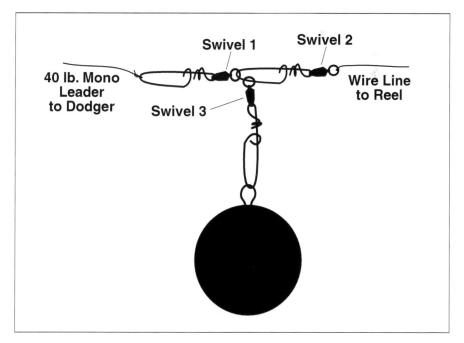

Captain Chip's 3-swivel wire line rig.

In Chapter 5 we will teach you how to apply tackle and delivery apparatus to a variety of seasonal fishing scenarios.

Electronics: Do You Really Need a Degree in Technology?

I confess, I am a data junkie. We do have a saying among us data junkies, "It's not the quantity of the information you receive, but the quality." In other words, hearing 100 times that the star quarterback for your team has six toes on each foot isn't as important as hearing it once from your best friend who happens to have the locker next to him. That's kind of the way it is with electronics. Electronics can be divided into three groups: the 'must have,' the cool and useful and finally, the gizmos.

Now, I have a tremendous friend, Captain Tim Dawidiuk, who I affectionately call, "the obsessive, compulsive, gizmo, gadget junkie." Tim probably knows more about boat set up, fishing accessories, and electronics than anyone I know. The reason is, he's bought all the stuff, tried it, and it saved me thousands! Rarely does something new come out on the market that Tim doesn't try. The great benefit for all of us is that Captain Tim is actually a stud fisherman and very practical in his ways (contrary to his buying habits). So through the mish mosh of the tangled wires that is our electronics jungle, Tim has helped enlighten us on the ever-changing world of fishing electronics. We should all give Captain Tim our praise and heartfelt thanks for his altruistic spending on our behalf.

Must Have Electronics

These are the electronics that will most directly lead you to fish. Let me introduce another Captain—Mike Smith. Mike is affectionately known around Northpoint Marina as, "The Mayor." Mike, who was chartering before many of us could spell the word, once told me, very early in my salmon fishing days, that the two most important pieces of electronics on his boat were his Loran and his surface temp gauge. He made this statement before the advent of GPS.

Upon questioning him about this, he explained that he could almost always find fish near a thermal break, hence the temp gauge. Once he found a school of fish, he wanted to mark the spot and work the school to produce more fish, hence the Loran. As I nodded in agreement and turned to walk away, I looked at The Mayor's boat and noticed that the depthfinder mounted in the cockpit had broken wires hanging from it making it inoperable. The moral to the story is that no matter how simple or sophisticated your electronic arsenal, you can use it to your advantage to locate and stay on biting fish. If you are short on electronics or lack sophisticated equipment, don't feel as though you are at an extreme disadvantage. My own co-author, the 'fly by the seat of your pants fisherman,' Captain Dan, is testimony to the fact that with some understanding of fish movement, environmental conditions, and application theory, nothing more than a decent graph is totally necessary.

Graphs

Call them what you want, graphs, fish locators, depth finders, sounders, etc., they all refer to the same gadget. A unit that emits a sonar signal and receives the echo and charts a picture of the bottom and anything in between the boat and the bottom. Volumes can and have been written on just that subject, including how to get increased performance from your graph with wiring, transducer location, blah, blah, blah. For the purpose of this discussion, we will simply refer to all of these as, "graphs."

A graph really performs five very vital functions:
1. It tells you your depth.
2. Illustrates bottom features.
3. Tells you if fish are present and their location in the water column.
4. Helps you locate schools of baitfish under power.
5. Tells you if fish are not present.

Learning to use your graph for finding schools of bait and gamefish is extremely important. We will address this very important issue in Chapter 5.

First, let's discuss sonar frequency. Frequencies are available all the way from 50 KHz on the low end to over 400 KHz on the high end. This is simply an expression of wavelength and unless you're Captain Tim, "just shut up because the definition is irrelevant." The basics of sonar frequencies are that lower frequencies are more suitable to deep water and higher frequencies, shallow water. The reason is that higher frequencies don't travel as far through water before they deteriorate. That being said, we generally don't fish over 700 feet of water and higher frequencies will read into the 300's. From here, we get into a long boring debate about wattage and whether we're measuring peak-to-peak or constant, more blah, blah, blah.

Here are the basic nuts and bolts of what you need to know. First, is cone angle. The sonar signal emanates from the transducer and shoots down in the form of a cone. The deeper the reading, the greater or larger the cone circumference of the sonar echo. Higher frequencies have narrower cones than lower frequencies. That means that lower frequencies

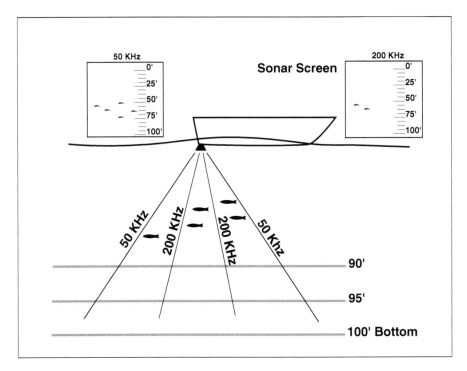

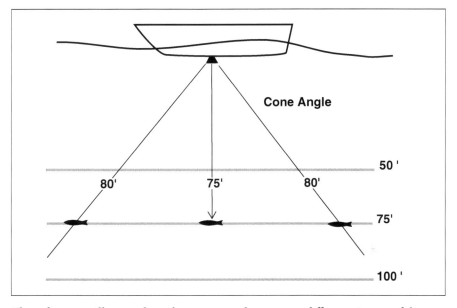

These diagrams illustrate how the two cones show us two different pictures of the same thing. First, understand that sonar marks the first thing it contacts and then measures how far from the transducer it contacted that item. It then relays this information to the graph and marks it on the screen. That means that although the 50 KHz cone shows us more fish underneath our boat because it scans more of the water, it is less accurate at showing us the depth of that fish because it is not measuring straight down, it is measuring distance from the transducer. For example, the graph may read a fish at 80 feet. With the wide cone we should not assume the fish is that deep. The reality is the fish may only be 75 feet down. If the fish referred to is on the outer edge of the cone angle, the sonar unit will read the linear distance between the transducer and the fish within the cone. The outer edge of the cone may be 80 linear feet from the transducer but in reality, the fish is 75 feet below the surface. A 50 KHz and a 200 KHz graph will each mark the bottom depth differently based on their cone angle. Remember that the sonar marks the first thing it contacts. This means that on a piece of structure that has an edge, the 50 KHz wide cone will tell you that you are just above that structure, when in fact, you may be quite a distance from it. The edge of your cone hits the top of that structure while your boat is still off of it, and your sonar marks that first ping of the structure as absolute bottom; therefore, you miss any detail deeper than that, which could be directly underneath your boat.

will show you more water underneath your boat, but higher frequencies will show you more accurately anything it displays (See diagram for explanations).

In general, most salmon anglers choose 50 KHz sonar's over higher frequencies, as they like to graph a broader range of water. When you consider all the open space Great Lakes anglers must search, that's an important aspect to consider. Ideally, a dual frequency unit, with 50 KHz and 200 KHz would allow us more accuracy.

Where you mount your transducer will also influence performance. You want to mount it in the 'cleanest' water available. Turbulence will minimize its effectiveness when running under power looking for bait. Ideally, mount the transducer in a through-hull fitting in an area that will remain underwater when motoring. If you mount the transducer on the transom, mount it where you have minimal prop and hull turbulence.

Speed and Temperature

I've lumped these two together because quite often they come in a combo unit. They can be found together in one unit or as part of a depthfinder. Speed is usually a paddlewheel that hangs off the transom or is built into a through hull or transom transducer. Temperature can be the same, a single probe attached to the transom below the waterline or as part of a transducer.

A speed paddlewheel is effective for two basic functions. The first is for duplication of presentation. That means, that I can reference my paddlewheel speed once I've started catching fish. Then I reference my direction, for instance SW, and I have a recipe for success. All I need to do is duplicate that paddlewheel speed on my southwest heading and I'm back to a productive troll. The downside to paddlewheels is that they are influenced highly by wind and waves. That means that if the wind kicks up on that SW troll, your previous speed-reading is worthless as the wind is going to affect the surface current and therefore impact your speed readout.

Temp probes measure the surface temp and at times can be absolutely the most important fish finding tool on your boat. Surface temp breaks, where the temperature changes radically over a short distance (this is a relative term that we'll discuss in more detail in Chapter 5), are key areas for fish to congregate. These temp breaks however, move around and without a good temp probe, one that reads in tenths of a degree, you will not be able to stay on the fish.

GPS (Global Positioning Systems)

How did I ever live or fish without one of these things? I'll be honest, thinking back to the days before LoranC (the predecessor to GPS), I wonder how I ever got back to port or stayed on a school of fish. Do you have to have one? No. Should you have one? Yes. Captain Dan likes to brag about how he's chartered for entire seasons without any GPS or LoranC. He claims it forces you to pay attention and builds character. Despite Dan's success, he would be the first to tell you to put a GPS on your boat!

GPS is simple. It's a device that receives multiple satellite signals from space, triangulates them, and determines your nearly exact position on God's great earth. The multitude of styles of units available is mind-boggling. All the way from the most basic hand-held unit storing a way-point and reading out digital Lat/Lon's, to Chartplotters which accept mapping cartridges and can show you detail all the way down to your slip in the marina and tell you how far you are from it and how long it will take you to get there based on your current speed.

GPS performs three critical functions for salmon and trout anglers:

1. Navigation.
2. Storing waypoints and hot spots.
3. Registering your speed and direction of movement over the bottom.

Navigating is everything from finding your way back to the harbor, returning to a hot school of fish, following a plot line, or showing you the path around dangerous obstacles. A plot line is a line generated on a screen called a plotter. It traces on the screen the path you have already taken, called a plot line.

Waypoints are points you either enter in manually in Lat/Lon form, or you enter in when you're exactly at the point you want to store. Let's say you just had a double on steelhead and want to be able to go back through the school. You would reach out and press a button on your GPS, usually marked 'quick store' or 'quick save,' and the GPS would mark the location on your plotter screen. All you have to do is pull up the reference number and your GPS will tell the heading and distance to return to the school of steelhead. This type of technology is the most precise way to return to the exact location where you caught fish. Sorry Dan, we all know you have an internal guidance system, but for most people, GPS is much easier!

GPS speed is the most precise way to reference your trolling speed. You can be in the right place, right time, right baits, right depths, but wrong speed and you won't catch fish. As you adjust your speed, you finally hit on what the fish want. How will you duplicate that speed? You must be able to accurately reference your speed. GPS allows you to reference and duplicate speed regardless of wind, waves or currents. GPS reads your speed in reference to the bottom of the Lake. It tells you how fast your boat is moving over the bottom. It also tells you in what direction your boat is moving or *slipping* over the bottom. GPS will help you identify when and how currents are impacting your trolling dynamic. We will explore the effects of currents in Chapter 5.

GPS units can perform dozens of other functions, including setting up routes to guide you on long cruises or interfacing with your autopilot to help steer the boat. The sky is really the limit when it comes to how much to spend on a GPS. As you look at all the different GPS functions available, ask yourself how many of those functions you will use?

Marine Radio

I remember the first day I arrived at my home marina with my 35-foot Viking. It was a 3-day journey through the Great Lakes from where I purchased the boat. I had traveled hundreds of miles alone in early April through frigid 9 to 12 foot seas, pounding and cursing the whole way home, sheets of ice everywhere on the boat. After showing off my new craft to all my Captain buddies on the dock, another Captain and I went for a spin. About 3 miles out on the lake, we decided to shut down the motors and listen for a mysterious noise.

Well, wouldn't ya know it, the old batteries that had been in the boat since I bought it, didn't have enough juice to start the big, twin 454 Crusader engines. They did have just enough juice to power the marine radio though, and soon three other Captains were on their way out to drop off some batteries for me to get going again. In true Coast Guard fashion, my buddy and I thought it would be funny if the other Captains arrived only to see us standing on the back deck wearing our Mae West's. Unfortunately, they had a camera, and well, that photo is out there somewhere, just waiting for the most inappropriate time to rear its ugly head.

Before you venture out on the Big Ponds, invest in a marine radio. Don't ever think that a cell phone will work, because many times they don't. If you get into trouble, your fellow boater will be your quickest response. The Great Lakes can get ugly fast: death has claimed more than one fisherman and a radio could save your life.

We recommend a fixed mount marine radio with an antenna over a hand held version. Hand held marine radios transmit on low power and have a limited range. This is done to conserve their battery life. Many anglers keep a hand-held radio on board as a back up.

A fixed mount radio is a relatively inexpensive item and easy to install. With a few screws, two power connections and screwing in the antenna wire in the back of the radio, you can rest assured that as long as you have power, someone, somewhere will be able to hear your call for distress. There are plenty of sources around to help you match the antenna and radio for your needs so further discussion isn't needed here. JUST GET ONE!

Autopilots

One of our Captain friends, Shawn Keulen, worked as a mate for many years before gaining his Captains license. On one of the boats, the

Captain would sit on the flybridge and drive the boat. The Captain was forced to stay on the bridge while Shawn ran all the rods and netted fish because the boat did not have an autopilot. This particular Captain also had a bad habit of watching the action on the back deck and not paying attention to his boat driving.

On one particular day, early in the spring when the coho were up high and Yellow Birds were hot, young Shawn learned just how important an autopilot really was. The action was fast and furious, Shawn was trying to keep up with the frantic coho bite when the Captain suddenly hollered down from the bridge, "Shawn, get the net, there's a bunch of Yellow Birds floating off the starboard side." Shawn looked off the starboard side, shook his head and hollered back to the Captain, "those are Yellow Birds!" Caught up in the excitement, the Captain had turned such a tight circle that he ran over an entire side of his own Yellow Birds!

The moral of the story is that with a good autopilot, situations like this should never occur. Dan and I are both very dependent upon our autopilots as neither of us runs with a mate. We let the auto drive the boat while we focus on other details. Autopilots come in a variety of makes and models. They are designed to steer boats based on the boat size and weight. It is quite easy to match the various brands to any size vessel.

Many of you may think that your boat is either too small or you will always have someone to drive. You think you don't need an autopilot. Well, driving the boat can be easy if you have someone that pays attention to the driving and the sea conditions are ideal. Driving the boat can be a pain for anyone if the seas are sloppy. Good autopilots simply master an otherwise tedious and sometimes stressful chore.

Many a friendship, and even a few marriages, could be saved by the addition of an autopilot. An autopilot keeps the boat going straight, minimizes tangles from unexpected turns and allows everyone to focus on the fish, lines and fellowship. Autopilots will help you catch more fish and more importantly, they will relieve a great deal of stress on any boat!

Having fished with and without them, I will never fish without an autopilot again.

Cool and Useful Stuff
Speed and Temperature at Depth
The first thing that comes to mind in the cool and useful category is speed and temp at depth monitors. There are a number of these available: Cannon Speed N Temp, Fish Hawk and Sub Troll. Although they use different resources to extrapolate and transmit the data, they all do the same thing. Use a paddlewheel and temp sensor on a probe that is attached to or near your downrigger weight to tell you the speed and temp at the depth of your downrigger ball.

Temperature at depth is vitally helpful. The reasons for this will be discussed later. Remember, finding the thermocline and cold water are keys to locating fish. The depth temp sensor can help you zero in on productive depth levels and it will help you catch more fish. The rigger temp sensor is the most precise way to monitor the water temperature at the depth your lures are running.

Speed at depth may be confusing to the uninitiated. In the most basic terms, each of the individual Great Lakes have currents. Notice that the word is plural, not singular. The reason currents is plural, is that there may be several current layers throughout the water column that you are fishing. The surface current is either a Corioles current, which is a clockwise rotation, or wind induced, which often overrides the Coriole's effect.

Below the surface there may be other currents, again plural, that travel in very different directions. We need to adjust our trolling speed to have our baits performing ideally based on the current in which they are traveling. As an example of this, if I am trolling into a current layer that is from 60 to 110 feet down, I need to travel much slower than I do if I am trolling with that same current in order to maintain productive bait actions. Bait action is the critical aspect here, not the speed at which the bait is traveling.

Speed at depth allows me to see a readout on my boat of what speed is being interpreted as being traveled at depth, based on my current surface speed. If I know the fish are responding well to dodgers presented at 2.4 knots at depth on a 180 degree heading, when I turn and go opposite on a 0 degree heading, I am going to use that 2.4 knots at depth as my starting point for speed. We will discuss this in more detail in Chapter 5, but at least you know now how this may benefit you.

Inexpensive Temperature at Depth Solutions

There are other devices that will measure temp for you that are much less expensive. They can be as simple as a cheap mercury thermometer that you clip to a downrigger weight, drop down, let it sit and retrieve. The most useful item I have seen in several years is a digital temp device that when lowered down and brought right back up, will give you a readout of the temp down to 10ths of a degree every 5 feet. This is the GMT 40. Many anglers claim this little device has made them a better fisherman.

One other great advantage to having this digital device is that it will tell you maximum depth achieved. For example, your downriggers have some blowback while trolling. Although your counter shows them at 85 feet, they do not really achieve that depth because of blowback. If you attach the digital readout device, and bring it back up, it will tell you that your downrigger ball is actually at 79 feet, or 81 feet, or 76 feet, depending on the circumstances.

This really is useful for determining the depth at which Dipsies or suspended wire lines are running. To do this let your Dipsy or wire line out to your intended target level. Allow it to settle down to achieve its stable depth at your trolling speed. Then attach the snap on the digital device around the line of the Dipsy or wire and let it slide down the line until you see the telltale bump in the rod tip that signals that it hit the Dipsy or lead ball. Then, bring the whole rig up and you now know the exact depth where your presentation was running based on the amount of line out at that trolling speed.

Radar

Strictly for the non-small boat crowd, radar can be extremely useful, especially in ports where there is significant boat traffic or fog. Being able to spot other boats in the vicinity, navigate through obstacles in low visibility, either fog or dark, and seeing approaching storms are all viable reasons to include radar in your electronics arsenal.

Most of the time, radar is used in applications where you are trying to avoid a collision with something. In periods of reduced visibility, or even in moderately clear weather, radar is extremely helpful. You can set the alarm on the radar to alert you when any object comes within a specified distance, usually set between one-quarter to one-half mile. Knowing when an obstacle looms that close allows you to make course adjustments to stay away from hazards, before you may even have visual contact with them.

That being said, radar is not flawless. I have had close calls with other boats in extreme fog when radar was in use on both boats. Don't ever get the false sense of security that radar will alert you to everything. Even with radar, it is still your duty as Captain of your vessel to maintain a vigilant watch for other craft or obstacles.

Foghorn/Hailer

It is required of all boats on the Great Lakes to have a sound-producing device aboard. I know that many small crafts possess the disposable air horns available at most boating outlets. The problem is that they are reluctant to use them, because that would mean replacement and more cost. However, if you plan on fishing in any inclement weather, I would advise carrying several of them so that you can signal other crafts in situations of reduced visibility to at least let them know that you are in the area. This is especially important for small craft, as the smaller the craft, the less likely it is to be picked up by radar. Letting another boat know you are there is the first key in collision avoidance.

Foghorn/Hailers are electronic devices that use a P.A. horn mounted on the boat, usually on the front somewhere. They automatically emit a specific sound at a specific interval. They look much like a marine radio with a mic attached to them, allowing you to communicate with another boat verbally. These are wonderful devices when used properly, to give regular warning sounds for other boats in the area, and do so automatically until turned off by the operator.

They are terrible units for some know it all knucklehead who wants to let the world know, in mostly profane language, that this is *his lake* and all the other boats should stay out of his way because he's trolling through. In all honesty, I do have a mental list of the people, who if I ever find their boat in the harbor, will have their microphone cords to their hailers clandestinely snipped off in the middle of the night, simply in the interest of maintaining some sort of civility on the lake.

Sidefinder

There are some graphs on the market that have the ability to scan out to the sides of the boat and let you know if there are fish there. They work quite differently than down looking sonar and have specific abilities and drawbacks. You will not be able to interpret the same depth of information from side finding units as down looking sonar, however, you may receive some incredibly valuable information.

Side finding is software controlled, so there is a computer algorithm that deciphers the size of the swim bladder that the sonar echo is bouncing off. This means that a sidefinder will not mark debris or small fish off to the side, but only fish over a certain predetermined size.

For all intents and purposes, sidefinder really has two major benefits. The first is that it will alert you to situations where there are fish near the surface, out to the side that you normally wouldn't consider being there. Salmon are famous for breaking all the rules and sometimes come into water temps where you wouldn't consider fishing for them. Steelhead especially, will cruise a wide range of water temps and without a side finding unit, they may go unnoticed and unfished.

The second benefit is the confidence factor. If for instance, you were going to set up in a good looking temp break and fish for steelhead, without side finding, you have no way of knowing if the fish are truly there or not (unless you see them visually, which is not uncommon). Let's say that you've fished in a slick for perhaps a half hour with no bites. Well, if you have sidefinding, you can determine if the fish are just not there by the lack of marks out to the side, or whether you have presentation problems because you are marking the fish, but can't get hit. It will help answer the age-old question of should I stay or should I go?

True Gizmos

The gizmo that tops the list is the Positive Ion Control emitter. Now you will find some top Captains around the Great Lakes who swear by these units, but personally, a well-grounded boat shouldn't have need of them.

Basically, every boat emits some form of electric current. This current can, and the operative word here is can, not will, can, carry excess current

The right boat set up, equipment and a little practice will help you catch more fish!

down through your downrigger cables and emit enough excess current to turn fish away.

Get out on the lake, put down your downriggers, attach one end of a voltmeter to a ground on the boat, and touch the other end to your downrigger cable. Experts tell us that anything less than .7 volts and you're in OK shape. If it's more than that, then you can either go through your boat, reground everything and look for current leaks, or you can add a positive ion control emitter and have the flexibility to adjust your voltage output. Cannon's electric downriggers come standard with positive ion control in them.

CHAPTER 3

Great Lakes Lure Selecton

How to enter a tackle store in the twenty-first century without losing your mind!

Picking the right lure is not a random process. It is part science, part art and part experience. Every time you place a lure in the water you need to filter a number of factors through your selection matrix. Target species? What lure group? What color? What size? Trolling speed? How far down will it run? What is the method of delivery; downrigger, side planer, Dipsy Diver lead core or wire line? Will it need an attractor? Sea conditions? Weather? Season? What is its compatibility factor with the other lures in the water?

If all this sounds complicated, let me illustrate lure selection another way. When you look at a football team what do you see? Are all the players the same shapes and sizes? Does the coach put 10 wide receivers and a center on the field at the same time? Or, does the coach insert a carefully crafted combination of players who fill a variety of functions with a common goal?

Lure selection is very similar to player selection for a football coach. A successful football coach manages a team made up of a variety of players that come in many shapes, sizes and qualifications. A fisherman is like a coach, managing a tackle box filled with an assortment of different types of lures. Lures come in a variety of shapes, sizes, colors and functions. Your job is to choose a combination of baits that, functioning as a team, will catch far more fish than a group of individual lures working independently. Just as a coach will understand his player's strengths and weaknesses, a fisherman needs to understand the qualities of the individual lures in the tackle box.

Variables Affecting Lure Selection
Target species
Lure group
Lure color
Bait size
Trolling speed
Target depth
Delivery method
Does it need an attractor?
Sea conditions
Local weather patterns
Season
Compatibility factor/group
Dynamic

Most anglers will troll with more than one lure at a time. For this reason lure selection needs to incorporate a team concept. Put a Heisman trophy fullback on the field by himself, and, while he may make some impressive runs, he won't win any games without his teammates on the field. Individual football players can't accomplish much on the field by themselves. Fishing lures are no different. As you place lures in the water, keep in mind that the lures are not alone down there. They are running in combination with the other baits in the water. If you just randomly select lures and place them in the water independently without consideration for the *group/trolling dynamic*, your time spent 'catching' will be greatly reduced.

So, let's approach lure selection with a team concept as our foundation. As you pick and choose individual lures, you are actually building a highly integrated pattern or *trolling dynamic*. The most consistently successful fishermen are the ones who choose lures with this 'team concept' in mind. Good lure selection leads you to craft a combination of lures that will play off each other and enhance their fish attracting tendencies. You are not running six individual baits; you are running a spread or group of lures. If all the baits are working in harmony, your chances of catching lots of fish will increase dramatically!

In this section we will categorize lures into three main groups: 1) spoons, 2) body baits and 3) flies, squids, dodgers and other attractors. We will highlight the attributes that distinguish the individual lure groups. Our goal in this chapter is to help you learn the differences between the major lure groups and give you some clues to help you determine when to reach for a spoon versus a crankbait. While our 'Hot Bait' lists are helpful guides, we think it is far more valuable for you to learn to read the water. If you can learn to read the water and factor in daily conditions then you will react appropriately to the ever-changing conditions of the Lakes and will choose the best combination of lures!

There is no magical formula that will lead you to choose the best lure all the time. Learning to pick the right lure for various scenarios is the result of hard work and experience. Creative thinking, a willingness to experiment and paying close attention to detail will help you build productive lure dynamics. For this reason we conclude this chapter with a discussion on how to integrate your lure selection into a complete, holistic pattern: *The group dynamic.*

Is lure selection important? While many variables influence a fishing trip, lure selection is one of the most critical aspects. Choosing lures is much more than walking into your local Wal-Mart and picking a handful of green spoons, two blue flies and a pair of orange crankbaits. Choosing lures involves reading the water, selecting the best bait for the job, placing it on the appropriate delivery device and then positioning it into a complete group dynamic.

Spoons

Spoons are one the easiest, idiot-proof lures to run. They can be incorporated into any position in your trolling dynamic, require minimal tuning and will catch fish all season long. They are easy to use in rough water and are less adversely affected by strong currents. Kings, steelhead, coho, lake and brown trout all readily strike spoons.

If you like choice, spoon manufacturers have not disappointed us in the past few years! Spoons come in just about every size, shape and color combination imaginable. They are all designed to display unique actions that will theoretically drive fish to commit suicide. Some spoons are very speed sensitive while other spoons maintain their action across a broad spectrum of speeds. Speed tolerant spoons are more forgiving and more productive over the course of the season. Spoons are a great mix and match bait. They can be used collectively with other spoons, mixed with crank baits or flies and dodgers.

We prefer to run spoons without a dodger or other attractor. This is referred to as "clean." There are occasional exceptions to this rule. I can remember an uncharacteristically slow August afternoon when one of my favorite clients was onboard. Just for kicks, I decided to put a silver with blue/pearl tape Mauler behind an O Luhr Jensen dodger on a fire line Dipsy Diver. This Dipsy hadn't been hit all afternoon. Was I ever shocked when I heard the drag start to sing as a nice steelhead hit the rig! As it turned out, that rig produced action for the remainder of the charter.

So, just *how* do you determine the right spoon for each situation? Trolling speed is one of the most critical aspects and often the defining factor in spoon selection. Every spoon has a speed range. Some individual spoons are more speed tolerant than others. In order to catch fish on spoons you not only need to place the right spoon in the water but you need to troll at the proper speed. A minute tenth of a knot difference in speed may make all the difference in the world.

Based on our experience we have found that the lighter and medium weight spoons tend to produce more salmon and trout than their heavier cousins. Heavier or thicker spoons such as Norwegians, Krocodiles and Pro Kings need to be run at higher speeds (2.5-3.2 knots). Thinner spoons such as Flutter spoons and Suttons will display their optimum action at slower speeds (1.5-2.1 knots). The medium weight spoons such as the Silver Streaks, Diamond Kings, Dream Weavers, Maulers, Stingers and Grizzlies are the most speed tolerant. Medium weight spoons, when used in conjunction with light line, will maintain fish catching qualities at all speeds (1.5-3.5 knots).

Spoon Techniques

Spoons can be incorporated into all locations within your trolling dynamic. Where you place a spoon in your trolling dynamic, however, will determine what spoon you reach for! As you gain experience you will find that not all spoons produce equally well in all locations. Some

Under tough conditions, big suspended lake trout will often strike a spoon on light line.

spoons are killers on a downrigger but they will choke on a Dipsy Diver. Line-up location is a critical factor in selection.

Let's look at downrigger and spoon techniques first. Before sending a spoon down on a downrigger you must first look at your line and swivel. When running a spoon on a rigger, use the lightest line possible. Spoons will achieve maximum action on light line! My standard spoon rod for charter fishing utilizes 12 lb. test line all season, even for big kings. It is a myth that you need heavy tackle and line to subdue trophy fish. You will catch far more big kings, steelhead and browns if you use light line on spoons! Occasionally we will drop down to 8 lb. test line on spoon rods if the water is super clear and calm.

Does line test really make a difference? If over 30 years of personal experience is not enough, let me make my point with an illustration from one of the times I won the Waukegan Salmon Classic Jackpot Tournament.

It was one of those typical early summer days on Lake Michigan, not a breath of wind and flat seas. We were on our way to a great looking box of fish but about mid morning, the action died. Nothing was getting hit. Even the spoon rods with 12 lb. test line were quiet. Before allowing Bill and Joe to hit the panic button I decided to try something different. I reached for an ultra-light rig with 8 lb. test line and sent it down off a downrigger with a clean spoon.

What happened next? Our last three fish were caught on this ultra-light rig. What is more amazing is that none of our other rods had a hit during that final period. Not only did we have the top weight for the tournament, we were the only boat to return with the 15 fish limit. If it wasn't for the 8 lb. test line, our victory may have been in jeopardy! Does light line make a difference when fishing with spoons? You bet!

What about swivels? Many anglers make the mistake of using a cheap swivel on an expensive spoon. A high quality ball bearing swivel will ensure that your spoon achieves maximum action, doesn't twist your line and 'comes home' when that trophy steelhead smacks the bait!

Swivel size is equally critical. As a general rule, use the smallest swivel possible. I have seen many an angler destroy the action of a good spoon by placing it on a swivel large enough to choke a horse. Why would you want to do this? We recommend using 20 or 30 lb. swivels for running spoons on downriggers in the Great Lakes.

Spoons are effective off corner, center and side riggers. Lead lengths for spoons off riggers will depend on a number of variables. So, let's begin with general guidelines. Spoon leads will be anywhere from 5-100 feet back. Most spoon bites off riggers, however, will occur from 10-40 behind the weight. When fish are below 80 feet in the water column, place the spoon 5-20 feet behind the downrigger weight. Conversely, if the fish are in the top 40 feet, spoons will usually need to be placed 20-50 feet behind the weight to attract strikes. There are exceptions, so experiment with lead lengths.

Spoons are very easy to run on Dipsy Divers. Clean spoons run off Dipsy Divers are dynamite for steelhead and brown trout. Your leader length off the Dipsy should be no longer than your rod length. I once watched an angler in a small boat battle a big king to the boat only to discover he had a problem. The angler, with the Dipsy at the rod tip, backed up as far as he could in the boat and the fish was still beyond the reach of the net handle! For this reason, spoons should be run no more than the rods length from the diver. I usually run the spoon six to eight feet behind the diver.

When using spoons on Dipsy Divers we recommend 20-30 lb. test leader line. Why not use the light line mentioned above? Two reasons. First, there is a tremendous amount of impact on the leader when a large fish slams a spoon/Dipsy Diver combo. If you try running 8-12 lb. test leader line, you will donate many spoons to the Lake. Secondly, a Dipsy Diver moves through the water with a great deal of action and creates turbulence in the water. The wild, jumping action of the diver imparts extra action to the spoon. Light line will not readily increase your spoons effectiveness in this situation.

Clean spoons work very well on inline and direct side planers as they track straight and clean. They are especially productive for surface oriented steelhead, brown trout and spring lake trout. Spoon leads off the side planers depend on target species, local conditions and fish temperament. We will discuss these details and how to incorporate spoons into a planer spread in Chapter 5.

No conversation about spoon fishing would be complete without talking about lead core lines. In some regions, lead cores are a major element in the trolling dynamic. Some fishermen rely on spoons and lead cores to catch the majority of their fish! In western Michigan anglers frequently run lead cores with clean spoons off side planers. A lead core will run deeper with a spoon than it will with a dodger/fly because a clean spoon has less drag.

Spoon Colors

As we said before, there is a huge selection of spoon varieties and colors available. Are some colors better than others? Yes, and it often depends on who you ask! Is there a magical formula that you can plug in to select the right color combinations? No! Choosing productive spoon colors is dependent primarily on fish temperament and local conditions. This requires you to read the water and experiment in light of past experience.

While some colors just seem to work year after year, the hot color of

Bill and Joe on another excellent adventure!

the day ultimately depends on what fish are willing to strike. From our vantage point above the waves we have to remember that the various spoon colors will look different in the water depending on how far down, sky and wave conditions, presentation method and any local influences that may tint the water.

How do we determine what colors to use? While Chip might say this is often the result of a deeper, internal feeling or "sixth sense," choosing the right color is often the combined result of experience, observation, experimentation and a dose of luck! Rather than theorize on spoon colors, we have included a side bar with our favorites. These are the spoons that have worked for many of our colleagues and us. One note: we are big fans of spoons that incorporate some silver or gold in their finish. In fact, many of the spoons listed in the "Top Ten" sidebars have silver backs.

Does spoon color make a difference? Absolutely! With over 20 years of charter experience I have seen many days where it was just a matter of finding the exact color combination fish wanted. Subtle differences in color can make the difference between a few fish and non-stop action. It may be a matter of changing to a spoon with a lime stripe rather than a bright green stripe. Or it may be a change from a glow stripe to no stripe. Spoon color is as important as spoon type.

Spoons and the Trolling Dynamic

Spoons are easy to use. Because of their clean tracking nature, they can be run exclusively with other spoons or in combination with other lure types. There are no rules as to the percentage of spoons to use versus other bait types. This is a variable that changes from day to day and requires you to react to conditions and choose the right baits. Choosing the right combination of spoons to flies and dodgers or body baits is critical to achieving maximum results.

As far as incorporating spoons into your trolling dynamic, you can run them on all delivery systems. On many days we will run a few spoons on downriggers and a few spoons on Dipsy Divers. The other riggers and Divers may have flies and dodgers.

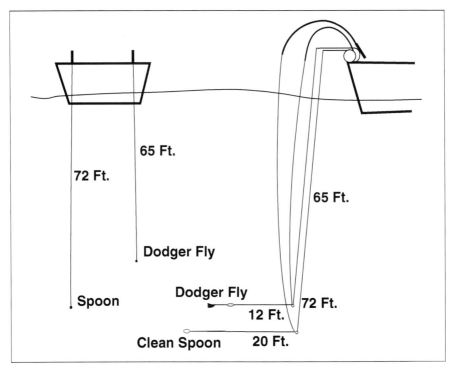

Integrating spoons and dodgers/flies into a group dynamic will lead you to some hot action. This simple pattern of placing a spoon just below and behind a dodger/fly is a favorite technique of Captain Dan Keating.

Similarly, when running a number of baits on side planers it is not uncommon to have an equal mix of spoons, body baits and flies and dodgers. When you hit on a productive combination, continue to duplicate your success! If one side of the boat is hot, duplicate the set-up combinations on the other side. Remember, all the lures are working together. Individual lures have two functions: first, they are to catch fish and secondly, they are to help pull and attract fish into your spread.

A simple, but deadly approach to mixing spoons and flies on downriggers is this: If you are using dodgers off the downriggers, try placing a clean spoon 5-10 feet behind the dodger set ups. Also, place the spoon 5-10 feet deeper in the water column than the dodger combo next to the spoon. Often, the dodgers will draw fish into your spread. Some fish may not strike the dodger but the clean spoon running a little deeper and behind the dodger will draw strikes!

If rough waves or a strong current are tangling your lines, try alternating clean spoons with dodgers and flies. By placing a clean spoon between the dodger rigs, you will greatly reduce tangles. This principle applies to downriggers, Dipsy Divers and side planers.

CRANKBAITS

What in the world is a crankbait? Is it a lure with a 'chip' on its shoulder? Or, is it a multi-dimensional lure group that really covers a multitude of categories? We could devote an entire chapter to crankbaits, as they are a fascinating topic! Without trying to give you a Ph.D. in crankbaitology, we will discuss the major differences within the crankbait family. We will look at crankbaits based on seasonal and species-specific applications.

For this discussion we will divide crankbaits into three categories:
1. Minnow imitators
2. Fat bodies
3. Lipless baits

The first two categories can be further divided into shallow and deep diving models. Before looking at these three individual groups, we need to define basic crankbait actions.

Basic Crankbait Actions

When choosing individual crankbaits, lure action should greatly influence your selection. Before you put a crank in the water, you need to ask yourself what type of crankbait action you want to show the fish. When you encounter fish, they may appear to be keyed on specific lures. The truth is they are usually keyed on a very specific bait action. When choosing crankbaits, let the fish tell you what crank-type to reach for.

The first general action is the roll, and we don't mean Danish. Straight minnow imitating plugs with a shallow lip feature one primary action, a roll. If you were to look at this bait either from the nose or the tail, as it is retrieved through the water, the bait would roll from one side to the other. This subtle action is usually associated with cold water situations or fish in neutral to negative feeding modes.

You can turn a subtle crankbait, like a rolling minnow imitator, into an aggressive crankbait by adding speed and erratic retrieve. The main action of the bait, however, is still a roll.

The second major action is a tail kick. Looking at the nose or tail of the bait as it moves through the water in a straight line, the tail of the bait kicks out to one side and then the other. The kick action is diminished at the nose of the bait because of the line attachment. The rate of tail kick is not uniform and can cover a spectrum of speeds and ranges. Some baits, like Cordell Spots or Rattle Traps have such an eccentric tail kick, they are known as tight vibrators.

> **Top Ten Great Lakes Spoons**
> 1. Green Dolphin Silver Streak
> 2. Old Yeller #5 Diamond King (silver/thin yellow edge)
> 3. Purple Stinger
> 4. Blue Dolphin Silver Streak
> 5. Silver Mauler w/green edge
> 6. Ludington Special Silver Streak
> 7. Orange Crush Mauler
> 8. Lemon Ice Dreamweaver
> 9. Sunrise Melon Grizzly
> 10. Hammered gold Mauler

With the exception of tight vibrators, cranks with tail kick are generally thought of as chase-down lures. These lures appeal to aggressive fish that are on the attack. Tight vibrators can fall into that category, but they can also elicit reaction strikes from less aggressive fish.

The third basic crankbait action is the wobble. This action is really a hybrid of roll and tail kick, but in and of itself, unique. Wobble is usually relegated to either deep bodied or fat bodied crankbaits. These cranks are generally associated with active, feeding fish, but they will draw occasional strikes from neutral fish.

The one mitigating factor in choosing a crankbait for trolling is speed. At some point, most crankbaits run out of speed. This means they lose their intended action and either begins rolling or sliding up on their sides. Tuning the bait properly or adding weight in front of the nose can neutralize some of this. Trolling speed is a primary consideration when choosing crankbaits. As a general rule, the larger the lip on the crankbait, the less speed it will tolerate.

Another consideration in choosing a crankbait is bait attitude. This refers to how horizontal the bait is when running through the water. For example, most shallow lipped minnow baits have a very horizontal attitude. If you outfitted the same bait with a deep lip it would acquire a nose down attitude. Generally, the nosed down bait will also have more tail kick than roll. The point is that fish can have a preference to the attitude of the bait. Frequently, a deep-lipped crank, run tight to the planer board, keeping it high in the water column, drastically outperformed the same shallow lipped bait and visa versa.

The size of a crankbait will also change not only the profile, but also the action of the bait. Therefore, the same crankbait in two different sizes does not necessarily have the same action. Lip size also impacts action. If you were to take a minnow imitator and replace the shallow lip with a deep diving lip, you would achieve two things. First, the attitude of the bait would be changed from horizontal with shallow lip, to nose down with the deep lip. Secondly, the action of the bait would move away from roll and into the tail kick.

Top Ten Great Lakes Crankbaits
1. Solid gold Fastrac
2. Black/silver Rebel Minnow
3. Bomber Long A, gold foil insert, black back, orange belly, black squiggles on sides
4. Orange/gold jointed Rapala
5. Silver/blue back/orange belly Rebel Fastrac
6. Bomber Long A, lime top clear sides, orange belly
7. Pearl #4 J-Plug
8. Silver #4 J-Plug
9. Orange/gold Fat Rap
10. Black/silver Shad Rap

Minnow Imitators

The definition of minnow imitators is simply a long, slender bait that is built in a tubular form. This category has hundreds of different brands, sizes and actions. Probably the three most common names in this category that you can relate to are the Rebel Minnow, Bomber Long A and Rapala Minnow. Over the years, millions of fish have succumbed to just these three baits! There are, however, many more baits and brands within this category that are applicable to Great Lakes salmon and trout fishing. Most shallow lipped minnow imitators are big in the roll property and offer very little to moderate tail kick.

Individual models of minnow imitators display a variety of actions. Through different shapes, (arched, straight, plump or skinny) subtle nuances in action can be achieved. Don't assume fish are not biting shallow lipped minnow baits just because you tried one brand and size. If the conditions are right and you believe there may be a minnow bait bite, run through some different brands and sizes and you might find the key to catching a bunch of fish!

Another general rule with minnow imitators is to go larger later. There is an escalating scale of size to crankbait choice throughout the Great Lakes season. Now this does not always hold true, as sometimes in very early spring a moderate to large crankbait can be just the ticket.

Learning to pick the right lure is critical when fishing for browns.

However, the increasing scale of size rule is a good guideline to lead you into the fall spawning migrations.

Fat Bodies
Fat bodies incorporate the wobble action that is so enticing at times to active fish. Typically, fat bodies are thought of as springtime and early summer baits. Generally fished in the 2¼-inch to 3½-inch sizes, seem to be exceptionally productive off flat lines and planer boards. The Cordell Big O, Bomber Fat A and Fat Rap are representative of this style

Lipless
Lipless lures encompass two major styles. Tight vibrating plugs like the Cordell Spot and cut plug imitators like the J-Plug. Other than their lipless heritage, these two baits have little in common.

Tight vibrators are best suited to fast trolling situations. Cut plugs do not tolerate speed well and do not mix well with high-speed baits. Cut plugs also exhibit a high degree of what we refer to as 'wander.' This means that they do not track in a straight line like tight vibrating or minnow baits. Cut plugs also have a tendency to run up and out to the sides and then return to their center position. Because of this wander, they can be frustrating to run in a tight downrigger/Dipsy set because of the probability of tangles.

Crankbait Philosophies
For years people swore by the old J-Plug as *the* bait to catch big salmon. Then, along came baits like the Rebel Fastrac and suddenly there was another top player in the salmon crankbait arena. Today, we have learned that cranks do have a time and place in our arsenal. When you encounter fish in the top 30 feet of the water column, they are susceptible to cranks.

Choose your cranks based on perceived fish attitude, water temperatures (colder usually means more roll, less tail kick) and the speed at which you intend to troll. Speed is a critical issue. You wouldn't want to fish a J-Plug in a set where you are pulling spoons at high speeds. Similarly, you may not want to run a Cordell Spot when you are crawling along with a full spread of dodgers. Flatlines, planer boards, lead core, Dipsies and downriggers all work with cranks, given the right circumstances.

Species wise, steelies love 'em all. Coho are definitely heavy on fat bodies and the tight vibrators. Lakers love cut plugs and fat bodies and brownies prefer minnow imitators. Kings prefer minnow imitators and cut plugs. Just remember that the things we have outlined here are only guidelines. In the world of fishing it seems like as soon as you make a rule, the fish break it. Crankbaits can be fascinating for catching fish. Develop an instinct of your own when it comes to choosing and using crankbaits and you will be a better fisherman for it.

Attractors: Do You Really Need Them?

When my Dad and I first started fishing on Lake Michigan back in 1972, we were under the popular misconception that before we put a lure in the water, we had to put some sort of attractor on the line. I remember putting fender-sized dodgers in front of J-Plugs and Schoolies in front of Flat Fish. My Dad and I often felt we just needed more hardware in the water! Was this a good idea? Some days it paid off, on other days? Well, that's another book.

If we want to be honest about the function of an attractor, we must first ask ourselves, "What is the purpose of an attractor?" Attractors are multi-dimensional. They affect more than just the trailing bait—They impact the entire trolling dynamic. Each individual attractor will impact every other lure in your entire lure spread or group dynamic.

Attractors impact the trolling dynamic in three ways:
1. They supply action to a lure such as a fly or squid, which have no action on their own.
2. They are a visual stimulant.
3. They "audibly" enhance (or detract) the "signature" your group dynamic puts off. Attractors give off sound vibrations that fish can sense or "feel" with their lateral line nervous system.

When properly used, attractors will enhance your overall fishing presentation. Attractors are deadly, but they don't work one hundred percent of the time. There is no prescribed formula for the percentage of lines that should have an attractor. In order to achieve the maximum results on any given day one must experiment to find the perfect combination of attractors and clean lines.

Attractors can be divided into two categories: direct attractors and indirect attractors. Direct attractors are those devices incorporated into the fishing line immediately ahead of a lure. They are intentionally used to attract and stimulate fish into striking a trailing lure. Most direct attractors will also function as an indirect attractor as they impact other lures in the group dynamic.

Indirect attractors are delivery devices that are not intentionally used to attract fish. The two dominant indirect attractors are downrigger weights and Dipsy Divers. The primary purpose of an indirect attractor is to deliver a bait to a specific location within the trolling dynamic. They have a secondary impact in that they do function as a sight, sound and action stimulant. Both types of attractors have a large impact on your group dynamic. Both give off a signature that can help or detract.

Direct Attractors

The three most popular direct attractors are dodgers or flashers, schoolies or six pacs, and cowbells. Of the three, dodgers and flashers are the most productive and commonly used attractors for salmon and trout fishing on the Great Lakes. Dodgers and flashers come in a variety of sizes ranging from super small kokanee flashers up to some saltwater versions that appear large enough to knock out a 10 lb. coho. The most popular sizes for Great Lakes angling are the OO and O sizes. These are 5 3/4 to 8 inches in length. We will take an in-depth look at fishing with flies, dodgers and flashers in the following section.

Six pacs are a collection of six metal "minnows" lined up in three pairs. Cowbells are a string of two to eight spinner blades. They come in a variety of sizes and were one of the original hot set-ups for lake trout.

These two attractors can be run off downriggers, Dipsy Divers, lead core and wire rigs.

Six pacs and cowbells are both visual and sound stimulants. However, they impart little if any additional action to the trailing lures. For this reason, only lures with their own independent action, such as spoons and plugs will work behind these two attractors. Anglers on the Great Lakes do not frequently use six pacs and cowbells today. In years past, both were popular tools in the arsenal of Great Lakes anglers.

Indirect Attractors

As mentioned earlier, downrigger weights and Dipsy Divers effectively function as sight and sound attractors. Visually, the fish can often see both downrigger weights and Dipsy Divers. The weights or divers going through the water often attract the fish's attention. Fish come over to investigate and find a snack close behind. Many anglers pay close attention to Dipsy colors and weight shapes and colors because of this fact.

Audibly, both downrigger weights and Dipsy Divers add their unique signature to the trolling dynamic. Both displace water, creating turbulence and give off vibrations that impact your trolling dynamic. Through their lateral line, fish can feel the disturbance of the weight or diver moving through the water. Depending on conditions, this may attract fish into a spread, or repulse them.

What many people fail to realize is that Dipsy Divers impart a tremendous amount of lure action. Dipsy Divers do not travel through the water in a straight line. In fact, they oscillate and jump around, imparting outstanding lure action to the trailing baits—even on a calm day! As your boat sways with the waves and makes turns, picture the diver erratically "jumping" up and down and side to side as it is pulled through the water. The additional lure action imparted to the trailing bait is often irresistible to fish! Many anglers ignore this critical, fish catching element.

On rough days downrigger weights will also impart additional action to lures. The closer the lure is to the weight, the more action supplied.

Learning how to mix attractors and clean spoons will lead you to tournament winning catches!

When you put a dodger or flasher behind a downrigger ball or Dipsy, you actually have a double attractor system.

Remember, many small tedious details will make the difference when using attractors. The most important thing is to be observant of what goes into the water and to fine-tune yourself to what is taking place beneath the surface and behind your boat. When incorporated properly, attractors will greatly enhance your trolling spread and increase your productivity.

DODGERS, FLASHERS AND FLIES: EVERYTHING YOU EVER WANTED TO KNOW AND MORE!

It has often been said that fishing is part luck, part science, part experience and part art. When it comes to successfully trolling dodgers (flashers) and flies, the artistic quality of the fisherman rises to the surface. Fishing dodgers and flies is truly an art! Consistently catching fish on dodgers and flies requires one to fine-tune their presentation to capture subtle nuances that often go undetected by mere mortals. For some anglers, this section may be the most important part of the book. For the balance of this section the term 'dodger' will signify both dodgers and flashers unless otherwise noted.

Most anglers are familiar with dodgers and flies. Many own an assortment of flies and dodgers and some even know how to use them with a fair amount of success. An even smaller percentage of anglers know how to use dodgers and flies to their fullest potential. Our goal in this section is to help you become a highly proficient dodger and fly angler.

Flies and dodgers can be run in just about any location in your trolling dynamic. They can be delivered off downriggers, Dipsy Divers, wire line, sinker drops, super line, flat lines, side planers and lead cores. Dodgers and flies are highly productive when mixed and matched with clean spoons and body baits. Yes, you can also run dodgers exclusively.

The "art" of being a great dodger and fly fisherman is multi-dimensional. Before we discuss the intricate dynamics of mixing and matching dodgers and flies in the trolling dynamic, we will first look at the selection process. Next, we will focus on the variables that dictate when, why and what. We will conclude this section with a comprehensive analysis of how to fish dodgers and flies!

Dodger and Flasher Fundamentals

Is there a difference between a dodger and a flasher? Yes. Can you use dodgers and flashers simultaneously? Yes, and both catch fish. There are a variety of individual brands available and each brand has a unique action that characterizes it from the rest. Personal preference, however, often dictates whether an angler reaches for a dodger or a flasher. Successful anglers will incorporate both into their trolling arsenal.

Dodgers and flashers have different properties that distinguish one from the other. The fundamental difference is the action of the attractor. Dodgers feature an erratic action with a side-to-side swishing or flipping action. When excessive speed is applied, dodgers will spin. Flashers are also known as rotators because they swing in a wide symmetric circle with little or no erratic action.

While dodgers are made out of metal, flashers are produced in both metal and plastic varieties. The plastic varieties are much lighter in weight. A typical dodger is flat with slight cupping angles at either end. Flashers come in a variety of shapes. Some are flat in the mid section with an angled bend at both ends. Some flashers, such as Spin Doctors and Becholds, are flat with fins. These brands have no bend in their bodies.

Not only does action vary between dodgers and flashers, but action also varies between brands. The general action of a dodger at slow to moderate speeds will be a side to side swishing with an occasional spin. At higher speeds and in strong currents the dodger will spin. Both actions will catch fish. The key to focus on is, what action is the dodger or flasher imparting on the fly? The side to side swishing will impart a different action to the trailing fly than a spinning action.

Many anglers believe flashers are more speed tolerant than dodgers, thinking that dodgers become less effective when they lose their wobble and start to spin. On some days, however, the fish will prefer a dodger that is spinning rather than wobbling. Dodgers and flashers will catch fish over a broad range of speeds from 1.5-3 knots.

To better understand the subtle differences between individual flasher and dodger brands, do a boat side experiment. Take individual dodgers and flashers and place them in the water. Watch their respective actions. Experiment with your trolling speed and watch what each one does as you slow down and speed up. As you change speeds, watch how the fly reacts to the various moves of the dodger and flasher. You will notice that slight alterations in speed will have a big impact on what the fly does in the water. Keep this mental image in your mind as you set lines over the balance of the day.

Choosing the Right Dodger or Flasher

Dodgers and flashers come in a variety of sizes from the super small four inch models used by kokanee anglers in the Rocky Mountain states up to salt water super flashers large enough to knock out a fish! Most Great Lakes anglers, however, will use dodgers in the 5-10 inch size.

The larger the dodger, the more action, sound vibration and sight stimulation produced.

During the spring months the 00 size (5 3/4 inches) is the most popular for fishing the top twenty feet. During the summer and fall months, or anytime the fish are deeper than 30 feet, the 0 size (8 inches) is the most productive. As the fish move deeper, light penetration becomes increasingly less. In effect, the deeper fish move the darker their environment. In the darker, deeper water anglers often need something "extra" to grab the fish's attention. The added sight and sound stimulant of the dodger is often just what is needed to tempt deep water fish into striking!

Today, a variety of dodgers and flashers are available. Metal dodgers and flashers are available from Luhr Jensen, OPTI Tackle, Action Flash and B & B Super Flashers to name a few. Plastic flashers are available from Hot Spots, Spin Doctors, Becholds and Luhr Jensen. Our personal preference for metal dodgers is the Luhr Jensen and OPTI dodger. Our favorite metal flasher is the Action Flash and our favorite plastic flasher is the Hot Spots and Spin Doctors. If fish are present and you feel a dodger bite is possible, experiment with various dodger and flasher brands until you start getting hit. Don't stick to one brand if things are slow.

Choosing the right dodger color depends on season, target species and water column target depth. For fishing from the surface to 20 feet down, red is our favorite color. For all other depths the silver, silver glow, white or pearl, yellow/yellow tape, yellow/silver tape, green, chartreuse, and blue/silver are popular. A general rule of thumb is that when fishing below 80 feet, white or silver tends to be the most productive. When targeting the 20-80 foot range, all colors can work. Dodger color is an area heavily dependent on daily conditions and fish temperament.

Fly Mechanics

Since we're trolling with a dodger, does fly selection really make a difference? A fly appears as just a flash of green or silver in the water, right? If you've spent any time fly fishing for stream trout, you know fly fishermen believe that minute differences in individual flies will make all the difference in the world whether a stream trout will take an offering or reject it. We believe that fly selection for trolling on the Great Lakes is equally critical!

Many people will look at a collection of ten different trolling flies and say they all look the same. To the average human eye, they may look *similar*; however, to Mr. Salmon there will be a world of difference to his palate! These differences may be in slight color alterations, the density of the fly or the dimensions in which the tinsel was cut. Various fly manufacturers will cut the tinsel they use at different widths. Our point, small or large, there is a difference.

While we could talk for days about fly selection, we will limit ourselves here. Season, target species, delivery system, water column target depth, sea/sky conditions and group dynamic heavily determine fly selection.

Great Lakes trolling flies come in three general sizes; the ½-1 inch peanut fly, the 1-2 inch models and finally the larger flies in the 3-4 inch range. Some anglers will use 4-6 inch flies for spring steelheads and summer lake trout. The majority of Great Lakes trolling flies are made

These are the three most common fly sizes used by Great Lakes anglers.

from mylar tinsel. Flies made from hair and similar materials are not as productive as tinsel. The exception to the rule is the super small peanut fly. Peanuts flies are equally productive in both tinsel and hair varieties (or a mix.)

Fly color is highly critical. General fly colors include green, blue, pearl, white, black, purple, red, yellow, silver and aqua. But within each color group you can find a variety of subtle differences and combinations. Take green for example, there are shades of green (crinkle green, flat green, metallic green, lime green, etc.) that may seem minor to us, but when viewed from the fish's angle under specific water and light conditions, the various shades of green will look different. On some days, these very subtle color shade nuances can make a huge difference. Pearl is another color that has a variety of shades within. Some are pure pearl, others have an iridescent or purple tint when put in the water and other pearls are closer to white.

When a fly is hot, look at it in the water. As you try to match the fly, look to see that the other flies look the same under the water. Look at color, size and density as the fly is snapped behind the dodger. Believe us when we say fish can detect the slightest variances. Choosing trolling flies can be as critical as matching the hatch on a Rocky Mountain trout stream.

One question we hear all the time is what about new flies versus old or "well worn" flies? Is there a difference? As a fly is used and catches fish, its character or nature will change. Take two identical flies, a green crinkle Howie for example. Take a new one, never used and lay it next to one that has caught 20 fish. You will see a noticeable difference between the two! Slight differences such as this can make a huge difference in the water! For this reason, savvy anglers don't throw "old" flies away—they save them and will use them to "match the hatch."

One final consideration for fly mechanics is beads. The larger 2-4 inch flies, such as Howies, are usually slipped onto the leader line. Ideally, you want the number one or number two treble hook to ride just beneath the tail end of the tinsel. To position the fly, anglers will use

Howie flies are one of the hottest lures on the Great Lakes. Basic rigging consists of running a 40 lb. mono leader through the fly body, adding 4 beads and then a number 2 treble hook.

beads. Three to four 6mm beads will ride immediately above the hook. The fly body rests on top of the beads, keeping the hook in the ideal strike position. Assortments of bead colors are available. Do bead colors make a difference? Yes. Chip and I favor green, yellow, black, glow, blue and white beads. Experiment with these colors and you will come up with some creative combinations.

Selecting the Right Fly

Now that we understand the mechanics of flies, how do you choose the right fly? Is it a blind game of chance, or is there something deeper that needs to be factored into the decision? Every time you put a fly in the water, four selection criteria should run through your selection matrix. These include fly size, color, construction material and density. The macro variables that impact our four section criteria include time of year, target species, target depth, sea/sky conditions and delivery system.

Seasonal variances are the easiest to deal with, as much depends on the month in which you are fishing. The smaller peanut flies are used during the spring months. The medium and large flies will catch fish spring, summer and fall. Our experience shows that the medium size flies work better during the spring and early summer. Mid summer through fall finds us using predominantly the two to four inch flies.

Color selection depends primarily on target species and target depth. Favorite fly colors for surface oriented fish include green, green/gold, green/silver, blue, blue/gold, blue/silver, purple, blue/green/gold and black/gold. For the mid ranges of the water column (40-80 feet) our favorite colors includes green, crinkle green, aqua, pearl/blue, aqua/green, green/white, powder blue and white. For fish deeper than 80 feet we prefer pearl, white, crinkle green and pearl/blue. There are many, many more color combinations. These are our favorite and most consistent color combinations.

What species of fish are you targeting? Kings love pearl/blue, aqua, pearl, white and crinkle green flies. Steelheads are fond of blues and pearls. Lake trout are suckers for greens, whites and yellows. Coho seem to favor greens. Browns like pearls, greens and yellow. These are general guidelines. As you gain experience with flies, take note of which colors catch which species. If one species is more prevalent on a given day, adapt your fly selection to the species available.

Water column target level is a major consideration in fly selection. Flies that work for surface oriented fish are not as productive 80 feet down. Peanut flies are great for coho and steelhead on the surface but catch few fish down deep. As you gain experience, make note of which flies produce fish at different water column depths. When you are targeting the various levels, use the flies that are known to catch fish at target levels.

Water clarity and sea conditions are silent factors that often determine which flies fish strike. Your flies and dodgers will show up or appear differently to the fish depending on how rough, clear or murky the water. Weather and sky conditions also impact fly selection. Different conditions will warrant using a different color and possibly size and density of fly. For example, a pearl/blue Howie fly may be red hot under a heavy overcast. Suddenly, the sun may come out and the pearl/blue shuts off and the crinkle green Howie starts producing. Pay attention to conditions and don't be afraid to experiment.

If we can revisit the banks of the stream let us offer another trick: "Match the hatch." Cut open a fish you catch (or look in his throat) and see what size alewives he is feeding on. If they are eating larger baits, go with the larger flies. If you have one rod popping fish consistently and want to match the other rods, look at the density of the fly on the hot rod. Is it a new fly or does it have a few miles under its belt? Little clues like this will pay big dividends.

Today, anglers can buy flies from a number of different manufacturers. Many anglers choose to make their own. Despite the tremendous variety between fly brands, many anglers think all flies are alike. With all the choices available, one has to ask, "Is there a difference? Should you buy one brand of fly over another?" Yes! Our favorite fly is the Howie Fly. We have been using Howies for ages and during the summer and fall months, no other fly will catch as many fish! This is the proven opinion of some of the best anglers across the Great Lakes region! When fish go deep, the Howie Fly really shines. For spring fishing our favorite fly for fishing the surface is the Cheddar Fly. When steelheads are on the surface, this fly catches more steelhead than any other fly!

Squids and Other Interesting Baits

Dodgers, flashers and attractors are nothing new to fishing. Although improvements and new designs have come and gone, one of the most critical aspects to using them is the trailing bait. While flies are the most popular entrees, squids and Yum tubes should not be ignored.

When salmon were first introduced to the Great Lakes, squids were all the rage. Today, flies have gained in popularity, as many anglers do not use squids. Do squids still work today? Yes, squids are still a productive bait and you should learn when to use a squid versus a fly. Smaller two-inch squids can be deadly on spring coho. Anglers targeting kings have used large glow squids for years.

If fish are not hitting flies, don't be afraid to try putting a few squids down in the water. Late one summer off North Point Marina we had big schools of mature kings staging in 180-250 feet of water. The problem was, these big kings were very deep in the water column and they were moody. One of my charter clients gave me a handful of glow squids he uses across the Lake. Wouldn't you know it, I put a squid out and we hooked a big king! The remainder of that summer, the glow squid was a solid producer for kings, and other species, in deep water.

Only through trial and error will you learn when to use squids to your advantage.

Yums are a recent newcomer to the Great Lakes trolling scene. Chip is a big fan of Yums. Yums are successful for two reasons—tube construction and scent. The tube is produced with ribs that give off vibrations. Secondly, the plastic is impregnated with an enzyme that stimulates the feeding sense in fish.

The key though to Yum success is in the rigging. The angle of the leader line through the solid head of the tube must be off center. To rig, take a hollow piece of plastic, (coffee stirrer straws) and push it through the head of the tube at an angle. Enter the head off center, and then exit the head inside the hollow cavity area of the tube, opposite the entry point. Now feed your leader line, the same as you'd use for flies, through the top of the tube and out through the hollow body cavity. String two 6mm beads onto the leader at the bottom to fill the hollow cavity of the tube so the hook hangs in the proper position in the tube tentacles, and tie on your hook.

A popular modification is to run a mylar fly like a Howie, over the top of the tube, using the tube as the body of the Howie fly instead of beads. When this is done, most fishermen pinch the tentacles off the tube so they don't tangle in the flowing mylar when fishing.

How to Run Dodgers and Flies

This is where science and instinct meet and become art. As we have seen above, there are a multitude of elements that influence the overall effectiveness of fishing with flies and dodgers. Where in the trolling dynamic do you place the set-up? How do you get the fly and dodger to the target level? What are the seas and weather like?

While these are all important, there is one variable that is easy to manipulate, but often ignored—fly leader length. Leader length may be the most important element in the entire scenario. Before we go any further, let me answer your question: How can a couple inches really make a difference? Remember, one of the functions of a dodger is to impart action to a fly. Simply put, a shorter fly lead will impart more 'snap, crackle and pop' to the fly. A longer lead will give it a more swishing or lazy action. If fish are super aggressive, a quicker snappy action may be needed. Dormant kings and lakers often are suckers for the lazy fly action of a long lead. Leader length determines fly action.

Arriving at productive leader lengths is the result of experimentation and observation. Each day is different. The mood of the fish will dictate how long your leads should be. Standard leads between the dodger and fly can vary between 9-37 inches. Dodger size plays a role in determining lead lengths. The smaller dodgers will require shorter leads of 9-18 inches while the larger dodgers are productive with leads of 15-37 inches.

A general rule of thumb is to begin the day with a variety of fly leader lengths. If you are using three rods with 0 size dodgers start with one short (16-19 inches), one medium (20-26 inches) and one long (27-37 inches). If one rod gets hit consistently, start changing the other lead lengths. If you

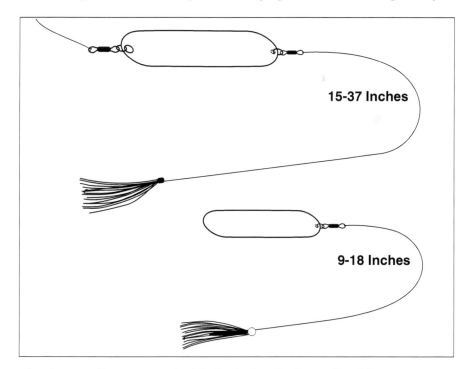

This diagram illustrates standard fly leader lengths for small and large dodgers/flashers.

are using smaller OO size dodgers, begin with a spread of lead lengths covering the 9-18 inch spectrum.

If anyone would know how important leader lengths are, it is Charter Captains. Because of their access to a wealth of daily fishing information from other Captains, a Charter Captain knows, first hand, the importance of leader length. If a Captain is not catching fish, but his friend is into a hot bite, an experienced Captain will always ask one question first: "How long are your leaders?" Don't underestimate the importance of leader lengths!

The next major factor impacting your success is the color combination of your flies and dodgers. Remember, salmon and trout can be temperamental. On most days you not only have to pick the right fly color but match it with the right dodger color. Flies and dodgers are a combination. Once you put them in the water, each set-up is a team. As you place a set-up into your trolling spread, try to visualize it as a "pearl fly/white dodger" rather than a pearl fly and a white dodger. This will help you keep track of what is drawing strikes.

Is this color combo jumbo really that important? YES! There will be days when the fish want a crinkle green fly behind a yellow dodger with silver prism tape. You can put the same crinkle green fly behind a yellow dodger with yellow tape and the fish won't look at it. It is a matter of picking the right fly color and combining it with the right dodger color. Anglers who can determine the proper combination of fly and dodger colors will catch more fish. Before changing a dodger color you may want to try several different fly colors behind the original dodger. If that doesn't draw strikes, then start changing the dodger brand or color.

How you deliver the fly/dodger combo into the water column is also part of the equation. As mentioned above, flies/dodgers can be deadly on most set-ups. Every time you go fishing you must determine which delivery set-ups will be the most productive with a fly and dodger combo. As you place the rigs into the water you have to keep in mind that the various delivery apparatuses will impart additional action to the dodgers.

First, lets look at Dipsy Divers. Dodgers on Dipsies (mono, super line or wire) will catch as many fish throughout the season as any set up on your boat! The reason is simple. As Dipsy Divers move through the water, they oscillate and jump around. As they move around, they are jerking and pulling that dodger up and down. It imparts a wild action to the dodger/fly that is hard to duplicate. Run the dodger four to eight feet behind the divers. On many days, dodgers behind Dipsies will out-fish all other set ups.

Dodgers and wire line go together like kids and McDonalds. They are a dynamite combination that result in many smiles! You can run the dodgers off wires with sinkers or wires with Dipsy Divers. Both types of wire line set-ups will impart additional action to the dodger. Dodgers will also catch fish when run off lead core lines.

Fly/dodger set ups are great on downriggers. Typical lead lengths off rigger weights fall in a range of 5-40 feet. The closer you run a dodger to the downrigger weight, the snappier and quicker the dodger action. The further back you place the dodger, the lazier and less snappy the action. A standard rule is to run dodgers tighter to the weight as you descend deeper in the water column.

> **Top Ten Spring Combos for Surface Lines**
> All dodgers/flashers in the 00 size
> 1. Red dodger/green-blue-gold fly
> 2. Red dodger/green-gold fly
> 3. Red dodger/blue-silver fly
> 4. Red dodger/aqua peanut fly
> 5. Red dodger/green two-tone peanut fly
> 6. Red dodger/blue-silver fly
> 7. Red dodger/blue-copper fly
> 8. Red dodger/green-silver fly
> 9. Red dodger/dark blue fly
> 10. Red dodger/purple fly

Determining downrigger lead lengths is often the result of trial and error. If your dodger/flies off Dipsy Divers are catching fish that tells you the fish may want a snappy, jumpy action. Try running your dodgers closer to the downrigger weight, say 5-12 feet. If the Dipsies are not producing, try lengthening your leads off the riggers back 15-30 feet. As you can see, there are a multiple of variables that will function as clues to help you zero in on the fish!

Sea and current conditions will also play a huge role in determining how you run dodgers. If seas are rough or you are fishing a strong sub surface current, you will have to pay close attention to lead lengths. Dodgers and flashers tend to "wander" more in the water than clean spoons. When two or more dodgers gather at the same point and time, a huge mess is likely!

Under adverse conditions you may have to experiment with lead lengths and you may have to reduce the number of dodgers in your trolling spread. Typically on rough days or in strong currents, you can't place downrigger dodgers right next to each other. For example, you may have to maintain at least 10 vertical feet and 10 horizontal feet between individual dodgers to prevent tangles in rough seas. You may find that by choking the dodger on the weight you reduce tangles, or by running every other one long, you eliminate tangles. By tweaking your lead lengths and depths you can often reduce tangles.

When running dodgers off downriggers you can put a dodger on every line or mix and match the dodgers with clean spoons and plugs. Captain Tim Dawidiuk of Sturgeon Bay, Wisconsin is an advocate of running all dodgers on downriggers and Dipsy Divers. Tim catches a ton of kings with this strategy. Other anglers, like Chip and I, prefer to run a mix of dodgers and clean spoons. Some days, the best mix might be 50 percent dodgers and 50 percent clean. On another day, a single dodger with two or three spoons will deliver maximum action. This is a daily factor that will change. Be flexible and experiment!

Dodgers and flashers can be used on inline and direct side planers. You will have to place a small weight ahead of many dodgers to keep them from surfing on the surface. For spring coho and steelhead it is hard to beat a 00 red dodger or flasher on the surface. Lead lengths are a matter of fish moods however; the standard distance off side planers is 8-30 feet. For surface oriented fish you can also run dodgers off mono flat lines. Running dodgers on the surface is examined in detail in Chapter 5.

Vertical and horizontal distances between fly and dodger combos and other lures are also a huge factor. There is no formula of inter-spatial distances that works every day. Daily fish temperaments, sea conditions, currents and lure mix determine inter-dynamic lead lengths. Lead lengths within the dynamic are a factor that is fine-tuned through experimentation and observation. Some days fish will want lures clustered together. Other days baits will need to be spread out or minimized.

No discussion of fly/dodger mechanics would be complete without mentioning the need for high quality ball bearing swivels. Remember what a dodger is doing under the water—it is spinning or rotating, sometimes madly out of control! If you don't have a high quality ball bearing swivel on the nose of your downrigger dodgers, you will spin your dodger off the line. A high quality ball bearing swivel is a must.

Just how important is trolling speed to dodger fishing? Does a dodger only work if it is swishing gently? Or will a dodger really catch fish if it is spinning along at 2.7 knots? Believe it or not, dodgers will catch fish over a much broader spectrum of speeds than most people realize. While side-to-side swishing may be the "ideal" action, it may not be the most productive action.

Trolling speed is super critical for flies, dodgers and flashers. On any

The author's Dad, Tom Keating, with a Great Lakes steelhead.

given day the fish will aggressively hit at only one speed! You better determine that speed if you want to catch fish. All we can say about speed is, "Pay attention and experiment." You can have the right color fly, with the proper fly leader, on the right color and type dodger on the right lead length and delivery device but if you are trolling too *fast* or too *slow*, all the other variables you worked so hard to isolate will be moot.

As you can see, fishing with dodgers and flies is much more involved than throwing your baits in the water. It requires a great deal of concentration and a willingness to experiment. Those who are willing to continually tweak and modify their trolling dynamic achieve success.

Dodgers, flashers and flies are some of the most productive lures to use for Great Lakes kings, coho, steelhead, lake and brown trout. On many days they will out-produce all other lures. Mix them into a trolling dynamic with spoons and you will find that your spoons become much more productive. If you take the time to learn how to properly run dodgers and flies, you will become a far more versatile angler. You will also catch more fish!

Top Ten Dodger/Fly Combos for Mid and Deep Levels
(Dodger or Flasher in the 0 size)
1. White dodger/green crinkle fly
2. White dodger/white fly
3. Yellow dodger/green crinkle fly
4. Smoke (silver glow) dodger/aqua-green fly
5. Silver dodger/green fly
6. Yellow dodger/aqua fly
7. White dodger/pearl blue fly
8. White dodger/pearl fly
9. Silver dodger/white fly
10. Smoke dodger/pearl blue fly

THE GROUP DYNAMIC: HOW TO BUILD AN IRRESISTIBLE LURE SPREAD

The Philosophy and Mechanics of The Group Dynamic

Every time you go fishing you will encounter a number of choices, many of them concerning what lures to run. We would like you to think about your philosophy of lure selection before you even choose your first lure. We're talking about whether your philosophy is one of a cohesive spread, or whether you just want to put a bunch of lures in the water. Sure, you can choose individual lures and place each one in the water and run each lure independently of the other lures. Or, you can consider the spread's *group dynamic*. Within the group dynamic, you choose individual lures and insert them into the collective trolling spread. Each individual lure functions in relation to the other lures beneath/behind your boat. The individual parts, when working together, form a complete group dynamic as they are working together toward a common goal—to attract and hook maximum numbers of fish!

To build a group dynamic, you must realign your focus and vision: To think collectively. You are not running a corner downrigger, a mono Dipsy Diver, or a port side planer. You are running a complete spread of baits, made up of multiple parts, moving through designated layers of the water column. You need to visualize what the spread looks like under the surface. For example, as you put a lure out behind a Dipsy, you should visualize how that Dipsy Diver and lure will impact the other lures within the group dynamic. Remember, a complete picture makes a greater impact than a fragment.

Let's go back to the beginning. Individual lure selection is based on a number of variables including target species, season, micro-weather, sea conditions, target depth, trolling speed, boat size, lure group, lure color, attractor and delivery method. The twelfth element in lure selection is integration. How will this lure work with other baits and delivery apparatuses?

Within this mind-set every lure change impacts the entire dynamic beneath the surface. Individual lures are not running in a vacuum. Therefore, your philosophy of lure selection should build upon a team concept. Let's return to the football field. Teams that win games use a combination of linemen, quarterbacks, running backs, receivers, defensive backs and kickers. If a team is weak in any one of these areas it may cost them the game.

A fisherman is like a coach. A successful angler knows how to choose and run a variety of lures. He/she is multi-dimensional and understands the subtle differences in how to mix and match lures. Yes, there will be days where you run all spoons or all flies and dodgers. On many days, however, you will run a combination of spoons, flies and body baits.

Can you run spoons with plugs? Can clean spoons be used with a group of dodgers? How do you mix and match lures to achieve maximum results? All three-lure groups can be mixed and matched together. Lines with dodgers or attractors can be mixed with clean lines. The key is to place the right combination of lures in the water to trigger the most strikes possible. This is an unknown variable that will require daily experimentation. As you spend time on the water you will notice that certain spoons work very well with flies and dodgers. Some body baits work well with spoons.

The key to building a productive group dynamic is to continually

Captain Dan with Rebecca and Ethan Daniel, two of his favorite fishing partners.

visualize what all the lures look like together from the fish's perspective. To do this you have to think three dimensionally. You will need to view the strike zone both vertically and horizontally. For example, on the vertical plain you may be running lures between 30 and 70 feet down. Horizontally, you are covering an area 50 feet across with Dipsy Divers. If you are fishing the surface layer you may be covering a horizontal layer that is several hundred feet wide. As you move lures around in the target zone you will have to keep the larger picture in mind: The vertical and horizontal strike zone.

Another factor determining the inter-spatial distance within the dynamic is how broad is the strike zone? Are you targeting a single species in a narrow band of the water column? Or, are you targeting multiple species over a broad cross section of the water column? For example, in some locations you may be targeting fish on the surface and fish 50 feet down, simultaneously.

Fish temperament will also determine the inter-spatial parameters of the group dynamic. Some days the fish will want the lures tightly packed into a narrow window. Other days, you will need to spread your offerings out or actually reduce the number of lines in the strike zone to draw strikes. As we unpack a typical fishing season in Chapter 5, we will discuss the inter-dynamic factor as it applies to individual situations.

The implication that follows three-dimensional thinking is that every lure and trolling device you place in the water affects every other lure and trolling device already in the water. As you set a downrigger with a dodger and fly, ask yourself how this will affect the other downrigger lines and Dipsy Divers. Often, an attractor on a corner downrigger may be attracting and pulling fish into your spread. The fish may be striking a clean spoon on a different rod. If you pull the dodger off the corner rigger and put another clean spoon out, you may stop getting strikes on the corner spoon on the opposite corner. Why? The dodger was attracting fish to your group dynamic but a clean spoon was triggering the fish's strike mechanism.

Dodgers and flashers are the linemen of the trolling dynamic. On many days they will do most of the work attracting fish. The dodgers will excite the fish and draw them into your lure spread. Once the fish are drawn into your dynamic, they may hit the fly behind the dodger. Some fish, however, will not strike the flies. These fish, which were excited by the dodgers, may strike a clean spoon or crankbait within the group dynamic. The group dynamic is a team effort.

On the flip side, maybe too many dodgers in the water are spooking fish. In this scenario you may begin the day with dodgers on half your lines. As you pull dodgers you may start to have more action. Is it possible that too many dodgers were chasing fish away?

Just as you have to pay close attention to the lures you put in the water, remember what you take out of the water. Whether you are aware of it or not, individual lures serve a dual function. Every lure you put in the water is intended to catch fish but, simultaneously, each individual bait and delivery system is impacting the surrounding group dynamic. Individual lures may impact the trolling dynamic by attracting fish into the lure spread or they may scare fish away. If you change a lure and this shuts down the other rods, ask yourself if the previous lure (or attractor) was pulling fish into your lure pattern. A set up that is attracting fish into your group dynamic and triggering strikes on other rods may be as valuable as the line drawing the strike. Remember, Walter Payton didn't gain all those yards without the linemen leading the charge.

Every time you troll for salmon and trout your goal should be to catch fish on every line. If you are running seven lines and only one or two of them are producing strikes is it because the other lines have the wrong lure? Are the other lines set at the wrong depth? Or, are the hot rods catching fish because one or more of the 'dead' baits are pulling fish into the group dynamic? If the dead rods are not contributing to the effectiveness of the group dynamic, then you should work on changing their baits, color combinations, lead lengths or depths. If you are using seven lines and one rod has eight strikes and the others none, you may catch eight fish. If you are using seven lines and each line has three strikes, you may catch 21 fish! I think you get the picture.

If you remember only one thing from this chapter, remember this—it is the lure combinations (group dynamic) that often trigger strikes, not just the individual lure being hit. Knowing when to change baits and when to leave the 'old reliable' in the water is as important as choosing lures. Some anglers will spend so much time changing lures that by the time they find active fish, they will have 'junk' on their lines that is more appealing to trinket collectors than to feeding salmon and trout. Top anglers around the Great Lakes know how to weave a combination of lures, attractors and delivery devices into a complete and effective group dynamic.

The next time you go fishing, focus on the three-dimensional group dynamic. You are not just running a green spoon 45 feet down. A white dodger/pearl fly 70 feet down. A Dipsy Diver with a yellow dodger and aqua fly at 55 feet. Think collectively! You are running a highly visible group of lures that are intentionally working together to cover a specific cross section of the water column. You'll never go fishing the same way again!

A well-crafted group dynamic will result in catches like this!

CHAPTER 4

Down And Out on The Great Lakes

Reaching the strike zone!

One of the biggest misnomers in fishing is that we need only deliver the right bait, in the right size and color, to the right depth, at the right speed, and we'll catch loads of fish. Believe me, having all those properties in your favor is a wonderful thing, but woefully incomplete. At times how we deliver the baits to the strike zone is of paramount importance to all other aspects. For Great Lakes salmon and trout fishing, *how we reach the strike zone* (delivery apparatus) is a very important component in the fish catching equation.

How you deliver lures to the strike zone makes a difference! Believe it or not, your lure's action and the *trolling dynamic* are greatly impacted by the method of deployment. For example, if you drop a dodger and fly down 55 feet, it will have a very different *look* and action, from the fish's perspective, based on whether you are running it on a downrigger, a Dipsy Diver, wire line or a lead core.

Rigging and delivery apparatus technique are the subject of this chapter. If you understand how to deploy your tackle, you will not only catch more fish, but you will greatly reduce stress. Most Great Lakes anglers will use a combination of delivery apparatuses including downriggers, side planers, Dipsy Divers, wire line, super line, lead core and flat lines to present baits to the fish. On any given day you may use a few of these elements or all of them in combination. As you gain experience, you will learn when to reach for a super line Dipsy Diver versus a wire line rig.

Before diving into the nuts and bolts of rigging and application, we need to first lay a foundation. This baseline data consists of theoretical concepts and definitions that will tie all the various delivery tools and strategies together to meld a complete picture of our objective—presenting a complete, irresistible, fish catching *trolling dynamic*.

Principle 1
All lures, delivery devices and equipment work off each other. None is independent. This is the basic principle of the trolling dynamic and you should have received a good dose of this from Chapter 2 and 3.

Principle 2
Great Lakes trolling is commonly referred to as controlled depth fishing. Simply put, the angler determines the target depth at which he/she wants to place their bait. That depth may be one foot under the surface or it could be hundreds of feet down. Having your lures in the strike zone is critical, but before the first strike you must ask yourself, "How am I going to get my bait to the position and depth I am targeting?" Today, anglers have a variety of different delivery devices to use to reach the strike zone. You have to choose which device or technique is best for every situation. At times this is of paramount importance to all other factors.

Let's look at the evidence. Have you ever been on the Lake when all the fish want are baits presented behind Dipsies and they won't touch the identical offering behind a rigger? To top that scenario, then the Dipsies absolutely die, but the riggers are now hotter than ten-cent pistols. The moral to the story is that our presentation apparatus is highly important and each one has a time and place where it shines above the others.

Principle 3
Patternistic (Just made that word up, and kinda like it!) thinking is where our head needs to be. Trolling patterns within our set, like V's and inverted W's have a method to the madness. Theoretically, trolling in a V pattern would feature a deep-set with your corner riggers and a shallow set with your boom riggers. On a vertical plane, this creates a V pattern underneath the boat. Some of what we do with patternistic thinking is for fish catching and some for maintaining order and avoiding nightmarisitc (I'm getting good at inventing words, this could get ugly!) tangles. In Chapter 4, we will tell you how to get your baits down and out to the strike zone. In Chapter 5, we will explain the philosophy behind "patternistic" fishing.

To get us all on the same page, let's begin by first understanding some basic terminology.

Terminology
Stretch: The distance behind a delivery apparatus that a bait will run. For example, a 20-foot stretch behind a downrigger means that 20 feet of line is separating the bait from the downrigger weight.

Signature: The amount or lack of turbulence, vibration, or other intrusive elements that a particular delivery device emits when trolled. Lines vibrate and sometimes audibly hum, when trolled, and this would be part of their signature in the water. The total signature would include any disturbance or emittence from the delivery device, i.e. downrigger ball or Dipsy, along with the actual signature of the bait itself.

Blowback: The distance behind the boat that a downrigger weight is taken rearward by the force of forward trolling motion. Downrigger cables and balls have resistance in the water therefore they don't hang straight down, they are blown backwards. The amount of blowback is dictated by speed, trolling depth and currents.

Shallow, Mid and Deep levels: Shallow is surface to 30 feet, mid level is 30 to 70 feet, and deep is beyond 70 feet.

Warm-Cool-Cold: Warm is 60 degrees and above, cool is 48-59 degrees and cold is any temp below 48 degrees.

With these basics under our belt, we're now ready to tackle the implementation of tackle. Just remember, every change makes a difference, sometimes minute, sometimes gigantic, sometimes preferable, sometimes not. So, thus changing things around is a good thing, and other times, changing things back is better.

Fishing with Downriggers

When it comes to controlled depth fishing, downriggers are the most popular presentation device on the Great Lakes. They offer us the most precise way to control bait delivery and to most people, that is very comforting. The reality of the human condition is that we like to have answers and be in control of variables. It is sometimes tough to answer how deep a suspended wire line is running, or how far off to the side a Dipsy presentation is carrying our baits. Downriggers, however, give us these data streams and allow us the greatest perceived precision.

A downrigger is really a very simple device. It is made up of three major components: a reel or spool, cable, and a weight with a line release attached. Beyond the basics, riggers come as simple or complex and sophisticated as you want. On the simple end, Dan remembers one of his first saltwater fishing experiences. He and his Dad took a charter off Ft. Lauderdale, Florida. The Captain took the head off a 15-pound king mackerel, stuck it on a hook and threw the line in the water. Next, the Captain attached the fishing line into a clothespin attached to a 20 pound piece of concrete. The Captain then threw the entire assembly into the water, let out a bunch of line, and hooked the line to a cleat. That block of concrete and mackerel head wasn't in the water very long. A 150-pound shark couldn't let it pass!

Now that Dan has enlightened us on the primitive side of downrig-

Downriggers are the most popular delivery device used by Great Lakes anglers for controlled depth fishing. Downriggers allow you to use light line and tackle to catch trophy fish, such as this 17 lb. steelhead, at pre-determined depths—without any weight on the line.

gers, let's move on. To start simple, there are the Riveara manuals. These are made from a metal spool, some pipe and some pulleys. On the other end of the spectrum are the Cannon Digitroll IV and Mag 20 DT's. These can read the bottom and automatically adjust downrigger depth, along with dozens of other high tech features. The net result is that they both carry a weight with release to a specific depth and maintain it there. The critical aspects of downriggers, outside of the proper placement of them on your craft, (see Chapter 2) are the components that make them work. A number of manufacturers make downriggers including Big John, Penn, Vector and Cannon to name a few.

Downrigger Weights

It is a simple fact that the heavier the downrigger weight, the more vertical it will be in the water and the less likely it is to tangle. This is a principle we call blowback. Simply put, blowback is how far behind the boat an object goes while being dragged in the water. Sitting still, lower a 10 lb. weight and it sits vertically, directly beneath the boat. Once you start moving, as you would in trolling, water resistance comes into play and the effect can be tremendous. Simple water resistance can cause the 10 lb. lead weight to drag back so far behind the boat, it rises 10 feet or more from the depth that the counter reads on the downrigger. This is blowback, the distance rearward that something is pushed based on water resistance from trolling.

Because of blowback, fishing deep (over 70 feet) with anything less than 10 lb. weights is asking for trouble (tangles) in many cases. Most fishermen opt for 10 to 12 lb. weights. If your arms or downriggers can handle it, heavier weights are better. We bring this up because not all electric downriggers (or arms) can easily handle heavy weights. If you plan on fishing heavy weights and are considering purchasing electric downriggers, check with the manufacturer to find out the maximum weight guideline for the particular riggers you are buying.

Another consideration regarding weights is the brand and style of weight. Weights come in a variety of styles, and much is personal preference with the exception of one. Pancake weights have an adjustable fin on the back that will help it track out to the side away from the boat. This gives us the advantage of a wider presentation swath through the water, along with preventing tangles. We highly recommend them for boom riggers. For corner and boom riggers, we recommend weights that are round (ball shaped) with a small tracking fin.

Anglers across the Great Lakes have debated the merits of colored weights versus unpainted, rubber coated weights versus uncoated weights—is there a difference? We feel that the greatest difference is not in downrigger performance but in the mind of the angler setting the downrigger. Now, there are some great fishermen who will argue weight color does make a difference. Based on our experience, however, we do not perceive any added fish catching attributes to the color of the weights. If you find that a painted weight works better for you, then by all means, continue to duplicate that element of your trolling dynamic.

An overlooked aspect, although less critical, is the brand. Lead is not uniform. Weights made from virgin lead, like Cannon Flash weights, instead of recycled lead; can be 40% smaller in size, for the same weight size. The reduced weight size features less surface area, resulting in less blowback due to water resistance. For an angler using a weaker motor on an electric, or a manual downrigger, this means they can use less weight to achieve a more vertical presentation than the angler buying weights made of recycled lead.

Releases

You can purchase the most expensive, technologically advanced downrigger on the market, but if your downrigger release fails to operate properly—your rigger system will break down. The downrigger release you choose is as important a component in your rigger system as the rigger itself. In the simplest terms, a release attaches your fishing line to the weight and holds the line until sufficient pressure is applied to the release. Once pressure is applied, the line is released from the bonding point. Pretty simple, right?

Now that we understand the 'function' of a downrigger release, let's address several key factors to help you choose an appropriate release. The first and most obvious criteria is that it needs to effectively release the line with a predetermined amount of pressure every time and flawlessly. Release tension should be adjustable because you will fish under a variety of conditions for fish of different sizes. If it is rough, you may want to set your release tighter so waves don't continuously trip the rigger. If small fish are present, you may want less tension on the release. When fishing deep, you will want to tighten a release because of the increased pressure exerted on the line and release. If fish are striking, but not hooking up, you may want to tighten your release. Adjustable release tension is critical and it will help you to catch more fish rather than talk about all the bites you missed!

The next release consideration is that it is non-damaging to the line. You may consider this silly, but there truly are releases out there that are hard on your line, and over time, they'll cause a break-off. This is very important, especially when using light line! The third factor, resilient or fixed, is where the proverbial can of worms opens up. The terms, resilient or fixed, imply movement or lack of for the release. A fixed release is a release that holds the line in a single position and allows no movement of any kind until the release disengages. A resilient release allows movement at the attachment point of the line (see photo below). This movement allows us the opportunity to interpret data that is happening at the depth of the release. For example, with a resilient release, you can see the action of the dodger on your rod tip because the bouncing of the dodger is not diminished by the release being fixed. You will also be able to see soft bites and small (shaker) fish if they are hanging on.

One of the most ubiquitous releases used on the Great Lakes today, and terrific as a resilient style, is the simple rubber band release. Size 12 rubber bands are the recommended ideal, although sizes 14 and 16 will work also. Rubber bands are also adjustable for release tension. In order to increase tension, just use two or three rubber bands together, as would be needed when fishing deep with big dodgers or in a strong current.

To use the rubber band release, simply take the rubber band, do two or three loops (half-hitches) around the fishing line. Pull the band tight

The release here, a Cannon Uni-Release, is a pinch pad release that is held to the downrigger ball by a cable tether. This tether allows the attachment point of the line to move without releasing the line, therefore creating a resilient style release. Resilient style release's come in many shapes, styles and sizes, from the sophisticated to the simple rubber band release.

(there should be no slippage, if the line slips, do another loop) and either place the band into a clip style release, such as a Black's, or loop the rubber band over the weight and allow it to settle under the lip of the clip holding the downrigger weight to the cable.

Stackers and Sliders

Stacking is the simple principle of running more than one line off a single downrigger. For anglers with only two downriggers, this technique allows two additional rigger lines to be deployed. Stacking is accomplished with a specialized stacker release. (See diagram page 134)

A stacker is quite simple to use. To illustrate, let's say that you wish to run your main line (the one attached at the ball) down 80 feet, and you'd like to stack another rod at 65 feet, 15 feet above it. To accomplish this, you would set your main line normally and send it down to 15 feet. At that point, you would attach your stacker release to your downrigger cable and then attach your stacker line to your stacker release. Next send the downrigger down to your predetermined depth, in this case 80 feet, and you'll have your two rods running off the same rigger. This is particularly useful in situations where only a couple of riggers can be utilized, either because of the size or style of your fishing craft. When stacking rods, keep both rods in holders positioned close to the downrigger deploying the lines.

The concept of downrigger sliders may appear simple, but to anyone who has spent much time around salmon anglers will attest, there are a multitude of different opinions on how to run a slider! Volumes could be written on the styles, techniques and virtues of sliders. Here's where things can start to get really complicated. There are many types of sliders. Some being free, fixed, pegged, etc. Because of space limitations, we are going to look at 'free sliders.' By definition, a free slider is one that can slide up and down the line unimpeded. A fixed slider, is set so that it will run at a specific point in the line without variance, until a fish hits and slides the rig down to the bottom.

A typical, and the operative word here is 'typical' slider as there are

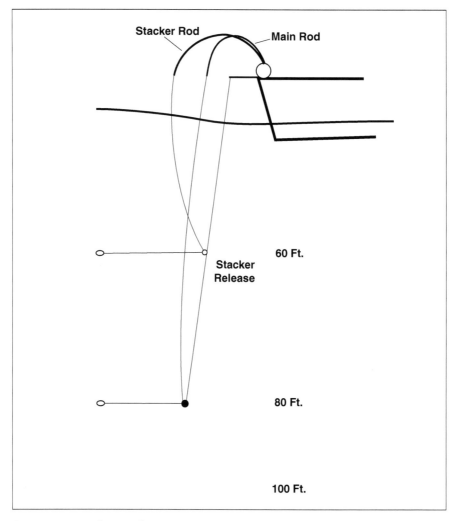

Downrigger stacking technique.

numerous atypical types, consists of a 3 to 6 foot piece of line with a snap swivel at both ends. To one swivel we attach the bait, then with the other, we attach it around the main fishing line of our other presentation, usually on a downrigger line. Clean spoons are used on free sliders. A free slider is a very simple way to add a second lure to your group dynamic.

Now that we've cleared that up, (yeah right, you're saying), here's what they are in practice. If you set your downrigger to 80 feet and then take your slider, attach the snap around the main line and throw the bait in the water, the slider rig will slide down the line somewhere between 50% and 75% to the bottom rig, therefore likely 40 to 60 feet down. (See diagram)

When a fish hits a slider, whether fixed or free, the theory is that the tug will release the line from the downrigger release and the slider will slide down until the swivel makes contact with the bait on the mainline and stops. For these reasons, sliders are highly desirable and less than desirable at the same time. Because they are running two thirds of the way down the line and standing off the downrigger cable significantly, they are running in what we term, 'clear or clean water,' meaning that there is no cable vibration or delivery apparatus signature nearby. This can be very desirable during times when fish are a bit shy. On the other

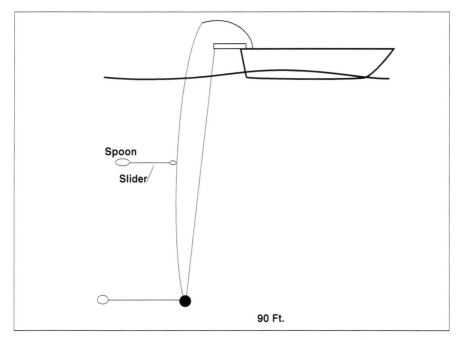

Downrigger free slider rig. Water resistance means that the main fishing line will not run straight down from the rod tip to the downrigger release. It creates what we call a "bow" in the line, with the apex of the bow usually occurring half, to two-thirds of the way down the line. The principle of a free slider is that the slider rig will slide down the line until it finds the apex of the bow.

hand, after the strike, the line releases and there can be a significant amount of time from the actual release, to when the slider rig actually makes contact with the lower main rig. This translates into a period of time when no tension can be maintained on the fish and he/she has slack line. This is a pitfall of using sliders. Plenty of days have been seen with many slider hits, yet only several fish in the net as a result.

Everything You Can Imagine About Using Dipsy Divers

I learned 'how to make fun of your charter client for being a dope and still have a good time with him,' from my buddy, Captain Al Johnson, this past summer. Dipsy Divers are great fish catching tools but to charter customers, they can be a bit confusing. On a typical charter, I get excited when a fish hits a Dipsy. A fish will crush one of the Dipsies, and I'll scream, "Fish on the Dipsy, fish on the Dipsy," while pointing to the bucking and dancing rod. Once in awhile, the guy whose turn it is will jump up and ask, "Which one?" You have to understand my boat set up. I've got two Dipsies running on each side of the boat and they are only about a foot and half apart.

Thanks to Captain Al, I can now pause and say, "That's a good question, let's think about that one for a minute. I've got my short Dipsy running nicely that doesn't appear to have much happening with it. My long Dipsy rod has line screaming out, the rod bouncing like a 4 wheeler without shocks, and the drag screaming for mercy, hmmmmmm? I'm gonna put my money on the long Dipsy, but what do you think?"

Invariably every other guy on the charter is just about wetting his pants laughing while the guy who asked the question is trying to cover his tracks by saying something clever like, "Thanks for clearing that up for me." The thing that makes the question so absolutely ludicrous for me is that there probably isn't an apparatus on the boat that receives a more crushing strike with more instant drama than a Dipsy. Fish don't just hit Dipsies, they smoke 'em!

For some reason, Dipsies seem to create more apprehension than any other delivery apparatus on the boat. Any apprehension, however, is completely unfounded as Dipsies are very easy to learn. Once learned, they are absolute stud producers for salmon and trout. On many, many days, Dipsy Divers will out-produce all other lines. Dipsy Divers can be run on mono, super line or wire line.

There are several varieties on the market including Slide Divers, Kastaway Magnetic Divers, and a few others in varying shapes and sizes, all with slightly different attributes. Dipsy however, has become the generic name for the Luhr Jensen Dipsy Diver, just the same as Kleenex has become generic for facial tissue.

The Mechanics of a Dipsy Diver

By definition, Dipsy Divers are called 'directional trolling sinkers.' Functionally, Dipsy Divers take your fishing line and bait down as well as out to the side, thus giving you vertical and horizontal control of the lure. You gain additional control over how deep and how wide a diver will dive through adjusting the diver and your line choice for deploying the Dipsy.

Dipsy Divers have a unique signature that is quite unlike any other delivery apparatus. What is the signature of the Dipsy? When used to reach the side, a Dipsy will run out to the side, away from the boat. Since the Dipsy is outside the trolling path of the boat, does this make it stealthy? Despite the angle, a Dipsy may quite possibly be the most intrusive and aggressive presentation apparatus available. It creates a high amount of water turbulence due to its angled attitude, movement and resistance in the water. The bait trailing the diver is running in the turbulence wake created by the Dipsy, similar to standing in the wake of a jet airplane engine. The diver also pulls tightly on the line holding it and increasing the vibration frequency. So, all in all, the signature of the Dipsy is quite loud and obnoxious.

Dipsy Divers angle left or right based on the adjustment made to the directional plate. The 'L' and 'R' markings on the bottom refer to the direction the Dipsy will travel, from the boat, as you troll through the water. The bottom plate of the Dipsy contains a lead weight. Moving the directional plate on the bottom of the Dipsy moves this weight to one side or the other causing the Dipsy to list to that side. A one setting creates very little list, while a three setting creates extreme list and carries it more to the side than down. As we continue our discussion of Dipsy Divers, we will address how and when to set the Divers.

Dipsy Choices

Dipsies come in a variety of sizes depending on manufacturer. For most applications, choose the large Dipsy, as it can do everything the small one can do and more. The basic M.O. of a Dipsy is that a larger surface area will create more displacement. This results in greater depth penetration and potentially, more side distance.

The equalizer in this is the fact that the Dipsy requires a nose down attitude to achieve diving plane status. By adding drag to the back end of the Dipsy, it pulls the rear down and the nose up, thereby losing some, or all, diving properties. Therefore, a large Dipsy will tow a bait that pulls more and still maintains a diving plane status. A smaller Dipsy will not be capable of achieving great depth with a dodger and fly.

The next choice you'll be forced to make is which color to choose, as there are a myriad of colors and patterns. We've fished with tons of them, some out of choice, some out of necessity. As a general rule on our boats, you'll only find three colors of Dipsies, orange, yellow, and green. Now, don't take this as law, as we hear of fishermen all the time who are having some sort of stupendous success with the key being some other or bizarre color of Dipsy. Our friend, Captain Bob Poteshman, is one of the most creative anglers when it comes to picking new color combinations of Dipsies, dodgers and flies. We do believe that Dipsy color does matter; however, we also believe that we can achieve wonderful results, day in and day out, with only those three colors in our arsenal. Orange is relegated to presentations in spring or high in the water column (above 40 feet), while yellow and green are our staple summertime colors for deeper fish. Kings seem particularly fond of green Dipsies and big lake trout seem to favor yellow Dipsies.

All Dipsies come with a power ring attached to them. Just because something comes attached to your apparatus doesn't mean you have to fish it. Quite often, you'll find us fishing without the power rings. The obvious exception to this is if we need to fish quite deep, over 100 feet down. Adding the power ring increases the surface area, which creates a larger diving plane and more depth. The downside is that because we increased the surface area without increasing the weight in the nose, the Dipsy can become more unstable and rock up from side to side. This can be problematic if we are trying to fish multiple Dipsies per side. There are also aftermarket products. One called a super ring is at least twice as large as the power ring that comes with the Dipsy. This will do what it claims and help achieve more depth, but again, the stability problem raises it's ugly head. There is a way to try and skirt the instability issue and potential tangles, and that's using multiple settings.

Running Dipsies

You've noticed that we used the plural, "Dipsies," to title this section. That's because many times we're running multiple Dipsies per side. The idea is that we can cover more than one depth to the side of the boat, thereby increasing our swath that we cut through the water, much like planer boards, except deeper.

We'll stick with the example of two Dipsies per side, but don't think that's the maximum achievable. We are going to use a combination of rod length and rod tip elevation as our first coordinating tools. The easiest choice to make is to run different length rods on the same side. Short to long rod differences of a couple of feet or more are normal. Something like seven and nine footers, or eight and ten foot six, is common. The short rod is run in the more rearward rod holder and parallel to the water. The longer rod needs to have the tip elevated slightly from the short rod, and this can be done by either elevating the angle of the rod holder slightly, usually 15 degrees, or by using a rod holder on a rail that is physically higher placed than the short rod holder. These two aspects create tip separation that prevents tangles.

The second criterion to running multiple Dipsies is the setting on the Dipsy. When running Dipsies out to the side, the dial generally needs a setting of at least one. For running two Divers a side, set the rearward rod to run the deepest. The rearward Dipsy should be set on a lower setting. This will cause the Dipsy to dig deeper. Set the forward Dipsy on a slightly higher setting than the rearward Dipsy. This Dipsy will dig out to the side at a more moderate angle than the deeper Dipsy, creating additional horizontal separation between the two Divers. To illustrate, you may set the deeper Dipsy on a '2' setting and the shallower Dipsy will be set on a '2.5' setting. For deep applications set the rearward Dipsy on '1' and the forward diver on '1.5.' There is no rule of thumb regarding

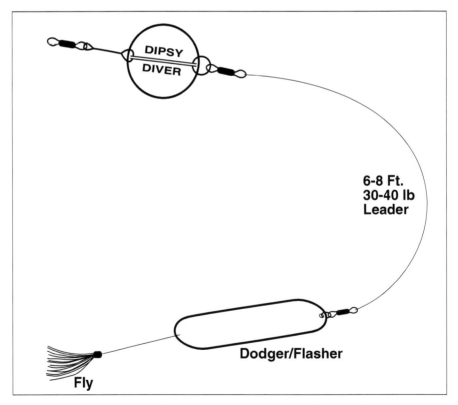

Rigging a Dipsy Diver is really quite simple. This rig will account for many, many fish across the Great Lakes.

which Dipsy should be run out further, but generally, the shorter, rearward rod will run deeper simply because of the setting.

One of the spots where Dipsies get overlooked is down the chute. Most anglers reserve the area down the middle for a suspended wire line, lead core or both. Although we are huge fans of the suspended wire line, there are times when fish just aren't biting it well. A good alternative is the center Dipsy. Run a Dipsy down the chute, on wire, super line or mono, on a zero setting. Even when Dipsies off to the side are only moderately productive, at times this center Dipsy can be the stud rod on your boat because it is being run internally in your spread instead of on the periphery.

Dipsy Line Choice

Another major factor impacting Dipsy performance is the line that you run them on. Anglers use mono, super lines and wire line to deliver Dipsy Divers to depth. By nature, Dipsies are designed to achieve depth. The larger diameter line we use as the attachment line to a Dipsy, the more water resistance it's going to have and that means blowback which translates into lost depth. Mono in that case will obviously have the largest diameter of the three lines. In addition, mono has tremendous stretch. The further out you put it, the larger the rubber band you are creating. This means that on long leads it can be very hard to detect small fish or tangles. Mono is ideal for achieving depths of about 30-40 feet, with 50 feet being the maximum depth.

Super lines, with their narrow line diameter and lack of stretch, are ideal for taking that next step into deeper water with Dipsies and can achieve depths of 90 feet. Add a power ring, and a super line Dipsy will continue to dive. Super line is the ideal line to use to deliver Dipsies in the 30-80 foot levels. Having said that, super line can also be used for targeting the upper layers of the water column as well.

Wire lines will carry you into the true deeps with Dipsies, as wire also sinks. Wire is ideal for hitting really deep fish beyond 80 feet. With all that being said, don't pigeonhole wire Dipsies into deepwater only, be open-minded.

You can inter-mix the various line types in your trolling dynamic. For example, you may want to run a mono Dipsy down 25 feet for steelhead and a super line Dipsy down 55 feet for kings. These two set-ups can be run off the same side with no trouble. Likewise, wire line Dipsies and super line Dipsies can also be run in tandem. We have also used all three-line types to run three Dipsies simultaneously off one side. Be creative and use the various line applications to deliver Dipsy Divers to the most productive strike zones when you are fishing.

One last thought: Each line type (mono, super, wire) delivers the Dipsy to a depth with a different *presentation*. Just this presentation factor alone can make all the difference in the world. If action is slow, experiment between the line types to achieve maximum results. If you are limited on rods or deck space, super line Dipsies offer the best of all worlds! Super line Dipsies can be used in most Great Lakes scenarios.

If you've never used a Dipsy Diver before, then try running one Dipsy per side first. As you become comfortable running one Dipsy per side, then try running multiple Dipsies. As you tweak your trolling dynamic, play with Dipsies and the various line-systems used within the parameters of your fishing platform. Dipsies are like the American Express card of delivery apparatuses; we never leave home without them—they catch a ton of fish, spring, summer and fall!

WIRE LINE—THE LEAST UNDERSTOOD DELIVERY DEVICE

Wire line is one of the most misunderstood delivery apparatus on the Great Lakes. Most days wire line is a quiet but steady producer, but on some days—watch out! When wire line gets hot, never put it in the water unattended because, "daddy, it's gonna fire off like right now!"

Anglers who know how to use wire will catch more fish, especially when other delivery apparatuses are slow or conditions are tough. Why? Simply put, wire is the pinnacle of all examples showing us that delivery apparatus can and will make a difference. How can it be, you wonder, that all things equal, with the exception of the fishing line, that one particular delivery apparatus can so drastically out produce the other delivery apparatus? The answer is simple, but two-fold.

First, from the fish's perspective (and we hope, by now, you are starting to think from the fish's perspective) delivery apparatus does influence lure action and presentation differently! Wire places the lure *into* the trolling dynamic differently than a downrigger, or other delivery device. It also imparts a unique action to the lure that cannot be duplicated with mono, super line, lead core or downriggers.

Secondly, the old signature and vibration factors. Think of your fishing lines as guitar strings. Is a classical guitar with nylon strings as loud as an acoustic guitar with metal strings? Nope. Well, the same happens with our fishing lines. Any line dragged through the water is going to create some form of vibration.

How much and what frequency the line vibrates depends on several factors. The first of which is the composition of the line. Wire simply emits stronger vibrations than cloth (like a super line fiber) or nylon (like a monofilament.)

The next factor influencing wire presentations is tension; which is usually static considering that all wire is run with similar resistance either from a Dipsy or a lead ball. After tension comes angle. How much something is going to vibrate is dependent on the angle at which it is in contact with the element causing the resistance. The steeper, or more vertical the angle, the more easily the vibration occurs. Therefore, a wire line with a 1 lb. weight will probably have a different vibration quotient than a wire line with a Dipsy because the angle of the wire has changed.

The last factor, but in some minds the most critical aspect of running wire lines, is line diameter. Just like the guitar string analogy, diameter is going to influence the pitch, or frequency of the vibration. Some people believe 'frequency' is the magic property behind a wire line.

This brings us to one of the most influential reasons of all to run wire on your boat—the information it will give you. Okay, Chip, are you telling us you 'communicate' or talk with your fishing rigs? In a typical year, not before Labor Day, however, I am talking about a different form of information that has saved many a fishing trip. Because there is no release and wire is very 'stiff' when compared with other lines, the wire is an information transmitter right to the rod tip. People spend years trying to understand the nuances of underwater currents. Thousands of dollars are spent on gadgets that read and interpret information at depth, attached to our downrigger balls, sending data streams back to our dash for us to interpret. Decades of experience have been invested in trying to quantify blowback in downriggers and bend in Dipsy rods. All of this to interpret one single thing—how our baits are performing in the underwater currents at the depth of presentation.

One quick look at a suspended wire line and you can have that answer just by *reading* the angle of the wire and the *vibration* or *bounce* in the rod tip. You can tell instantly whether your presentations are hanging dead because you're trolling with a current. Likewise, you'll know if you need to slow down because everything is spinning wildly out of control as you troll against an underwater jet stream. Simply put, a suspended wire line can give you incredible, instant speed recognition for interpreting the bait action in the current layer at the depth that you are fishing.

Well, now in our eighth paragraph of what seems to be a pretty heavy discussion about wire line let me tell you a story before we go on. This story is testimony to the reasons that beatings by charter captains on their clients should remain illegal.

A couple of years ago, a family came out with me during early August for an eight-hour charter. Their two grown teenage sons accompanied mom and dad on this outing. We had really big fish around, but we were struggling to catch anything but small to medium fish. Every delivery device was popping fish, but not the big fish we were marking all around the boat.

After moving lines around and tweaking our trolling dynamic, it became apparent that the really big ones only wanted to eat baits off wire lines! Well, being the shy and reserved Captain that I am, three riggers, two wire Dipsies and three suspended wire lines went out in the mix. About three hours, and 14 big kings (12 of which bit wire) into the charter, the boys, no not boys, fit and strapping young men, began groaning about how it was too hard to reel in these big fish. They inquired if there wasn't another spot we could go to catch smaller fish? Let the beatings begin.

This story just illustrates a point that sometimes wire is the answer. It is not meant to replace other techniques, just supplement them. Some day's wire is all they'll eat. Conversely, there have been entire weeks where fish wouldn't touch anything presented on wire. In a normal year however, wire lines can account for over 50% of the really large fish on your boat. There is something special and magical about wire, when it comes to really tripping the trigger of behemoth fish.

Wire and its Rigging

Before we meander down the wire path any further, let's first clarify what wire is. Many folks' only recollection of wire line is a single strand wire, known as Monel. The wire we now fish with on the Great Lakes is quite different, in that it is a braided wire and has properties more consistent with regular fishing lines than it does a single strand Monel.

There is an upside and downside to the features of braided wire.

Great Lakes anglers can deliver baits to multiple strike zones through the use of downriggers, Dipsy Divers, wire line, specialty lines and planer boards. When you integrate the various delivery devices, great catches can be expected!

The upside is that it is very supple, lays nicely on the reel, can be easily cut and retied, and is of thin diameter. The downside is that unlike Monel, which is smooth, braided wire is as abrasive as a hack saw. That means that we need specialized equipment to fish it with, as outlined in Chapter 2.

Wire line is suitable for fishing with a couple of different delivery techniques; either the suspended wire with a lead weight known as a 'thumper' rig, a lead ball bouncing the bottom, or with a Dipsy Diver. As a thumper rig you can fish a single wire down the middle or you can run two thumpers, one off each corner. Some anglers will run three of these suspended wires, one in each corner and one down the middle. You can even add a pair of outrigger poles to drop wire thumpers.

In all applications, wire will deliver two distinct things: A high degree of vibration and more depth. Wire, because of its narrow diameter and the fact that it sinks, will absolutely help any device achieve greater depth. However, many fishermen consider wire as only that; a device to achieve greater depth and never consider it when fishing higher in the water column. As an example, steelhead love wire high in the water column delivering baits. There are days when a suspended wire, run right down the chute with a 16-ounce ball and 30 feet of line out is a stud setup. That bait is probably only running 8 to 14 feet down, yet the same baits on a different setup, will not achieve the same results. The moral is that wire is a versatile tool that can be implemented in a variety of ways and circumstances.

Rigging wire is extremely simple, since we can actually tie knots in the wire. To attach something to wire, like a Dipsy or a swivel, all you need do is thread the wire through the item (like the eye of the swivel) bring it back to form a loop and then tie an overhand knot in the wire, creating a loop. This is the same knot you use to terminate a fly to attach it to the dodger. Because the wire is highly abrasive, the knot will never slip. For attaching the lead balls we use the three-swivel rig diagrammed in Chapter 2. Basically, this rig consists of three swivels. The first is attached to the end of the wire. A second swivel holding the lead ball is hooked to the first swivel. A third swivel hangs off the first swivel. You can attach your leader line to this swivel.

Running Wire

Because of the highly abrasive nature of wire, it's imperative that you know precisely where your other line presentations are in the water column and within your trolling dynamic. A wire running between a boom and a corner downrigger is very much at peace until a huge king slams one of the riggers and heads straight for the wire. Just be ready to move the wire rig and keep it from rubbing up against other lines.

Running wire Dipsies is really nothing more than running a regular Dipsy, so we won't spend much time on that here. Wire Dipsies off the side are dynamite for targeting fish from 60-140 feet down. Running thumper wires however, is a completely different ball game. Let's start with the basics—bait presentation. Wire is generally run with dodgers or flashers and a trailer. Although you can catch plenty of fish on crankbaits and spoons off wire, using it with a dodger helps give you the speed data that we talked about previously.

In order to avoid tangles setting a thumper, you must put the rig into your spread in key locations. Basically, on a boat with four riggers, there are 5 usable holes through which to drop wire rigs. They occur outside either boom rigger or between the corner and boom rigger. The most obvious and largest location to set a wire, however, is generally the center between the corners. You can use any hole you like as every boat fishes differently. To send the wire down, drop the dodger in the water and then free spool the ball into the water slowly, maintaining tension on the spool with your thumb. Once in the water, maintain some pressure on the spool with your thumb as you let the rig down, otherwise the dodger will cause resistance and float back up into the wire creating a tangle.

Once you have let the wire out the desired distance, rod holder angle can be important. For suspended wires where you are going to want to read the rod tip, a 45-degree angle or lower is preferable towards the stern. In a set heavy in wires, running four or five simultaneously, you may have wires laying over to the sides and flattened out some, but generally leave one in a position where you can read the tip easily to judge speeds.

One thing we can tell you for sure is that once you start running wire, you're taking a quantum leap forward in advancing your knowledge of your environment and the little idiosyncrasies that govern it. You will see quickly how current layers change your presentations and small changes in course, as little as 10 degrees, can change how your baits are running. In a period of time you will be transformed into a person who understands the nuances of subtle changes in open water and become a master of throttle and boat control. On top of all this, you'll develop forearms like Popeye from reeling in all those giant fish on your suspended wire!

Get the Lead Out: Fishing Lead Core

Depending on where you fish, you may think lead core is the best way to catch salmon and trout, or you may view it as the scourge of trolling, fishing it only under protest. Either way, one thing is surely true—lead core catches fish, even when other techniques don't!

The term 'lead core fishing' refers to the line that is being used in the technique. Lead core line is a Dacron sheath surrounding a filament of lead that runs through the line to make it sink and achieve depth. It is segmented into a different color every 10 yards so that you may always know how much lead core you have out. A 'single core' is 100 yards, or 10 colors, while a double core is 200 yards. A half core is 50 yards. Most fishermen consider a single core as a standard lead core technique. To the business end of the lead, attach a 20-yard monofilament leader.

A single lead core (10 colors out) will reach a maximum depth of about 40-55 feet. A double lead core (20 colors) will reach depths of 55-70 feet. Now, actual depth a lead runs at is heavily dependent on lure selection, trolling speed and lead core test. A dodger or flasher, because of the added drag, will not run as deep as a clean spoon. If you troll fast, lead lines rise up in the water. If you make slow, loopy turns, the lead will sink.

To fish lead core, you simply let the lead line out a great distance behind the boat. If you were to fish all the colors, meaning all 10 colors of lead, your lure would be running 100 yards astern. Add a 20 yard mono leader to the business end, and an additional 30 yards of backing (to keep all the lead in the water) and your lure is now running 150 yards behind the boat in the absolute cleanest water available with nothing else around it. Lead core is the epitome of a stealth technique. It is running out there all by itself. The line is a huge diameter at a very shallow angle so there is almost no perceptible vibration, and there is no signature in the water from any delivery apparatus, only the lure.

Now you need to understand the nuances of lead core in order to understand which lead core you need and how to fish it. Lead core line is the most speed dependent presentation we have. Because of its thick diameter, it is subject to water resistance. At faster trolling speeds, the lead core encounters more resistance and actually rises in the water column. Conversely, the slower we troll, the less resistance we create and the deeper the lead core will travel.

With that knowledge under our belts, now we need to tackle the issue of which lead core to use. We have choices like 18 lb. test, 27 lb., 36 lb., etc. Quite simply, lead has no strength, so that means that the Dacron sheath achieves all the strength. The higher the test rating, the heavier the sheath, which translates into a thicker diameter, which means more lift which means less depth achieved. Greater depth is achieved only if there is more lead within the Dacron sheath. The reality is that some manufacturers have more lead in 27 lb. test than in 18 lb. test. Others don't. The only way to know is to put the different brands and pound test lead cores on a postal scale and weigh them to determine lead content. Generally however, 27 lb. test does not contain more lead than 18 lb. test, therefore the thinner diameter of 18 lb. test will allow it to achieve more depth.

Delivery of lead core can be as a flat line, off planer boards, or outrigger poles. If fishing multiple lead cores, it's advisable to use planer boards, as trying to run them as flatlines will only cause grief and headaches when fish hooked on other apparatuses find their way into tangling with the lead core. Believe us, there is no tangle that is worse than a lead core tangle.

Be advised that when fishing lead core off boards it is best to attach the release to the backing and not directly to the lead core. The lead inside the Dacron sheath causes the sheath to wear excessively fast when in a release. For this reason, many fishermen that wish to fish less than a full lead core, or a half core, spool a reel with only 5 colors of lead. This allows them to attach the release for the planer board to the backing and not directly on the lead core.

Reaching Out With Planer Boards

Generally speaking, a planer board refers to a device that tracks out to the side of your boat and carries your bait along for the ride. Used with mono line and little or no weight, these devices are dynamite tools for fishing the surface layers of the water column. Utilized with unconventional methods, they can be used to target deeper layers of the water column.

Today, there are a great number of different devices that achieve this goal; all with different properties and periods of success. The main principle at work when using planer boards is that it gives us the opportunity to cover more water as boards present baits in a wide swath of water. This increases our chances of contact with active and biting fish as we can run additional lines as well as reach fish that are spooked by the boat or fish not in the direct path of the boat.

Specifically, planer boards fall under two distinct categories: inline planer boards and 'Mast and Ski' Planer Systems (direct planers.) Inline planers are smaller and are attached to the individual fishing line. Mast and Ski Systems utilize a larger board or ski on a separate towline. We will look at both types of planers in the following pages. You may want to refer to Chapter 2 for rigging tips on the rods and reels that are used with both planer board systems.

Mast and Ski Systems

These are a pole or mast, or even a large specialized reel like a downrigger reel, mounted forward on the front third of the boat. From this runs a clothesline type cord that attaches to a large ski, or double ski. When you begin setting lines, you let the large ski out to its desired trolling location. The ski line is then locked in place.

To set fishing lines off the ski, your next step is to let out the individual fishing lines to the desired lead length. Attach the fishing line to a 'shower curtain' release that will slide down the ski cord and carry your lure out to the side. You control how far to the side the line will run (on the ski tether) by the amount of line you let out on the individual fishing reels.

You can run multiple lines off of one ski and when the fish hits, it pulls it out of the release, and the release slides down to the ski. When you reset the line, you do not pull the ski back to the boat. Simply re-set

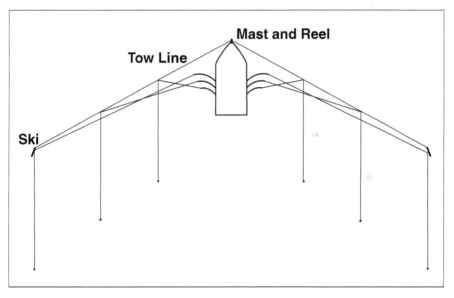

Mast and Ski System. Here you can see 3 lines running in the water off each ski. When a fish strikes, slack line is introduced because of the angle from rod tip to fish. If a fish were to hit line three, in our three line set, the only way we could reset that line in its original position, to recreate the exact same trolling dynamic, is to pull lines one and two, reset line three, and then reset lines one and two. What usually happens is most fisherman slide line two out to become line three, slide line one out to become line two and reset line three on the inside, now becoming line one. This practice destroys any semblance of maintaining order with your trolling dynamic.

the fishing line to the productive lead length and attach another 'shower curtain' release to the towline and away it goes.

Rigging a rod for a Mast and Ski System is nothing more than rigging for a downrigger. Either tie directly to the lure or tie to a swivel and attach your bait. The advantage of a Mast and Ski System is that it is just you and the fish after the fish pulls the line free of the release. The disadvantages of a Mast and Ski System are threefold.

First, the Mast and Ski System simply imparts less erratic action to the bait. Although ski's still stall going up waves and speed up going down waves, and jump and dance much like inline planer boards, the fact that your lure is attached between the ski and the boat diminishes that erratic action, which in many cases, is detrimental. Secondly, upon release, there is a great deal of slack introduced into the line. This slack will many times result in more lost fish. The third reason is the inability to recreate the trolling dynamic that was just productive. (You'll read more about the trolling dynamic in Chapter 5).

There is one particular situation where, at times, Mast and Ski Systems do seem to have an advantage. That is the early spring, near shore brown trout fishery. Browns can sometimes be very spooky and when in ultra clear shallow water, inline planer boards sometimes give them lockjaw. Running a Mast and Ski System, keeps the boards from going over their heads and still maintains the baits in the strike zone where the fish are.

Inline Planer Boards

These are the bread and butter of most Great Lakes salmon trollers. Inline refers to a device that carries the bait out to the side. This device is attached directly to the main fishing line. For each line you run off the side, you will need to attach an individual planer board. Some popular brands include Wille Sideliner, Big Jon Otter, Cannon Rover, Off-Shore, and the most famous of all, The Yellow Bird. Inline planers are smaller and less costly than a mast and ski system.

There are two ways you can rig an inline planer board: fixed or releasable. Fixed boards are the style used by most walleye trollers where

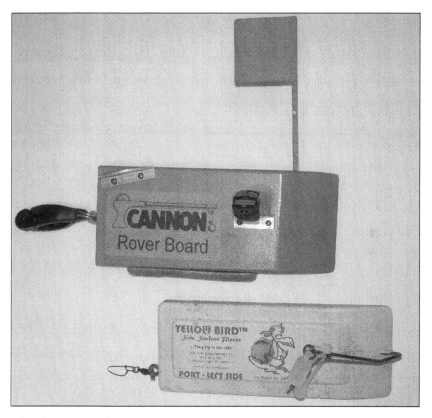

This shows two different sizes of inline boards and styles of release. The smaller is the famous Yellow Bird. In contrast to the Cannon Rover, it is light, smaller, and has a pin and cylinder release that will allow release of the board when a strike occurs. The Yellow Bird is ideal for most salmon trolling exercises when fish are in the top portion of the water column. The larger board is a Cannon Rover board. This particular style is heavy, large (about as large as inline boards get) and has a pinch pad release, which actually doesn't release until you take it off the line. The advantages to boards of this ilk, are that they track extremely well out to the side, run nicely in rough water because of their weight, and can carry a pretty good load behind them. The Rover is ideal for use with heavy loads like trolling lead core line. If you notice the release system of these two examples, the Yellow Bird has a snap at the tail end of the board that the line goes through and holds the Yellow Bird on the line after the release has given way. The Cannon Rover has two pinch pads on it, thereby holding the line in a fixed position behind the board until someone manually releases it from the line.

the board never releases from the line until it is reeled up to boat side and your fishing partner takes it off the line manually. There are circumstances where we want to use a fixed board, in particular, when we fish lead core on boards. Most of the time however, we'll want to fish releasable boards, for a variety of reasons.

Inline planers are also very easy to rig and deploy. For rigging suggestions, you may want to refer to Chapter 2. When setting inline planer boards for surface fishing, lead length (stretch) behind the planers is very important. The pattern we recommend will minimize tangles and increase your productivity. Simply put, the outside planer lines will be stretched longer distances than the boards to the inside. This greatly reduces tangles when a fish is hooked and releases the board! Lead lengths off planer boards will be addressed in detail in Chapter 5.

Planer Releases

All planer board systems employ some form of line release. All inline boards you purchase come with releases. The Mast and Ski Systems do not come with line releases. For the larger skis you can use the same releases as inline boards, just hung from shower curtain hangers. Which release system is best for you?

Just because a release comes with the board however, is not necessarily a good reason to use it. Pinch pad style releases are generally considered non-releasable. Ideally, for releasable boards, you'd like a release that is adjustable. The easier it is to adjust, the better as we fish in a constantly changing environment for different species and sizes of fish. If a flat calm day turns windy and wavy, I can quickly increase the tension on my planer board release so that the release doesn't keep tripping from action in heavy waves.

Our favorite release in this category is the pin and cylinder release. The line is placed in the notch in the pin (or threaded through the opening) and then the pin is inserted into the cylinder that is attached to the board. Gaining tension on the release is simply a matter of greater insertion into the cylinder. If you want more tension, push the pin in further.

There is no simpler release to use as setting these releases is really a matter of feel to find the right tensions for the right circumstances. The most commonly used releases these days are the Jettison, Big Jon Otter releases and the Yellow Bird Osprey release.

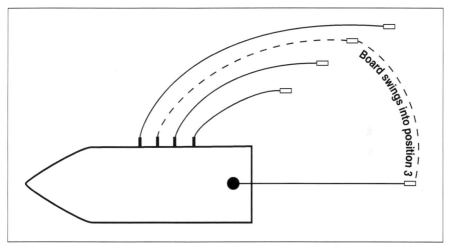

When running more than two boards per side, it is advisable to use releasable boards. When fish hit, if the board doesn't release, you need to bring in any board to the inside of the board connected to the fighting fish, otherwise, it may tangle with the inside planer line. The other major reason is that running releasable boards allows us to put the bait back in the same slot that it was running at when the fish hit, thereby preserving our group dynamic. From a rod running perspective, notice how the most rearward planer board rod is the closest to the boat and the most forward rod is the furthest from the boat. In this scenario, when a fish hits any of the rods, you simply lift it out of the rod holder, and go over the tops of the other lines towards the center of the boat.

CHAPTER 5

Putting It All Together

How to find and catch fish all season long!

Great Lakes anglers fish some of the most awesome, yet challenging waters on the face of the earth. Weather and Lake conditions seem to change on an almost daily basis. Fish migration patterns vary from year to year; and as we all know, the Lakes are open to a variety of external influences. To catch fish all season long, anglers need to draw upon a wide variety of skills and techniques. This is where we put all the pieces together!

We do not approach the lake in a chaotic or random fashion. Neither should you. Our goal is to help you look at the Lakes systematically. To simplify our discussion of finding and catching salmon and trout we will divide our fishing into three periods: spring, summer and fall. By dividing the fishing season into periods, we believe you can gain a better understanding of the target species and the season-specific fishing techniques used to catch salmon and trout. If you understand your adversary and grasp the techniques needed to catch them, you can be more intentional and productive at locating and catching salmon and trout.

As we said in Chapter 1, success is built on understanding. You must understand both your prey and the methods needed to catch fish. Technique applications need to be built on the nature and characteristics of salmon and trout, and the environment in which they swim. There is a great deal of variety between the individual lakes but there are many aspects that remain constant. Our target species are identical whether you find them in Lake Michigan or Lake Ontario. They have behavioral and feeding tendencies that remain constant.

If you understand the behavior patterns of salmon and trout, the waters in which they swim, and learn to adapt your fish finding skills and techniques to the various seasons, you will become a better angler. Chapter 5 is designed to function like a road map. It will serve as a guide to help you locate and catch fish all season long. The principles and techniques are applicable to all Great Lakes waters where salmon and trout

Captain Dan Keating with a 17 lb. steelhead taken from the surface waters of Lake Michigan.

swim. As you spend time on the water it is our hope that the information here will lead you to more fish!

Spring Fishing

Winters across the Great Lakes can be long and brutal. As winter loosens its grip on the Lakes, the metabolism of salmon and trout accelerates as icy cold waters begin to thaw. During the cold winter months salmon and trout feed sporadically. As the days lengthen, fish become more active. The spring fishing season gets under way between early April and mid May, depending on geographical location and local weather patterns (microclimate).

After a brief discussion on early spring fishing, we will approach spring fishing by dividing the playing field into two zones: Shallow water and deep, offshore water. We will define shallow water as the zone extending from the beach out to 70 feet. Deep water will be all water beyond 70 feet. Both shallow water and deep water can provide excellent spring action. Techniques vary between the two zones as do species availability within each zone.

Early Spring Coho and Brown Trout

In some locations, anglers begin fishing for coho and brown trout as early as March 1st! We have heard of anglers on southern Lake Michigan getting into a hot coho bite in Indiana in late January! Early spring fishing occurs close to shore from the beach out to 30 feet of water. This makes it an ideal small boat option. Because it is spring and small boats are involved, extreme caution with the weather is a must. When on the water, monitor the winds and any Lake ice that may be in the area. Don't take any chances with the weather.

The dominant early season targets are coho and brown trout. When the waters begin to thaw, schools of coho will move into warmer shoreline regions. After a long winter, coho are hungry! As the waters warm they will become more aggressive and are usually easy to catch. Brown trout, who prefer the shoreline shallows all year, become active as the days lengthen. You will occasionally catch a king, steelhead or rare lake trout during early spring fishing.

Early spring fishing is characterized by very cold water. Water temperatures will range between 32-38 degrees. Remember, salmon and trout prefer 42-56 degree water in general. Finding and catching early season coho and brown trout is quite elementary. Locate the warmest water available and fish the top 10 feet. Areas that warm quicker include river mouths, harbor mouths, shallow bays and protected breakwall regions. Once you have identified the areas that will warm first, use a surface temperature gauge to find pockets of water that may be a degree or two warmer than surrounding Lake water. This is where you begin fishing.

Some of the fastest early fishing will occur at power plant discharges. These discharges on the Great Lakes attract fish like magnets! If you have the luxury of fishing off a power plant, you may find water 10, 15 or even 20 degrees warmer than the surrounding areas.

Presentations during the early spring are not complicated. Deepwater trolling gear can be left in the garage, as most of the fish will be caught on surface lines including side planers, flat lines and shallow set Dipsy Divers. Most active fish will be close to the surface so you don't want baits diving below the fish.

Crankbaits are often the most productive lures for 34-44 degree water. Popular plugs include jointed J-7 and J-9 Rapalas, Fat Raps, Thunder Stiks, Tiny Tadpollies and small Shad Raps. If coho are the target, you may already own a tackle box full of assorted crankbaits that will catch fish. Remember, these fish are hungry! Flies and dodgers and spoons will also catch fish. The coho and brown trout application techniques discussed in the following shallow water section are applicable to most early spring scenarios.

Shallow Water Techniques

The months of April, May and early June find large numbers of salmon and trout frolicking in the nearshore waters. Because the fish are often close to shore, this is an excellent period for small boat anglers to sample salmon and trout fishing. Spring fish are also highly aggressive and can be found in large schools. This makes them ideal targets for anglers who may have limited experience fishing for salmon and trout. It also makes them ideal targets for anyone who just wants to get out on the water and catch fish!

Coho, brown trout and kings are the species most commonly found in shallow water during the spring. Coho and browns will often move into very shallow water, sometimes as shallow as 5-10 feet! The kings venturing shoreward prefer to stay out in the 30-70 foot range. Occasionally you will encounter steelhead and lake trout in the springtime shallows.

Why do we find so many fish in shallow water during the spring? Salmon and trout are cold blooded but they have a preferred temperature range of 42-56 degree water. As winter loosens its grip on the Lakes, the average Great Lakes water temperature will often be in the 34-42 degree range! As the Lakes begin to warm the shallows will warm first. Bait and gamefish will often move into shoreline areas in pursuit of warmer water.

Shallow water regions warm earlier and quicker than deep water for a variety of reasons. In terms of volume, the shallows contain less water, therefore the effects of spring warming make a quicker impact on the shallow water. Shallow water is often murkier. Darker waters absorb light and heat at a faster rate than deep, clear water. Wind also impacts shoreline warming. If a region features extended periods of onshore winds, this will drive the warmer surface waters into the shoreline. Shallow water areas behind points and long breakwalls will also trap pockets of water that will collect and hold heat.

Locating Spring Salmon and Trout in Shallow Water

The two keys to locating fish will be water temperature and structure. Water temperature is often the defining element of success. If the average lake temperature were only 34-42 degrees, then any water warmer than that would be a good place to begin looking for fish. For this reason, a surface temperature gauge is invaluable in helping you locate pockets of warmer water. On many spring days the secret to success will be to locate the warmest water available.

Are some shallow water areas warmer than others or do Lake shallows warm uniformly? There are a number of variables that will accelerate shoreline warming including power plant discharges, river and stream outflows, harbor mouths, concrete breakwalls and shallow sandy stretches of beach. These areas have a pronounced influence on the surrounding Lake waters and are the areas to target.

Power plant and large river outflows are two of the most productive nearshore locations. Both discharge large quantities of warmer water into the Lake. This functions as a giant magnet and draws baitfish as well as salmon and trout into the warmer waters. Power plants and river mouths also wash large amounts of food into the lake and this helps nourish the bottom end of the food chain in the local region. Just how big of an influence do these outflows have on a local region? The impact of these outflows will extend for miles out into the Lake and along the shoreline. The end result is that they draw bait and gamefish into the shoreline.

Harbor mouths and breakwaters are also dynamite locations to look for fish. These provide shelter for baitfish as well as trapping water that can be warmed by the sun. The concrete and rocks that form breakwalls absorb heat on sunny days. This warmth is transferred to the surrounding waters. Brown trout are particularly fond of hanging around harbor mouths and breakwaters. While all breakwalls can attract fish, those that extend further out into deep water will draw the most attention. Breakwalls can also provide areas of sheltered water where small boat anglers are likely to find fish.

Productive spring bottom structure includes near shore drop-offs, river and stream channels, rock riprap and wave troughs. Kings and brown trout will often relate to these features in shallow water. Coho are less sensitive to bottom structure during the spring months than kings and brown trout.

Shallow water salmon and trout are not difficult to catch. In fact, anglers employ a wide variety of methods across the Great Lakes. In order to help you isolate the various techniques required to consistently catch spring fish in shallow water we will break this technique "conversation" down by species. We will look at our favorite methods for catching coho, brown trout and king salmon in shallow water.

Shallow Water Coho Strategies

Spring coho fishing is not rocket science! When looking for coho in the shallows, remember coho are coho. They prefer water in the 48-54 degree range. Therefore, your first objective is to locate water in this range. On many spring days, however, 48-54 degree water may not be available. If the surrounding surface water is colder than 48 degrees, you will be looking for the warmest water in the area. For example, if you are running under power and the Lake water is 40-42 degrees and suddenly the temperature jumps to 45 degrees . . . slow down! This is where you will find coho. A surface temperature gauge that you can monitor while under power is invaluable when looking for warm water.

In shallow water or deep water, spring coho tend to orient themselves to the surface. For this reason you should concentrate your fishing presentations on the top 20 feet. Typically, this is the warmest layer of water.

Where do we find spring coho? A favorite place to locate shallow water coho is along color lines. Spring winds tend to stir up shallow shoreline water. This often results in a marked contrast between a band of murky or off color water shore-side and cleaner water lakeside. This color change will often feature a temperature transition as well. Coho love to hang on the edges of these changes! Color breaks are not stationary. They may set up for one day or one week. Breaks such as these will often move perpendicular to the shoreline depending on winds and currents.

As spring advances, local waters will gradually warm. Typically the water nearest the shoreline will be warmest. As you move offshore the water will progressively cool. As the waters warm, 48-54 degrees is still the target range. As nearshore waters warm, you may have to start working out from the shoreline to locate 48-54 degree water. Coho movements off the shoreline are not always uniform in nature. If local wind regimes are chaotic or swirling, coho may be in 25 feet one week, 45 feet the next and back in 30 feet the following week.

Spring coho techniques are very elementary. During the spring months, coho are very aggressive feeders. This aggressive behavior makes them an ideal fish to target! A combination of side planers, Dipsy Divers, flat lines and downriggers can be employed to catch spring coho. Side planers and Dipsy Divers, however, are usually the most potent.

Coho will strike a variety of lures throughout the day including flies and dodgers, spoons and body baits. Inland anglers are often surprised by the numbers of coho they catch on lures designed for inland species. The most productive lures to use for shallow water coho are flies and dodgers and body baits.

If we had to pick only one lure to use for shallow water coho, it would be a 00 red dodger or flasher followed by a small tinsel fly. Nothing catches more coho! The smaller peanut fly and the 1 to 2 inch tinsel flies are equally productive. On any given day, either of the two fly types may be more productive. Fly color is often irrelevant; however, the four most popular coho colors include green/gold, blue/green/gold, aqua and blue/gold. Other hot coho colors include blue, green, green/silver, blue/silver, black/gold, dark blue and red/blue/gold.

Fly leader length is critical. For spring coho, flies are run anywhere from 9-18 inches behind the 00 dodgers. If coho are present but not striking, the first element to change is your leader length. Let's go back to a crisp May morning on southwestern Lake Michigan to illustrate. I was struggling to catch a few fish. A good friend of mine, Captain Jerry Nied of the Spendthrift, who is probably *the* premier coho fisherman on the Great Lakes, was fishing several miles to the south. As usual, Jerry was on his way to a quick limit catch. Now, you have to know Jerry. Jerry has an unmistakable voice, more energy and enthusiasm for salmon fishing than the town of Milwaukee and he catches more coho than anyone walking the face of the earth!

A quick radio conversation revealed Jerry and I were using the same flies, same dodgers and fishing in the same depth of water. What was the difference? Jerry asked me one question, "Dan, how long are your fly leaders?" That was the key! After lengthening the leaders by three inches we started catching coho one after the other. I didn't have to change fishing locations, baits or delivery devices. Simply making a minor adjustment in leader lengths made all the difference in the world. When pursuing spring coho, leader adjustments are crucial. It does make a difference!

Where can you run the 00 red dodger and fly? On some days it almost appears that you could catch coho before the dodgers hit the water. We recommend, however, that you run them on Dipsy Divers, side planers, downriggers and flat lines. If Chip and I could run only one coho set-up, it would be a shallow running Dipsy Diver followed by the 00 red dodger and fly. The Dipsy, without the power ring, is run out on 15-30 feet of line. The dodger is placed 4-6 feet behind the Diver, which is set on the 2.5-3 setting. If coho are present, they will have a hard time letting one of these rigs pass them by!

Body baits are also very popular and productive spring coho lures. When water colder than 43 degrees is present, body baits are often the most productive lures. Some of our favorites include Shad Raps, jointed J-9 Rapalas, Fat Raps, Bomber Long-A's and jointed Rebels. Hot colors include orange/gold, red, blue/silver, gold, black/gold, black/silver and the rainbow finish. Minnow imitators should be attached to the line via a loop knot. All crankbaits will work better on light line. Crankbait lines or leaders should be no heavier than 14 lb. test for spring fishing.

Crankbaits will catch coho on flat lines, side planers, Dipsy Divers and downriggers. When run on flat lines place them 50-150 feet behind the boat. We recommend using 6-12 lb. test for flatlining body baits. For planer action, set them back from 15-50 feet. Usually a shorter lead will keep them closer to the surface. For downriggers, experiment with lead lengths between 10-50 feet.

Side planers, direct and inline, are a favorite tool for anglers prowling the shallows. Flies/dodgers and cranks are the lures of choice for planer boards. These are run back from 8-30 feet depending on conditions. Again, the 00 red dodger and fly is the standard fly combo. When running a 00 dodger or flasher behind a side planer you may have to add a little weight to keep the dodger from skipping on the surface. Usually a $1/4$ or $3/8$ ounce keel sinker will do the trick. When running body baits off side planers you may want to experiment with keel sinker size. Cranks without any weight will produce one day, and at times you may need $1/4$ ounce of weight to draw strikes.

Since spring coho are aggressive, lures running close to the boat will often be the most productive. Believe it or not, coho are often attracted to the noise and commotion created by a spinning propeller! When this happens, the lines run closest to the propeller will out-fish all other lines. That is why a shallow set Dipsy Diver off the side or a boom-downrigger in or near the prop wash is so deadly.

If you need a compelling reason to fish for spring coho you may want to consider the taste factor. When taken from ice-cold water, small spring coho make excellent table fare! Many anglers consider small spring coho to be the tastiest Great Lakes fish! Grilled, fried, baked or smoked they are hard to beat. If you catch spring coho, you will definitely want to sample our recipe secrets at the end of the book! Many people have commented that eating fried coho fingers is like eating potato chips.

Shallow Water King Strategies

If spring kings are your targets, think baitfish and bottom structure. Kings are big, hungry fish. They need lots of food to survive. Spring kings love bottom structure. They will occasionally venture into warm water discharges, harbor mouths and river outflows, however larger numbers of kings can usually be found in deeper water. Kings will key off drop-offs, rock piles, humps and troughs in 30-70 feet of water. Bottom relief with as little variation as three to five feet may be enough to attract and hold kings. You will frequently find spring kings just outside and below schools of coho.

If you are not familiar with the topography of a region, you may want to consult a topo chart before hitting the water. Look for bottom relief in the 30-70 foot range. When fishing structure such as humps and drop-offs, make trolling passes across the structure from different directions. The kings may hang right on the structure or they may hold a quarter mile away from the structure. The point is they will concentrate in the vicinity of bottom structure.

When working bottom structure be aware that spring kings will often hold tight to the bottom. When this happens you may have to place your lures within several feet of the bottom. As you are working a piece of structure try raising and lowering your downriggers to keep your lure running along the bottom. Don't be afraid to occasionally tap the bottom with a rigger or wire line.

Spring kings can be taken off downriggers, Dipsy Divers, wire line, side planers and even flat lines. It is our experience, however, that downriggers produce the most spring kings. For the most part, lure delivery for spring kings is very similar to summer king fishing.

Spoons are the most productive lure group off downriggers during the spring months. Spoons are usually run from 10-50 feet off the weight. The most productive spring king spoon is the Silver Streak. Favorite spring colors include the green alewife, blue dolphin and green dolphin. Another top spring king spoon is the silver hammered Mauler in the small and medium size. When running spoons in the spring light line will greatly increase your action. We recommend 12 lb. test line. A small, quality ball bearing swivel is a must.

Body baits account for many spring kings. In areas where smelt are spawning long minnow imitators are hard to beat. Favorite spring king plugs include the Bomber Long A, jointed Rebels in the 2000 series and Thunderstiks. A variety of colors work but some of the more popular are rainbow finish, orange/gold, black/gold and green/yellow. Body baits will catch more kings on 12 lb. pound test line. Attach minnow type plugs to the line by use of a loop knot for maximum lure action.

Shallow Water Brown Trout Strategies

The spring months are a great time to target brown trout. Browns are a shallow water fish that are frequently caught within a mile of the

Brown trout are a shallow water fish, making them excellent targets for small boat anglers.

shoreline, making them an ideal target for small boat anglers. Browns are not as migratory as the other species. Certain locations will often produce great action week after week, year after year. Regions that receive large plantings of brown trout will frequently hold browns year round.

If you want to catch browns, think structure. Key locations to look for spring browns include warm water discharges, river and stream outflows, wave troughs and along rocky shorelines. Have you ever noticed that shore fishermen catch loads of brown trout? Harbor mouths and along breakwaters are also excellent areas for boaters to target. When fishing in the area of these major structure forms, pay close attention to detail. Look for smaller or microstructures in the vicinity of harbors mouths, river mouths and power plant discharges. These microstructures include corners and bends in breakwalls, underwater humps, near shore drop-offs, rock riprap, trenches, color lines and temperature breaks.

Browns like warmer water than coho and kings. If you can combine structure and warmer water, you will greatly increase your odds of catching browns. Most spring brown trout fishing will occur in 10-35 feet of water.

While brown trout can be caught on a variety of delivery systems, side planers are the most effective delivery tools to use in shallow water. Spring browns will often be found in the warmer surface waters. The boards allow you to present your baits to fish that have not been spooked by the boat. Side planers also allow you to place your lures in very shallow water and along breakwaters and pier heads.

Anglers use both the inline planers and direct planers (mast and ski.) The direct planers allow you to use lighter line. With inline planers you can splice in a 6-8 foot leader of 6 or 8 pound test line. This allows you to run the inline planer on your standard 17-20 pound test, but still place your bait on light line. If you are fishing in calm, clear water, the mast and ski planers may be more effective. These planers offer an added degree of stealth as the lures are not trailing directly behind the board.

Lead distance off planers depends on several factors including water clarity, wave action, depth at which fish are holding and the mood of the fish. Start each day by placing several baits long, 50-100 feet and several baits closer to the boards, say from 10-50 feet back. As you begin catching fish you can systematically determine the ideal lead length and adjust accordingly.

Dipsy Divers, flat lines and downriggers are also productive. When browns are holding tight to bottom structure, as they frequently do, downriggers and Dipsies will be your most effective presentation tool. The riggers and Dipsy Divers can produce anywhere from a few feet below the surface down to the bottom. Since most of the fishing is done in less than 35 feet of water, it usually doesn't take long to zero in on productive levels. Lead length for the riggers will vary from day to day, but typical leads are from 10-70 feet back. Water clarity and fish temperament are usually the determining factors in lead length.

Clean spoons and body baits are the dominant spring baits. Occasionally, the 00 and 0 dodgers and flies will take spring browns. Our favorite spoons for catching brown trout include: Mauler spoons in silver/blue and silver/green, Diamond Kings in the #4 green/glow and mongoose, Stingers, Sutton Spoons, small rattle spoons, Gold Stars in gold/rose and silver/purple, Pro Kings in blue/pearl and green/black and Silver Streaks in shades of green or orange. Proven spring cranks include Shad Raps, jointed Rebels and Rapalas, Thunder Stiks and Bomber Long A's. Favorite plug colors include shades of silver, gold, orange, brown, rainbow, copper, green and yellow.

Browns are a cautious fish. For this reason stealth, is a major contributor to success. Light line and small swivels are important. For clean spoons and body baits, 6-12 pound test line is optimum. Captain Ernie Lantiegne, one of the top brown trout anglers on Lake Ontario, recommends 8 pound test line for browns.

Offshore Action—Deepwater, It's Better Than You Think!

The deep, mysterious waters of the Great Lakes can be a very exciting place to visit during the spring months. This is steelhead country! Along with the high-flying silver bullet, the spring deeps will be home to roving schools of kings and coho salmon. If this is not enough to get your attention, some of the biggest lake trout of the year are caught each spring from the surface waters of the deeps. A 15-25 pound lake trout caught on light line off the cold surface is a very worthy opponent! In many locations you can catch four or five different species of fish a day.

Despite the great fishing available in offshore waters, many anglers never give the deeps a chance. Many anglers are satisfied with the action available in shallow water regions. Others are intimidated by the thought of fishing over 'deep' water. Admittedly, deep water can be intimidating. Yes, there is a great deal of water *out there*. Yes, there is a great deal of *empty* water *out there*. Yes, you can get *lost* in the deeps!

Yet, these factors should not keep you from exploring offshore fishing opportunities. The degree to which you are successful in fishing deep water often depends on how you approach deep water. You can approach the deeps randomly or you can approach the deeps with a plan. We recommend you head offshore with a plan.

Before heading offshore we will look at some basic elements of deep-water fishing. Then we will break this discussion down by species. We'll look at how to locate each species and then address specific angling techniques. Following that, we will tie it all together and take a brief look at the highly productive multi-species offshore presentation. The multi-species tactics can be used together, or the individual elements may be used separately.

Basic Elements of Offshore Fishing

Any time you fish offshore, five rules should govern your offshore strategies and techniques:

1. Identify your target species.
2. Be prepared to *hunt* for schools of fish.
3. Fine tune your trolling speed throughout the day.
4. Experiment with trolling direction.
5. When you locate active fish, stay with them.

Deep water is home to a variety of fish, identify your target species first. This will help you determine where you begin fishing (hunting) and how far a field you may want to wander. If kings are your primary targets, often the 70-140 foot band of water can produce dynamite results. If steelhead are your primary quarry, then anywhere beyond 140 feet of water is fair game. Once you determine a range, be prepared to cover some water as you search for active fish. Remember, while you may have a primary target species, your lure spread can still be multi-dimensional and tweaked to capitalize on local conditions.

Offshore fishing on the Great Lakes requires anglers to fine-tune their presentations. Pay close attention to trolling speed, trolling direction and stay with active fish. Success is often determined by your ability to focus on these three elements. These three intangibles are often ignored or dismissed as insignificant by many anglers.

Deep water fish are very speed and direction sensitive. The two are often tied together. Many of you have experienced days where you can't keep the lines in the water when you are trolling to the north. You spin around and make the same pass, through the same water but in the opposite trolling direction (south) and you don't have a single hit! You turn around and the north run produces fish again!

Why do we catch fish going in only one direction? Are the fish facing one direction? Often, the currents or wind will dictate a subtle difference on the world beneath the surface. It may have to do with some element of the baitfish's natural movement. It may be the unseen effect of currents on your trolling dynamic. The point is, the water and fish beneath the surface are reacting to their environment. Your trolling dynamic must appeal to the fish.

While we may not understand why fish behave this way, we need to compensate. The easiest and quickest way to react to 'one directional' fish

During the spring months lake trout can show up anywhere from the surface to the bottom.

is to experiment with trolling speed. Altering your trolling speed impacts your entire trolling dynamic, immediately. Remember, when fishing over open water, the productive trolling speed for one direction may not be productive in the opposite direction. As you change trolling direction to work back through a school of fish, don't be afraid to adjust trolling speed if the action slows. The speed you go in one direction may not be the most productive speed in another direction.

When fishing over deep water there are a number of variables that will affect your trolling speed including wind, waves, currents and trolling direction. The general speed range falls between 1.5 and 3 knots. Incremental speed differences of only a tenth of a knot can make a difference. If you are not getting action, you need to experiment with speed. Under tough conditions, the ability to fine-tune your speed will make the difference between a few fish and limit catches.

If you think fish are in a specific area, don't limit yourself to a one-directional fishing pass. You may pass southbound through a huge area of fish and not have your speed right. If you keep on trolling, you may leave the best fishing of the day! If you think fish are in an area, work the water from multiple angles. Make trolling passes from two to four different directions. This approach will improve your deepwater catches!

Another element of open water success is your ability to stay with active fish! When you take a section of deep, open water, the fish will often be concentrated in a few key areas. These "hot spots" often represent areas holding baitfish. If you find one of these hot spots, don't leave. Learn how to use your GPS or Loran so you can return to active fish.

Offshore Steelhead Strategies
Location, Location, Location...
Of all Great Lakes gamefish, steelheads exhibit the most nomadic nature and have the reputation of a heartbreaker. Schools of steelhead are known to show up in an area, provide several days of sizzling action and then vanish overnight! The big "bug-eaters," as Chip affectionately refers to them, have a rich history of doing the unexpected.

Despite the unpredictability of this fishery, some of the best steelhead fishing of the year occurs each spring over deep, open water. The key to catching spring steelhead is finding them. Hunting is as much a part of offshore steelhead fishing as lure selection. Be prepared to cover some water in your quest to locate fish. Once you find them, hang on as bone jarring strikes and aerial dynamics will be the fruit of your labor!

Steelheads are usually associated with deep open water. During the 1980's and early 1990's, it seemed that you had to run 10, 15 or 20 plus miles offshore to find the big concentrations of spring steelhead. Ever since zebra mussels have cleared up the water, large schools of steelhead can often be found much closer to shore. Some days the three to eight mile range will feature hot steelhead action. This does not mean there are not any steelheads in the more distant offshore waters. Steelhead like clear, cold water and today you can often find clear cold water closer to shore, unlike 15 years ago. In a typical year, you will find the major schools of steelhead over deeper water and outside the main schools of coho and kings.

We know steelheads are highly migratory, but do they relate to anything or do they just swim around randomly? To locate steelhead, look to the surface for signs of life. During the spring months, steelhead movements will be oriented toward the surface. Surface temperature breaks are the dominant features that will lead you to Mr. Steelhead.

Spring steelhead will concentrate along temperature breaks, current lines and color changes. Under normal conditions, you will find temperature breaks running parallel to the shoreline. Typically, water temperatures will get cooler as you travel further out onto the Lake. While all temperatures may hold steelhead, we have found that the three most productive breaks, in order of productivity, are the 42-44 degree band, the 47-48 degree band and the break that falls off into 39-degree water.

What is a temperature break? What does a temperature break look like? Temperature breaks can be classified into three categories; sharp, moderate and gradual.

A sharp break features a temperature inversion of three to ten plus degrees. The temperature inversion occurs within a 100 yards to a quarter mile stretch. These are the breaks seasoned offshore steelhead veterans dream about. These breaks are very easy to spot and often represent a current line as well. If you find a break such as this, hang on . . . steelhead love to load up on these breaks!

A moderate break will feature a temperature drop of two to ten degrees over a half a mile to one-mile expanse. This type of break is the most common type of break in many regions.

A gradual break displays a temperature change of one to seven degrees. It is really not a pronounced temperature inversion but rather a very gradual drop in water temperature over a one to two mile distance.

Steelhead will be more concentrated along sharp and moderate breaks. If you fish along the edge of a sharp or moderate break, you can expect to locate some thick schools of steelhead. If sharp or moderate breaks are not present, steelhead will usually show up along the gradual breaks. In this scenario you will typically find the steelhead scattered in loose schools or 'pockets.'

What is the origin of surface temperature breaks? These breaks are the result of lake warming, winds and currents. Surface breaks are transitory and will be moved by winds and currents. They may set up for a day or a week. Some breaks may drift offshore, others shoreward. A period of onshore winds will tend to concentrate the breaks and fish during the spring. If onshore winds prevail, you can expect to find sharp or moderate breaks offshore. Prolonged offshore winds will spread the surface water out and diffuse strong breaks. Under an offshore wind regime, you will find more gradual and moderate breaks.

How do you find temperature breaks? While you can spot dramatic surface breaks with the naked eye, two devices will help you locate surface breaks more efficiently. No serious offshore steelhead angler should leave port without a dash mounted surface temperature gauge. This is your key to locating and monitoring temperature breaks. A common technique is to run offshore and monitor your temperature gauge. Once you locate a fishy looking break, set up and begin trolling.

Sea surface temperature charts are your second tools. These charts are generated by satellite imagery and actually will show you before you even clear the pier heads a profile of the surface temperatures. These charts can help you determine general areas to begin searching for breaks and fish. If you don't have access to a satellite generated temperature chart, don't panic! Some of the best steelhead fishermen we know have never even looked at these charts. We won't ask Chip to mention any names.

How many temperature breaks will you find under normal conditions? Will there be one big break or a series of many smaller breaks? Typically, you will find a series of temperature breaks as you head offshore. The various individual breaks may not be the same size nor will they feature the same degree of temperature variations. As we can see from the diagram of surface temperature plots, some breaks will be con-

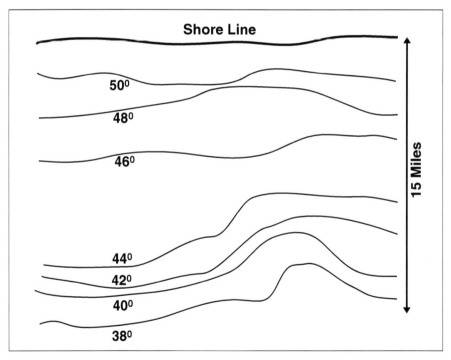

In a typical spring, water temperatures will drop as you head offshore. This diagram illustrates how temperature breaks can form. Notice the various distances between the breaks.

centrated in one location, but more diffused further up the shoreline. Some breaks will also hold more fish than others. Again, the hunting element appears!

If you encounter a series of temperature breaks, where should you begin fishing? Is there any way to identify the break holding the most steelhead? No, steelheads are a mysterious fish and if you want to catch steelhead, you may have to spend some time trolling around looking for them. One day you may set up on top of a big school, another day you may spend hours looking for them. Begin your search on the three most productive breaks; 42-43 degrees, 47-48 degrees and 39 degrees.

Here are a few general guidelines on how to approach temperature breaks with a plan. If we know a series of breaks extends offshore, we will often set up on the inside break and zigzag our way offshore. This gives us peace of mind that we haven't over-shot the fish. Once we locate a break with multiple strikes, we'll level off and begin working that break. Others, however, will go to the outside, or distant break, and work back to the shoreline.

Okay, you've picked a break to start on, how do you fish a temperature break for steelhead? Fish may hold right on the break, immediately to either side of it, or they may be half a mile inside or outside of the break. Remember, temperature breaks often function like a 'highway' within the lake. It is a point of reference for the fish as well as a feeding station.

Begin by trolling a zigzag pattern back and forth over the break. If that doesn't produce, try trolling parallel to the break or make perpendicular passes back and forth across the break, getting further and further beyond the break on each pass. If you are on a sharp break but not popping fish, try moving several miles up or down the break. Often a change in location along a break will bring results.

Trolling direction can make a difference. Before leaving an area try trolling in all directions. Sometimes trolling at a 120-degree angle rather than a straight 90-degrees will keep your lines popping! Trolling direction and speed go together. Both are hypercritical. As you adjust your trolling angle, making frequent looping turns, experiment with trolling speed. If you make a turn and your outside line gets hit, try trolling faster. If the inside planer line takes off on a turn, try a slow trolling speed. Be observant, and react to your environment and the moods of the fish!

What happens if you are offshore and there are no temperature breaks within a reasonable range? Under these conditions set up in 100-140 feet of water and begin working your way offshore until you locate fish. Believe it or not, this is a very productive way to locate rapidly moving schools of steelhead. Some people have compared this approach to "mowing the lawn." Make a plan, pick a pattern and start covering the water!

Offshore Steelhead Techniques

Now that you know where to find offshore steelhead, how do you catch them? There is no precise formula that will guarantee record catches of steelhead on every trip. Remember, steelheads are a very psychotic,

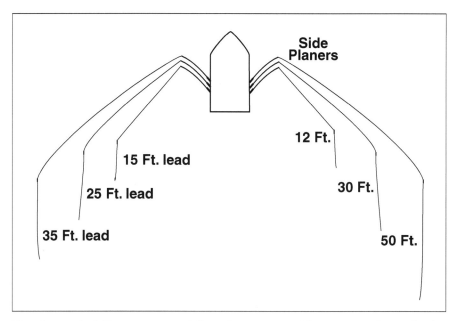

Here is a typical V pattern on an inline planer system. This pattern, shorter leads on the inside, will greatly reduce tangles from hooked fish. This pattern is also very productive for catching surface oriented fish.

unpredictable fish! Creativity and experimentation are often the trademarks of great offshore steelhead fishermen.

Most spring steelhead will be caught in the top 10 feet of water so you should concentrate your firepower on that range. The most effective tools for presenting your lures will be side planers (direct and inline), Dipsy Divers and flat lines. Usually a combination of the three will produce maximum results. Downriggers will catch spring steelhead, but they tend to be less effective.

Side planers are great tools to help you explore temperature breaks. They greatly expand your reach and they present baits to spooky fish. Spoons, body baits and flies and dodgers/flashers will work equally well off side planers. All three-lure groups can be mixed and matched.

On a horizontal perspective, a typical steelhead side planer pattern will look like an inverted V moving through the water. The outside planer lines will be run back further than the inside planer lines. Lead length is very important for side planers. Some days the baits will need to be 8-15 feet behind the boards. Other days the longer leads of 35-75 feet will draw strikes. Lead length depends on fish temperament and sea conditions. Best results and minimal tangles are achieved by placing the longer leads off the outside planer lines. Progressively shorten your leads as you move into the boat.

There is no science behind running Dipsy Divers for steelhead. Dipsies, without the power ring, are generally set out on 20-50 feet of line. The Diver is set on the 2.5 to 3.5 setting. If side planers are popping fish but Dipsies are slow, try setting the Divers on the 4 or 4.5 setting. As previously mentioned, steelhead are very unpredictable. Thus, some days they are drawn in to the turbulence created by the prop wash while other days finds them very skittish and spooky. When steelheads are curious, as they often are, short Dipsy lines will keep you on your toes! When in steelhead country, it often pays to have a Dipsy Diver set within 20-30 feet of the boat. One of our favorite spoons to run on a short Dipsy for steelhead is the magnum green dolphin Silver Streak.

Trolling speed is a key variable. Steelheads are not afraid of chasing fast moving baits. Many anglers will set up and troll at speeds of 2.5-3.2 knots to try and locate fish. If the faster speeds don't produce, don't be afraid to lower your speed. Steelheads are a highly unpredictable fish and you never know what to expect from them!

Steelheads exhibit a wide range in lure preference. On any given day, one lure group may out-produce the others. Hot spoons include Maulers, Silver Streaks, Gold Stars, Pro Kings, Finn Spoons, Pro Shiners, Grizzlies, Yuks, and Stingers. Productive color patterns include plain hammered gold, plain hammered silver, copper, gold/orange belly, silver/orange belly, red, blue/pearl, silver/blue, blue/yellow, watermelon, green/yellow, purple and gold/strawberry. As you can tell, bright flashy colors seem to draw the most strikes.

The most popular 'blades' for surface steelies are the 00 red Action Flash flasher and the 00 red Luhr Jensen dodger. The Action Flash works better at higher speeds. Tinsel flies from 2 to 4 inches long produce best. Our favorite steelhead fly is the Cheddar Fly. Fly size can be a critical factor in drawing strikes. At times a 4-inch fly will out produce a 2-inch fly and visa versa. Hot steelhead fly colors include medium blue/copper, medium blue/silver, purple, dark blue/gold, green/silver and red/black.

Body baits produce plenty of steelhead each spring. Productive plugs include the ever popular jointed J-9 and J-11 Rapala, Bomber Long-A, jointed J-2000 or J-3000 Rebels and Fastrac's. Again, stick with the brighter colors.

One final word on offshore steelhead: They prefer one another's company. In other words, steelheads like to swim with other steelhead. If you catch one or two steelhead in an area, thoroughly work the immediate area. Deepwater steelies frequently school by size. If you are catching four to six pound fish, you may want to search for a school of larger fish.

Offshore King Strategies

Spring kings can show up just about anywhere over deep water. Our experience, however, finds peak numbers of concentrated kings will be found in the 70-140 foot range. Spring kings will also suspend beyond this range over open water. The spring kings found suspended over 200 foot plus depths are often difficult to locate. If you are targeting steelhead over the wild blue yonder, it often pays to take your favorite spring king bait and run it down 60-120 feet. You may be surprised by the line-screaming run of an unexpected king in the middle of nowhere!

During the spring there is no established thermocline to concentrate deep water kings along. Frequently, the entire offshore water column may be less than 44 degrees. This creates a very broad strike zone! With cold water filling the entire water column, bottom structure will often be the clue leading you to spring kings. In many regions the 70-140 foot range is where you should zero in on drop-offs, hills, humps, rocky reefs and ledges. The drop-offs may be subtle, varying only two to three feet, or they may be more drastic. Kings holding on structure may suspend or hold tight to the bottom.

When fishing bottom structure for kings, approach the structure from multiple angles. Work parallel to drop-offs. If that doesn't produce, try trolling back and forth across a drop-off or work offshore from the drop. If the bottom structure is large in size, look for smaller features within the larger piece of structure. These nooks and crannies will often attract kings.

Spring kings are frequently the deepest fish in the water column.

To catch bottom-oriented kings, you may need to put your lures in the bottom five feet of water. Sometimes the bait must occasionally "tap" the bottom to trigger these bottom-oriented kings into striking. This can best be accomplished with downriggers or a wire line with a ball weight. Frequently very slow trolling speeds will be required to tempt these bottom dwelling kings into striking. Baitfish will also lead you to spring kings. If you find bait pods, chances are you will find kings lurking nearby.

If you want to catch kings in the spring, you need to fish for them. Once you make the decision to put some baits into the king's target range, your chances of catching spring kings improves dramatically. Spring kings can be taken on a variety of baits from all three-lure groups. Some anglers will have excellent action with spoons, others with body baits and some with flies and dodgers.

While you will catch some spring kings on the surface, most deepwater kings will be caught on downriggers and Dipsy Divers. Clean spoons are the most productive for downrigger fishing. These are run back 10-70 feet depending on target depth, sea conditions, water clarity and fish temperament. Top spoons include the medium and large Silver Streak in blue dolphin, green alewife, green dolphin and the Ludington Special. Small and medium Maulers in silver/green edge, hammered silver, black/pearl Yuks, black/silver Northport Nailers, gold or purple Gold Star's and the Stinger in silver/green, silver/purple also account for many spring kings.

Dipsy Divers run on super line and monofilament will also put many spring kings on ice. While clean spoons will work on Dipsy Divers, we have found that the 0 dodger followed by a Howie Fly is deadly over deepwater! The same colors used for summer kings work in the spring. Some anglers will use a suspended wire down the middle to target spring kings. An 0 dodger and Howie Fly will catch many kings when it is run as the deepest line, shotgun, over deep water. If I am fishing steelhead in the 'wild blue yonder,' I will frequently put a single wire with a one-pound ball down the middle on 200-400 feet of wire. This rig does not interfere with my steelhead presentation and it will let me know if there are any kings downstairs. A deadly deep water spring king set up on a suspended wire is a West River Sutton 36 inches behind an O silver dodger.

If kings are on the surface, clean spoons and body baits will draw strikes. The same spoons used for surface steelhead will produce kings. It is our experience that longer leads off the side planers will draw more king strikes. Run spoons and plugs with $1/4$ to 1 ounce of weight back 40-100 feet off planers.

Offshore Lake Trout Strategies

When most people think of lake trout, they think of heavy tackle and big sinkers bouncing the bottom in deep water. Did you know lake trout can often be found cruising the upper layers of the water column, mingling with coho and steelhead during the spring months? We've even seen hooked lake trout leaping from the water! Obviously associating with steelhead is inspiring to a lake trout! If you want to catch lake trout during the spring, you will have to re-calibrate your thinking.

During the months of April, May and early June lakers in the 15-25 pound range can be caught at or just below the surface. A 15 pound laker caught from ice-cold surface waters on light line can be a very worthy opponent!

Where do you find surface-oriented spring lake trout? Are they randomly scattered across the surface? While some lakers will be caught randomly across the surface, anglers targeting key areas will catch many more lakers. If you want to increase your odds of catching surface lakers in the spring, there are a few clues that will lead you to concentrations of lake trout.

Whether you find lake trout on the bottom, suspended or at the surface, lakers are a structure-oriented fish. Even when they are cruising the surface layers, chances are, bottom structure will still influence their location. During the spring, lakers will often suspend in the upper layers of the water column near their favorite summer haunts. Go to your favorite bottom structure and look for the lakers in the upper layers of the water column. If the water is less than 50 degrees from the surface to the bottom, Mr. Lake Trout may be anywhere from the surface to the bottom over drop-offs, hills and deepwater humps.

Spring lake trout are also attracted to surface breaks. The same temperature breaks we discussed for steelhead will also attract and hold lakers. The colder breaks of 38-44 degrees are most attractive to lake trout. On many days you will find lakers mixed in amongst the steelhead along these breaks. In some locations, however, the lake trout will not be mixed in with other fish. Generally speaking, you can find lake trout on the surface from 100 feet of water and beyond. On Lake Michigan we catch many spring lakers in 200-400 feet of water.

Lake trout are a school fish and when one laker heads up to the surface, others will follow. Once you start catching lakers, mark the spot as other lakers will be in the area. Lake trout are opportunistic feeders. Once you locate lakers, catching them often just becomes a matter of being in the right spot at the right time. In other words, you *can* catch spring lake trout on just about any lure if they are feeding.

The same baits and tactics used to catch steelhead will also produce surface oriented lake trout with two major differences. First, downriggers set from 20-50 feet down will produce many suspended spring lakers. Second, clean spoons run back 50-100 plus feet off side planers are the most productive set-ups for surface trout. While side planers are the most productive delivery system, flat lines, Dipsy Divers, wire line, lead core and downriggers will also produce spring lakers.

The most productive spoon is the Mauler in gold/hammered belly, gold with an orange belly, silver with an orange belly and silver/hammered belly. Other productive spoons to run on the surface include Gold Stars, Pro Kings, the Big Red Spoon, Finn spoons, Stingers, Grizzlies, Pro Shiners and Silver Streaks. Gold, red and orange are the best colors. A $1/4$ to 1-ounce weight is added ahead of the spoon.

Body baits such as Bomber Long A's, jointed Rapalas and Rebels and other similar plugs account for many surface oriented lakers. The OO red blades and flies used for steelhead will also take lake trout on the surface. When running downriggers for suspended trout 20-50 feet down, run the riggers just as you would in summer. Try a mix of clean spoons and 0 dodgers and flies. Spring lake trout are known to strike lures at a variety of trolling speeds. Some days slow, other days fast. Experiment with trolling speed until you connect with consistent action.

Offshore Coho Strategies

Deepwater coho fishing is very similar to shallow water coho fishing. The primary difference is fishing location. The techniques used to catch coho are very similar whether you are in 33 feet of water or 220 feet of water. Lure selection may be influenced by the diet of deepwater coho. Deepwater coho will feed on insects as well as alewives. As always, coho are a highly social creature.

There is no exact science for locating schools of deepwater coho. Coho can turn up just about anywhere in cold water. Typically, you will find them in the top 30 feet. Surface temperature breaks are often the clues that will reveal these schools. Many times, however, schools of coho will randomly roam open areas in search of the next meal. We recommend placing a few coho baits in the water when searching for offshore steelhead, lake trout or kings. Coho will let you know if they are present!

Deepwater coho are just as easy to catch as their shallow water cousins. The same baits run off the same set-ups will draw strikes. The techniques discussed in the spring shallow water section will work over deep water. The only noticeable difference is that the deepwater coho will strike spoons more readily. For this reason, many anglers will fish for steelhead and lake trout, and if coho are present, they will take them on the spoons. If spoons start popping coho, you may want to add more red dodgers and flies to your spread, capitalizing on the coho bite.

Go Long for Great Mixed Bag Action!

One of our favorite attributes of offshore spring fishing is the variety of fish you can encounter. When fishing offshore waters, it is not uncommon to return to the dock with three, four or five species of fish on one outing. If shallow water fishing is slow, deepwater will often provide you with more opportunities to battle fish because of the variety of species offshore. By targeting multiple species simultaneously, you increase your catching odds.

Steelheads are a favorite target of offshore anglers across the Great Lakes.

To consistently catch a variety of species, you must target all species simultaneously. You must approach deep waters with a multi-species focus or mindset. You will draw from experience and methods utilized for steelhead, lakers, kings and coho. The tricks and techniques used to catch the individual species will be woven into a comprehensive and complete trolling dynamic. Successful mixed bag anglers incorporate side planers, flat lines, downriggers and Dipsy Divers into their spring presentation matrix. Occasionally, a suspended wire line or lead core will find its way into the water.

Before you begin setting lines for a springtime mixed bag, you need to divide the water column into two target zones. First is the surface layer. This layer, the top 10 or 20 feet, is where you will encounter most of your steelhead, coho and lake trout. The second zone is the 30-120 foot layer. This is the zone where you will find most of your spring kings and occasionally some big lake trout and coho. When targeting a mixed bag, your thinking should be focused on these two distinct zones.

We will use side planers, a pair of Dipsy Divers and a flat line to target zone one. These lines are targeting steelhead, lake trout and coho. We will set our downriggers and a pair of deep Dipsy Divers for kings, in zone two. The depth range on the riggers and Divers will depend on depth of water being fished and local conditions. The typical range will be from 30-70 feet down.

Let's dissect zone two first. This is king country! Think kings when setting these lines. The king rods may look something like this: two Fire Line Dipsy Divers set to run 30 and 40 feet deep. Next, we'll place one downrigger at 45 feet, one at 55, one at 65 and the deepest one will be 70 feet deep. If conditions permit, we will run a suspended wire line down the middle. This will be run out on 200-400 feet of line. Either a one-pound weight or a Dipsy Diver may be used with the suspended wire. Standard king baits should be used.

As you can see, we begin by spreading our deep lines to cover a wide swath of the water column. The deeper lines will be adjusted throughout the day as we look for active kings or zero in on the strike zone. If you are fishing on a smaller or mid-size boat, you may elect to only place one or two downriggers down for kings. You may also scale back to only one deep Dipsy Diver. Again, as we unpack the mixed bag dynamic, you can use pieces or elements of each individual aspect.

If you are trolling at a fast clip or have found a hot steelhead bite, six or seven deep lines may interfere with your ability to capitalize on the steelhead bite. During these conditions we may scale back our king presentation and run only one or two downriggers off the back for kings. As the day unfolds, concentrate on the species the Lake gives you!

The surface zone is where you will encounter most of your active offshore fish. The mixed bag surface program is very easy to run. One monofilament Dipsy Diver is set off each side. These are run out on 15-30 feet of line with the Diver set on the $2^1/_2$ setting. These two rods can take anything with a clean spoon or the 00 red dodger/fly combo. Typically, we may put a dodger on one shallow Dipsy for coho and a clean spoon on the other side for steelhead. Some anglers will elect to run a second set of Dipsy Divers set out on 30-60 feet of line in lieu of the deeper king Dipsies.

A flat line using six or eight pound test is let out off the back between

75-200 feet. A jointed minnow imitator is deadly for big lake trout and steelhead. The light line is critical when running plugs in clear, cold surface water.

Side planers (inline or direct) are next. We run a combination of flies and dodgers/flashers, spoons and body baits off side planers. On any given day, one of the preceding lure groups may be more effective. You may also find you catch more steelhead on spoons and lakers on plugs on a given day. You need to experiment with your lure mix each day to achieve maximum results.

Most anglers run anywhere from one to five lines (side planers) per side. The number of side planers will depend on sea conditions, boat size and body count. With the advent of clearer water in the Great Lakes, we have found that sometimes less is more. Usually two to four side planers is more than adequate. The advantage of running additional planer board lines is that you can experiment with lure selection.

When setting lines off planers, Chip and I like to run the outside lines farther back behind the planer. As you move into the boat, the lines will be set progressively shorter or closer to the planer. The reason for setting planer lines in this pattern has to do with lure presentation and trolling efficiency. This pattern will minimize tangles when fighting fish and trolling in sloppy seas. For example, if you run your inside planer longer than the outside planer, when you hook a big fish on the outside planer, he will probably swim across and tangle the long, inside planer line.

Lure selection and distance off the side planers allows us to target different species with individual lines. When running spoons off the planers, these will be run back anywhere from 20-70 feet. Dodgers and flies are run on shorter leads from 8-30 feet back. Body baits are most effective on calm days and these are set back anywhere from 20-100 feet.

In a typical mixed bag spread we will run either a clean spoon or body bait off each outside planer. Next we will set a mix of fly/dodgers and spoons. These lines will be set progressively shorter as we move into the boat. To illustrate this concept, a typical three line side planer set-up would include a clean spoon or plug 50-70 feet behind the outside planer, a fly/dodger or spoon 20-30 feet off the middle planer and a fly/dodger or spoon 10-20 feet behind the inside planer. There is no exact percentage of spoons to flies to cranks, so experiment! Alter lead lengths until you start catching fish. We will attach a ¼-ounce weight six feet ahead of all lures. If lake trout are present, we may add up to an ounce of weight on the outside planers.

When targeting a mixed bag on the surface, you need to use lures that all species will find appetizing. Our favorite spoon for mixed bag surface action is the Mauler spoon. The Mauler is a great spoon because it catches all species over a wide range of trolling speeds. A variety of colors work but our favorites incorporate gold, silver, orange, purple, copper or blue. Other multi-species spoons include the Gold Star, Pro Kings, and Silver Streaks.

Good multi-species dodger combos include a 00 red Action Flash flasher or a Luhr Jensen dodger followed by a tinsel fly. Favorite mixed bag fly colors include medium blue, medium blue/silver, dark blue/gold and green/silver. The flies are run 9-17 inches behind the dodgers. As always, fly leader length is critical!

When using the Dipsy Divers to target the 30-80 foot range, we tend to favor the 0 dodger followed by a Howie Fly. This set up will take kings, coho and the occasional laker and steelhead during the spring. Productive spring dodger colors include silver glow, white, silver and yellow. Favorite fly colors include crinkle green, green, pearl blue and white.

Okay, you're running offshore, and you've spotted that fishy looking corner in the middle of nowhere over 180 feet of water; now what? Actually, this is the easy part! Put out a spread of lures that are speed tolerant and begin to cover some water. Remember, while you may be targeting kings or steelhead, lake trout, coho and the occasional brown trout are fair game!

THE SUMMER TRANSITION

No discussion of seasonal fishing would be complete without addressing the summer transition period. What is the summer transition? Basically, it is the period where the Great Lakes fish transition from spring schooling and feeding habits to summer habits. The implication for fishermen is that change is immanent. If salmon and trout are adapting their feeding habits and changing locations, anglers will need to react and transition from spring techniques and locations to summer methods.

The summer transition is never identical from one year to the next. How does one know when they are fishing in the summer transition period? In a typical year, the summer transition is characterized by a handful of features. Surface waters begin to heat up and a thermocline starts to develop. Fish tend to move offshore and deeper in the water column.

You may encounter a window of time where game fish scatter as they adapt to a changing lake. Salmon and trout will also start acting differently. For this reason, the techniques and locations that produced fish during May will often be less productive during the summer. Techniques and locations that produced fish during the spring begin to diminish in effectiveness. Some species may begin to disappear and others may move into the area. Typically, this transition occurs during the month of June. The transition period will normally last anywhere from one to three weeks.

The summer transition period can provide some extremely challenging fishing. Anglers need to be flexible and try spring and summer lures, techniques and locations. On tough days during the transition we have often felt like we were trapped in a time warp between spring and summer. This leads to an identity crisis for the boat as half the lines are set up for spring and half for summer!

Don't panic! Plenty of great fishing is still had during this period. Being able to identify when you are in the transition period is half the battle. Success comes to those anglers who can fish a variety of methods simultaneously and adapt to fast changing conditions.

Summer Fishing on The Great Lakes—Big Fish Time!

If you could only sample one fishing period or season on the Great Lakes, it should be the summer months. Not only are some of the biggest fish of the season caught during the summer months, but also calm seas and a variety of species can be found in many locations. The summer months provide some of the most exciting salmon and trout action of the year.

Our discussion of summer fishing will be broken down into two sections. First, we will look at the hunt; how do you locate fish during the summer. Secondly, we will unpack summer techniques. We will examine proven summer techniques used to catch salmon and trout around the Great Lakes. These fish finding methods and techniques can be adapted and applied to any large body of water that holds salmon and trout. We will use the *group/trolling dynamic* as our framework to analyze summer fishing strategies.

We approach our discussion of locating summer salmon and trout from a theoretical angle. A wise old fisherman once said, "You can't catch them, if you don't find them." It doesn't matter how many lines you have in the water or how good your trolling dynamic looks; if there are no fish under or around your boat, you won't catch fish! It's like baseball. Babe

The king salmon is the pinnacle of the Great Lakes food chain. It is also the prize catch for anglers across the Lakes.

Ruth never hit a home run without a pitcher tossing a ball across the plate. You have to find the fish before you can catch them!

Summer fishing on the Great Lakes features a wide degree of variation. Each individual Lake and region has its own set of unique characteristics and microclimates. These factors will impact local fish movements and techniques. Some regions will require you to target fish suspending from 80 to 120 feet deep. Other ports will hold cold water and summer anglers will target a thermocline that is only 30 to 50 feet down. Multiple scenarios will unfold around the Great Lakes each summer. This chapter will equip you to face a variety of scenarios wherever you fish on the Great Lakes!

LOCATING SUMMER SALMON AND TROUT

A Theoretical Discussion

How many of you men have ever had your wife ask you to go to the grocery store to pick up "just a couple of items?" You know the routine, it "will only take you 15 minutes, dear?" You know what happens next... 30 minutes later, and you still have no clues where the French's French Fried Onions are. You know what I'm talking about? The crispy onions you put on green bean casserole... the red, white and blue can that could be hiding in almost any aisle of the local grocery store, depending on the whims of the grocery stockers.

Fishing can be a lot like shopping for groceries. We know what we're looking for out there... they are silver, have beady little eyes, fins and come in a variety of sizes? The problem is, we often don't know *where* the fish *are*. Just like the French's Onions that we know are in the grocery store, we know the fish are in the Lake, but where?

In this section we are going to teach you the theoretical aspects of salmon and trout fishing—how do you find fish? How do we find anything? Typically, there are two ways of finding something. We look for things that are somewhere outside our scope of knowledge, like the French's onions, or we just intuitively *know* where something is. We all know the location of the chips and snacks in a grocery store! Fishing is a combination of the two approaches. While every fishing trip involves some hunting, intuition should be lurking in the background, ready to help guide the hunt!

The individual Great Lakes are each a little bigger than your average farm pond. Where does one begin looking for fish? When heading out into the wild blue yonder we are not approaching the Lakes in a chaotic fashion. Believe it or not, the Lakes give us clues, both beneath the surface and above, which will point us toward fish. The clues can be divided into two categories: physical structure and seasonal or temporal variables. Physical structure is defined as water temperature (vertical and horizontal breaks), baitfish, currents (surface and sub-surface) and bottom contours. Variables include time of year, local weather and port of departure.

Summer fishing on the Great Lakes is the most challenging, yet most rewarding season. All four structure elements come into play and in fact, the intersection of the four structure elements is often the point where feeding salmon and trout can be found! During the summer months, more than any other period of the year, you will find all five species of salmon and trout utilizing the same water. They may segregate within the water column, but they will often be found in the same general regions. When these intersections are located over deep water, you will often find multiple species feeding on the same schools of baitfish.

Summer Salmon Essentials

What do salmon and trout spend their entire life doing? Are they reading the newspaper? Looking into retirement plans? Focusing on raising good little salmon? NO! From birth to death, the primary activity of salmon is locating and consuming the next meal. They try to do this within their optimum temperature range! Salmon and trout are high-octane fish. They can't afford to sit around and enjoy the scenery. If that is their outlook on life, they will perish.

Do you understand the implications of the preceding paragraph? Find baitfish and cold water together in the summer and your chances of catching a lot of big fish dramatically increases! Summer salmon and trout will always find the bait and the cold water. You better find them too!

Water Temperature

Salmon and trout have ideal water temperature ranges. Yes, they are cold blooded and can survive under a variety of conditions. Fish that thrive, however, will seek out their ideal temperature ranges. In order to be a successful summer angler you need to know the preferred temperature ranges of your targets. Once you know where this ideal water temperature is located, you've just eliminated vast areas of dead water!

Let's review the preferred temperature ranges for Great Lakes salmon and trout: coho 48-54 degrees, chinook 42-44 degrees, lake trout 44-48 degrees, steelhead 42-56 degrees and brown trout 54-62 degrees. As you will notice, kings prefer the coldest water of the five species.

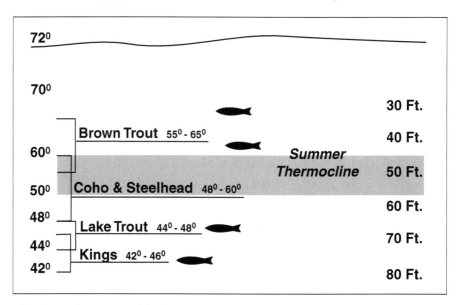

The thermocline is one of the keys to locating fish during the summer months. Once you locate the thermocline, you can zero in on the individual species of fish. This diagram shows the general temperature ranges, with respect to the thermocline, you are most likely to encounter salmon and trout during the summer. While fish do have preferred comfort ranges, they will occasionally cross temperature boundaries to feed.

Some may debate this temperature preference. We, however, consistently catch more and bigger kings in 42-44 degree water. We are not alone in this. Our good friend Captain Ernie Lantiegne agrees with our temperature analysis. His results also show that kings in the Eastern Great Lakes basin prefer 42-44 degree water. As you will notice, steelheads have the widest temperature range and browns prefer the warmest water.

By focusing on ideal temperature zones, you eliminate huge areas of real estate. During the summer months, the Lakes are stratified. Once you know the ideal temperature range or 'comfort zone,' you can use process of elimination to guide you in where to begin fishing. In order to do this, you must look at the Lake vertically and horizontally. Horizontally, you will eliminate areas that are too shallow for peak feeding temperature zones. Vertically, you will know what levels of the water column to target.

Depending on the target species available in your fishing destination, you now have a very specific water target. Now that we know the ideal temperature ranges of our target species, how do we go about locating comfort zones? You begin by finding the thermocline. The summer thermocline is one of the dominant factors impacting salmon and trout movements. At times the thermocline will function as a "superhighway" for active fish. Once you find the thermocline, everything is up and down from it.

Why does the thermocline attract and hold fish? First, it is a physical boundary separating masses of warm and cold water. Second, it holds zooplankton and phytoplankton. Both of these attract baitfish, which draw predators. A very simple key to using the thermocline to locate fish is to remember that typically coho, steelhead and browns will feed just below the thermocline to just above it. Kings and lake trout will usually hold below the thermocline from 48-degree water down to the 42-degree layer.

How Do You Locate the Thermocline?

There are three general ways to locate a thermocline. The most precise way is to use a sub-surface temperature probe. Today many downriggers have temp probes built into them. These are great tools for summer anglers as they allow you to pinpoint ideal temperatures at exact depths. If you don't have downriggers with built-in temperature sensors, don't worry. There are also a variety of less costly temperature probes. These devices, which are relatively inexpensive, can be attached to your downrigger and sent to depth. You can learn more about these devices in Chapter 2.

Did you know you can locate the thermocline before you even put a line in the water? Many graphs will actually pick up and show the thermocline on their screens. Many experienced anglers will run under power and monitor their graphs. By watching the level of the thermocline on their graph, they will know at what depth to place their lines before they even slow down.

What exactly is happening when we say the graph 'marks' the thermocline? Is the sonar picking up and registering a signal off cold water? No. As we mentioned above, a thermocline attracts and collects large amounts of plankton, baitfish and what we call a "debris field." The dead matter that sinks down in the water column and collects along the thermocline creates the debris field. The sound signal emitted by many graphs will actually bounce off the debris field and the plankton and baitfish in the thermocline. What is registering on the graph is the result of these echoes. Typically, the plankton, debris field and baitfish will run in horizontal layers upon the thermocline. At times a thermocline will also feature some form of sub-surface current. The turbulence and clutter in strong currents will also register on the graph.

Some graphs are better than others at marking a thermocline. See Chip's discussion of electronics in Chapter 2 to learn about today's high-powered sonar machines! The performance of your graph will be enhanced if you mount the transducer amidships in a through-hull fitting. This reduces turbulence. This is especially true when running under power and scouting for bait pods and monitoring the thermocline.

A third way to locate the thermocline is through the super highway of fishing information. A quick stop at a local baitshop or a phone call from a friend who has fished recently can reveal the depths and locations of a local thermocline.

Thermocline Movement

Before moving on, we need to realize that thermoclines are not static. Depending on where you fish on the Great Lakes, thermoclines may feature rapid movement or gradual transitions. As you move offshore, you will also notice that the thermocline may be at different levels in the water column. Also, as the summer progresses, a thermocline will typically move deeper in the water column.

What causes the thermocline to move and shift levels in the water column? The Great Lakes are large bodies of water. They are not large enough, however, to escape the effects of wind. Wind driven currents have a tremendous effect on thermocline location. As the winds shift direction, increase and decrease, a local thermocline may move up and down in the water column over the course of the summer. Typically, extended periods of onshore winds will drive a thermocline deeper on the

When you target the water column by temperature preferences, great mixed bag catches become a frequent occurrence.

windward shore. Extended periods of offshore winds will move a thermocline higher up in the water column in the lee of the shoreline.

General Lake warming and cooling will also impact thermocline formation and movements. Each geographical region has subtle differences influencing movements. An observant angler will pay attention to the conditions leading up to an outing and will make notes of how it affects the location and movements of the thermocline. This information should be recorded for future reference.

Baitfish

One fish, two fish, red fish, blue fish . . .you know the rhyme. For summer fishing on the Great Lakes think baitfish, baitfish, baitfish. These silvery little guys are a key ingredient to hot summer action. The preferred baitfish of Great Lakes salmon and trout are alewives. As we said earlier, salmon and trout are high-octane fish. They must find the bait to survive.

During the summer months, alewives can be found in schools or 'pods.' Alewife schools come in many sizes. They can be small, and rather isolated like an oasis in a desert. Or, the smaller schools are fragments of a larger group of alewives. These "loose" schools may cover a small or large area. Last is the super school. These are massive schools of alewives that we have charted up to a half-mile in length.

Regardless of school size, anglers need to find the bait. The key to locating bait pods is a good graph with mid to high-speed resolution. Many charter captains and top tournament anglers will simply run under power watching their graphs for signs of bait. Once bait pods are marked, they will slow down and begin to look for game fish marks, or just begin fishing.

Once you locate bait, there are a number of different ways to approach the pods. When you mark schools of bait in conjunction with structure and ideal water temperatures, you can slow down and monitor your graph for predator marks. Circle or run a zigzag pattern through the general area. If marks are there, the answer is simple—time to fish! If you don't mark predators but you think fish are present, you can begin to fish. If you set up on bait, try trolling over and around the baitfish from all different angles.

If game fish are not in or near the bait, store the location and return to the area later in your fishing trip. If alewives are schooled up, the salmon and trout will find them. Chances are also good that feeding salmon and trout have already concentrated the bait into pods. The game fish will return. If bait is scarce in a region, we may choose to fish around bait pods and wait for the fish to begin feeding.

Bait schools, or 'stacks,' as they call them in Florida, are tremendous pieces of non-traditional structure. These schools have a huge bearing on salmon and trout movements. If you understand how salmon and trout relate to bait stacks, you can take full advantage of any baitfish schools you encounter. The posture of salmon and trout to the bait will be; 1) aggressive or feeding, 2) dormant or 3) gamefish will be in the process of chasing the bait into tight schools or pods.

Obviously, feeding fish are the easiest to catch. When you encounter this situation you will mark balls or stacks of bait on your sonar and you will see predator marks in, around and slashing through the bait pods. This situation often results in fast action but many short hook-ups.

If fish are dormant, you will mark gamefish outside and below the bait pods. You may not mark any gamefish around the bait. In this scenario don't hesitate to send a few lines down around the bottom. Fish may sit just outside the bait pods and hold close to the bottom. Kings, lake trout and browns are known to lay so tight to the bottom that most graphs will not pick them up. These fish may not show up on your graph but they are very catchable! In this situation you may have to scratch the bottom to trigger strikes.

Another situation frequently encountered during mid-day is when salmon and trout are 'shadowing' the bait balls. These fish are not actively feeding; but, if bait is in the area, they will stay close to the bait. When the fish are ready to feed, they don't have far to travel. Patient anglers will work the schools of bait and pick off the predators that are staying close to the bait. These fish may require a bit more finesse to trigger into striking than the feeding fish.

Currents

When we think of ocean fishing, we know currents play a huge role in dictating fish locations. Did you know the Great Lakes contain currents? Do you realize that these currents not only steer water stratification, but they also play a major role in fish movements and locations? Great Lakes currents are one of the least understood areas of fishing.

Many experienced charter captains don't fully understand the impact of currents on Great Lakes fishing. Currents,

1. move fish around and
2. impact your trolling dynamic.

Your ability to locate and catch salmon and trout will improve dramatically when you understand this principle! No matter where you fish on the Great Lakes, it's impossible to escape the influence of currents.

The Great Lakes feature both surface and sub-surface currents. Our currents are the result of wind and the Coriolis effect. Space limits us here, so we will focus on wind driven currents. Before looking at wind-driven currents, let's look briefly at the Coriolis effect. It is produced by the earth's rotation. In the northern hemisphere it produces a clock-wise rotation of water in large bodies of water. The currents resulting from the Coriolis effect is subtle, but seasoned anglers learn to factor them into their fishing plan. The Coriolis effect often results in a strong reverse current in less than 150 feet of water.

Wind driven currents play a huge role in fish locations and fishing presentations. Across the Great Lakes, the wind generates surface and sub-surface currents. In many locations the surface and sub-surface currents will be moving in different or opposite directions. This is referred to as a 'reverse current.'

To better understand how currents impact our Lakes, let's take a brief look at water in the Great Lakes. This will help us understand the impact of currents on fish. Water in the Great Lakes often moves in masses or bands. The currents, which are predominantly driven by the winds, will steer the location of these water masses. Alewives, which are weak swimmers, will frequently get caught or stuck in a band of water. When the band of water moves, the baitfish moves with the water.

Let me illustrate this point. On the western shore of Lake Michigan we often find fish holding in bands of water running parallel to the shoreline. As you move offshore, you will find schools of fish 5-6 miles out, another major school 8 miles offshore and yet another band of fish 12 miles offshore. Frequently, you will find schools of fish holding the same distance from the shoreline at ports 20 miles up and down the shoreline. These bands of water will hold large amounts of active fish, but the water between the bands will often be barren and void of gamefish or bait fish. After the wind and currents shift, these bands of water and their fish will frequently change location.

Understanding currents is complicated. Before moving forward let's review the basics. The Great Lakes are full of surface and sub-surface currents. These currents move masses of water and greatly influence predator and bait locations. Let's move forward and examine how wind driven currents impact fishing.

Wind has a huge effect on summer fish location, because the winds determine the depth of the thermocline. Remember, the thermocline is one of the major features determining fish locations. Summer onshore winds will drive warm surface water in along the shoreline. Extended periods of onshore winds will pile warm water up along a shoreline. This will drive the colder water out and down deeper into the Lake. This scenario tends to drive the thermocline deeper in the water column. If it is later in the summer, this may also drive the thermocline further offshore.

Offshore winds have the opposite effect. Extended periods of offshore winds will push the warmer surface waters out and away from the shoreline. This will cause the deeper, colder water to move up and shoreward. The cold water will hit the shoreline or near-shore drop-offs and move up in the water column. This is often referred to as *rolling* or an *upwelling*. In this scenario, the thermocline will be higher in the water column closer

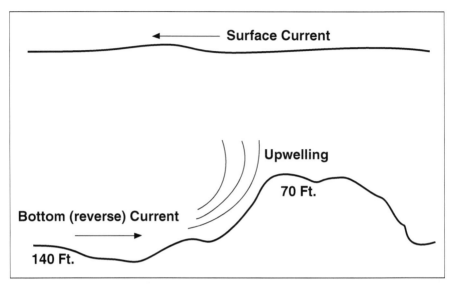

Reverse currents moving along the bottom in the Great Lakes frequently result in an upwelling where the current hits drop-offs and bottom structure. Upwellings are good locations to locate salmon and trout.

to the shoreline. As you move offshore, the thermocline will descend. If a strong summer upwelling occurs, the cold water will come all the way into the beach. You may have 44-50 degree water on the surface against the shoreline in July or August.

A wind that is swirling or shifting directions on a daily basis will often mix up the water. During spring and fall months a swirling wind pattern will produce large areas where there are no drastic temperature changes. During the summer months it may break up strong thermoclines and may scatter fish.

A stable wind regime will concentrate fish. Stability is usually good for fishing. It encourages layers of water to set up and allows bait and gamefish to settle into patterns. During the summer months a stable wind pattern will often result in a strong thermocline set up. Stable wind patterns make it easier to locate feeding salmon and trout on a daily basis.

Not only do currents play a role in water column stratification, they also have a huge impact on alewives. Alewives are weak swimmers. If a strong current is in an area, they won't fight it. They tend to be pushed along by currents. This is also true of the plankton alewives feed on.

Here is a simple hint for anglers who have not been on the water for an extended period of time: When you plan a fishing trip, monitor wind direction and velocity several days prior to your trip. This information will frequently give you clues as to thermocline and fish locations before you even leave the harbor! If you fish once a week or bi-weekly, this trick can help you to theoretically track fish movements from home. It will save you valuable time on the water.

This discussion of currents has been admittedly short. It is a huge topic that deserves greater attention but the limitations of space and the scope of this book prohibit that. It is our hope that this introduction to currents will open your eyes to an often-ignored element of Great Lakes fishing. When you go fishing, pay close attention to how the water, both on the surface and below, is moving.

Currents have a huge impact on fish locations. Remember, currents move masses of water, influence the formation and location of a thermocline, move baitfish and ultimately, impact the location of feeding salmon and trout. Experience is the best teacher when it comes to learning to read the water. We will examine the impact of currents on the trolling dynamic in *Summer Techniques*.

Bottom Contour

For years inland fisherman and saltwater anglers have focused on bottom structure when looking for fish. Great Lakes salmon anglers, however, have a reputation for minimizing the role of bottom structure. It is our belief that bottom contour plays a huge role in locating salmon and trout. Kings, lake trout and brown trout are the most structure sensitive, but coho and steelhead also key off bottom contours.

What forms of bottom structure impact summer salmon and trout movements? The Great Lakes feature a variety of different bottom contours. Yes, any form of bottom variation may attract fish. Certain features, however, will draw fish year after year. The dominant bottom features in the Great Lakes that concentrate salmon, trout and alewives are drop-offs, hills, humps, trenches, depressions, reefs and rocky shoals.

Why do these structures attract fish? While the individual features themselves may attract and hold bait and game fish, the structure often has a larger impact on the surrounding area. As we previously mentioned, currents are often moving along the bottom. When these bottom currents hit drop-offs, hills and humps, they deflect the current causing a local upwelling. This mechanism will attract baitfish and hold the bait in a specific location.

How large or small does a piece of bottom structure need to be to attract fish? I learned to appreciate subtle bottom detail from fishing off the Southwestern coastline of Florida. This portion of the Gulf of Mexico appears featureless to the untrained eye. What I learned from Gulf Coast anglers was that incredibly minor variations in the bottom often attracted and held bait and pelagic species in big numbers!

I applied this new thinking to the Great Lakes and began fishing structure previously ignored. By studying charts and my sonar, I discovered a number of new locations to fish. Much of this structure was in 100-250 feet of water and was water I had ignored or passed over for years. My catch rate improved because I had expanded my fishing horizon without traveling to a new location.

Obviously, the larger the structure, the more area that is impacted and the more fish attracted. When you locate larger bottom structures look for smaller or microstructures on or in the vicinity of the dominant piece of structure. These smaller features will often hold fish and go unfished by most anglers. An example of this would be a bank or drop off that runs parallel to the shoreline. If the drop runs north and south but takes a thirty-degree angle in one location, that bend will attract fish. Bumps on drop-offs or where two troughs or ridges intersect will also concentrate fish.

If a region tends to have little bottom structure, even the smallest nooks and crannies will function as fish magnets. Drop-offs and humps that only have 3-7 feet of relief will often hold fish if the surrounding bottom is relatively flat.

Does deepwater structure impact fishing for suspended fish? Yes, bottom features will impact the surrounding water whether they are in 20 feet of water or 200 feet. In the area we fish, there is a small rise or hump in 240 feet of water. It is affectionately called the "Big A Reef" in honor of Captain Arnie Arredondo. Arnie is one of the very best salmon fishermen alive! On a quiet day, he announced over the radio that he had discovered a "new reef." After a great deal of heckling, a number of us ventured out to the area. Not only was there a nice piece of structure, it was covered with fish!

This particular hump rises about 15 feet off the bottom and is about a half mile long. In a typical summer you will find suspended kings, coho, steelhead and lake trout within a mile of this hump in every direction. As you move away from the region, you may go for miles without encountering a fish! This small deepwater hump obviously impacts the surrounding water and holds fish.

Variables: Weather, Season and Port of Departure

Weather, season and port of departure all play a role in daily fishing activity. Seasonal aspects will determine overall patterns. Your degree of success is influenced by which Lake you fish on and which harbor you are using. Port of departure is something individual anglers can control and alter based on current fishing results and information. Stocking figures will often dictate what type of season individual regions will have. We will discuss how to use stocking records to your advantage in the fall fishing section. Local weather has a huge influence on fishing success. A sudden change in the weather can turn fish on or 'pull the plug' on a local bite. As we mentioned earlier, by monitoring the weather from home, you can frequently have a rough idea of where to begin looking for fish.

The Great Lakes feature a great deal of variety between and within the individual Lakes. Our targets, however, remain the same. When you are fishing, pay attention to detail. Explore all forms of structure. Look for the intersection of bottom structure, currents, thermoclines and baitfish. The intersection of these four elements is often the location of hot summer salmon and trout action!

This 17 lb. coho was taken suspended over deep water. Children enjoy catching big salmon just as much as adults.

SUMMER TECHNIQUES

Now that we know how to find summer salmon and trout, lets discuss some technique and delivery principles. Before we even put a line in the water, we need to align our thinking or 'vision.' When we approach the Lakes during the summer months, where are the fish? This is not a trick question. They are in the water, beneath the surface. Guess what! That's where *you* need to be focused. In order to consistently catch fish during the summer months, you need to visualize what is going on beneath the surface of the water.

As your boat is moving through the water, try to keep your *vision* focused on what the water and lures beneath your boat are doing, the *trolling dynamic*. Think about what all the delivery devices and lures look like, together under the surface. Mentally, view your lures from the fish's perspective. Your entire lure spread and all the devices you are using to deliver your baits to the fish need to be working together. They are a system, or more specifically, a team. As you add and subtract lures from your trolling dynamic, try and view them in a group dynamic. How do they look as a group? You will catch far more fish if all your baits are working together rather than independently.

The key to focusing on the sub-surface group dynamic is to be observant. Be aware of every lure that goes in the water, color changes, leader adjustments, lure depth, trolling course and speed, and remember what you tried 20 minutes ago. You get the picture. You need to *pay close attention* and make a mental note of everything you do. As you troll, you will constantly be fine-tuning your baits as you mix and match your trolling spread.

The summer season will typically find salmon and trout suspending over large sections of the water column. To narrow down your search ranges identify your target species first. What species of fish are available in your region? If only one or two species are in the region this will help you identify temperature and depth targets. If multiple species are available, you will need to cover more of the water column. Knowing who your opponent is will also help you in lure selection.

Summer anglers use a combination of downriggers, Dipsy Divers on super line, mono and wire line, lead core and wire line to reach the strike zone. Occasionally you will find fish on the surface but for the most part you will be targeting sub-surface layers. Depending on the day and conditions anglers may use a combination of the various delivery devices.

Trolling Dynamic: Macro Perspective

Before looking at specific summer techniques let's look at the trolling dynamic from the macro perspective. If we could view the water column as a slice, where would the downrigger weights, Dipsy Divers and wire line be in the water? As we start to build the trolling or group dynamic, lets begin with the area directly below and behind the boat. As our downriggers move through the water, they would form a V or an inverted V pattern.

As you add Dipsy Divers to the dynamic, you can maintain the V pattern within your dynamic if the Dipsy are run higher in the water column

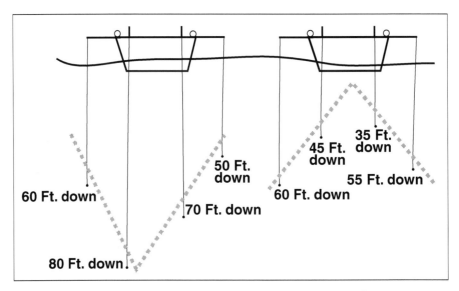

The macro-trolling dynamic can be diagrammed as a V or inverted V pattern.

than your downriggers (wing pattern). If you drop one set of Dipsies deep in the water column, a 'deep drop' pattern, then your group dynamic would appear as an inverted W on a vertical plane. The diagrams under 'Trolling Dynamic Presentations' will help to illustrate these two concepts.

For summer fishing most Great Lakes pros will use four or five downriggers, one or two Dipsy Divers per side and one or two wire lines suspended down the middle. Anglers in Michigan like to run multiple lead core lines off side planers. These anglers may run up to three lead cores per side.

Numbers of lines used will often depend on boat size, angler count and sea conditions. As you are reading this, don't feel like you need to run a ton of lines to catch fish. Years ago we ran more lines; however, since zebra muscles have cleared up the water we have found that less is often more! I know one Wisconsin recreational angler who fish's with only two downriggers, a couple of Dipsy Divers and out fishes most charter boats.

The depth at which you are targeting fish will determine what combination of delivery devices to use. If the fish are in the top 50 feet, you will want to use downriggers and Dipsy Divers with monofilament or super line. A single lead core is also effective for the top 60 feet. If the fish are holding from 50 to 80 feet down you will want to use downriggers, Dipsy Divers on super line or wire line and wire line thumpers. When the fish are deeper than 80 feet downriggers and wire line with a sinker or Dipsy Diver are the best tools for reaching target depths.

Trolling Dynamic: Micro Perspective
Individual Lure Placement Within the Dynamic
Now that we understand the summer trolling dynamic from the macro perspective, where do you set your individual lines within the trolling dynamic? Remember, the trolling dynamic is three-dimensional. We will examine the trolling dynamic from a vertical and horizontal perspective.

The Group Dynamic Viewed from the Vertical Perspective
Let's look at the vertical element first, how deep do you set a line? This depends a great deal upon species availability and thermocline depth. Remember, water temperature is critical to summer success! Locate the thermocline first; everything else is up or down from this depth.

If coho, steelhead or brown trout are the dominant species we will typically start the day by setting lines from 10 feet above the thermocline to 20 feet below the thermocline. If kings and lake trout are the target species, we will set lines from just below the thermocline all the way down till we hit 42-degree water. This may be anywhere from 20 to 50 or more feet below the thermocline. If four or five species are available, our target zone will be greatly expanded.

How much vertical distance should you place between individual baits? There is no guaranteed formula but we can give you a few guidelines. Ask yourself, "How broad or deep is the strike zone?" The strike zone is the band of water with the preferred water temperature of your target species. This will dictate the ideal window of opportunity for summer success. On a vertical perspective you may want to begin by setting your lines to cover 5-10 foot increments within the strike zone. Remember, water temperature is key.

As you search for active fish you may widen or narrow your spread as you zero in on the fish. Some days the fish may be spooky and you will need to spread out your offerings. On these days less lines cluttering the strike zone may actually result in more fish. Other days, you will find grouping your baits into a narrow window will trigger the fish.

Currents and sea conditions also impact vertical spacing within the group dynamic. On rough days or in strong currents, you cannot place your lures too close. This will result in tangles. On these days you may have to place extra vertical distance between your lures or reduce the amount of lines you are using. In choppy seas or a strong cross current, you may want to keep at least 10 feet of vertical distance between your lines.

The Group Dynamic Viewed from the Horizontal Perspective

Does the degree of horizontal distance between individual baits impact your trolling dynamic? Absolutely! Most anglers think they can only control vertical separation within the group dynamic but they can also control and manipulate the horizontal dimensions. Horizontal distance can be controlled by two factors:

1. The use of delivery apparatuses that create horizontal distance, separating individual rigs at the trolling depth and
2. lead lengths off delivery apparatuses.

The horizontal distance between rigs in the water can be increased through the use of Dipsy Divers, pancake (downrigger) weights, wire line and lead core. The first two devices pull your lines to the side by varying degrees. The second two delivery devices run significantly further astern of the boat at depth.

Dipsy Divers can be adjusted to plane farther to the side or angle down at a sharper descent. If you set the dial on $2^1/_2$, there will be additional side pull compared to a Dipsy set on a 1 setting. The type of line the Dipsy is riding on will also add or subtract horizontal distance. For example, wire line enables the Dipsy to dive at a steeper angle, placing them closer to your rigger lines. Super line and mono Dipsies will have more horizontal separation from the rigger baits as they will not dive down at the same angle as wire Dipsy. Mono and super line Dipsies will also run further astern. Of the three line types, mono will allow the Dipsy more horizontal movement.

Downriggers are rather limited as the weights go down from the rigger. Some anglers have started using 'pancake' weights on their boom riggers to spread out their lines. The pancake weight pulls out to the side and adds some horizontal distance between the boom riggers and corner downrigger baits. In strong currents and when fishing a narrow strike range, pancakes will reduce tangles.

Wire line and lead core rigs offer a presentation method that adds a great deal of horizontal distance within your trolling dynamic. Suspended wires and lead cores hang well behind the group dynamic created below the stern of your boat. Placing lead cores off side planers ads yet another layer of horizontal separation.

You can also gain a great deal of horizontal control within your trolling dynamic through the adjustment of downrigger lead lengths. As you set your rigger lines, remember where, horizontally, within the group dynamic each lure will be running. Your rigger baits may all be down between 45 and 65 feet, giving you a total vertical separation of 20 feet. They will, however, also have a horizontal adjustment within that 20-foot layer of water. For example, lures may be spread across a horizontal layer covering 15 feet or 50 feet. You determine the horizontal level of space by lead lengths off the riggers.

The general range for summer fishing is to set rigger baits back from 5-70 feet. Isn't that a big help? A general rule of thumb is that the deeper you are setting lines, the closer to the downrigger weight you need to run your offering. When fishing below 80 feet we like to set dodgers from 7 to 15 feet behind the weights. Clean spoons will be set back 10-20 feet. When fishing the 40-80 ranges we still like dodgers set back 7-20 feet. Spoons will be set from 10-40 feet back. When fish are above 40 feet we set dodgers from 7-30 feet back and spoons will have a range of 10-70 feet.

What is the determining factor in lead lengths? Would you believe the mood of the fish and sea conditions? A couple of factors to keep in mind; if fish are spooky, you need longer leads. The closer you set a dodger to the weight, the "snappier" the action. A dodger set back 30 feet will have a lazy action and less snap. In rough seas or strong currents you may have to run baits close to the weights to minimize tangles. Lead length off downriggers is not science. It is a process that requires you to react to the moods of the fish and the local conditions. Experimentation is crucial! When you hit on something that works, repeat the process until results diminish.

Here are a few examples to better illustrate the horizontal plane. On many days we will set a dodger/fly combo back 10 feet from the weight. We will then set a clean spoon on the downrigger next to the dodger/fly down-

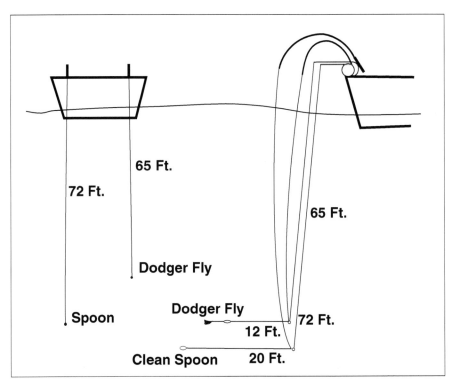

This diagram illustrates the vertical and horizontal separation between two downrigger baits. Vertical and horizontal separations within the group dynamic are critical.

rigger. This spoon will be set 5-10 feet behind the dodger/fly. The clean spoon will be placed in the trolling dynamic 5-8 feet below the dodger. You can expand the horizontal plain by running a boom rigger with a dodger rig back 15 feet. Then, take a corner rigger and put the lure back 40 feet. This boom may attract a fish into the spread, but the lure trailing just behind the other baits may tempt the fish. The potential combinations of horizontal adjustments within the trolling dynamic are quite broad.

A shotgun wire line down the middle is deadly. On a horizontal perspective, the lone wire hangs so far back in the trolling dynamic that it is often viewed in isolation by the fish. Big kings and lakers love this single lure presentation. Lead core lines have a similar presentation since they are so far astern of the trolling dynamic. Suspended wire lines and lead core lines allow you to run additional baits in a target layer of water without crowding the downrigger and Dipsy baits.

Experiment with various combinations of vertical and horizontal leads. As you set lines down in the water column, remember how far back each lure is as well as how far down. Fish are moody and sea and sky conditions can alter the way a trolling dynamic appears to fish. If you hit on a pattern of vertical and horizontal significance, duplicate the effect. That is why you must reset productive rods at the exact vertical and horizontal positions within the trolling dynamic! This is true of downriggers, Dipsy Divers, wire lines and lead core. We cannot emphasize this point enough.

Trolling Dynamic Presentations

Downriggers are the simplest element to set within the dynamic. To illustrate an overall summer trolling dynamic, let's look at a traditional V pattern. Place your two corner riggers deepest. The outside or boom downriggers will be placed higher in the water column. Let's assume the thermocline is at 70 feet. You have a mixed bag of kings, steelhead and lake trout in the area. You would set one corner rigger at 95 feet and the other corner at 83 feet. You would place one side rigger at 73 feet and the other side rigger at 67 feet. Chip and I both favor the V pattern for setting riggers. If you wanted to run an inverted V, set the boom riggers down in the

80-90 foot range and run the corners higher up. Obviously, if the strike range is narrower, your riggers will be closer.

Lead lengths off the riggers will vary depending on the day. In the typical V pattern we will run the two corner riggers shorter than the outside or boom riggers. There are exceptions to this rule. Frequently, we will set a boom rigger with a dodger choked 5-10 feet back. The corner rigger next to and below the boom will be run 5-15 feet further back than the boom.

When fishing an inverted V we like to run the corners longer and the booms shorter. The reason for this is that if the booms are the deepest riggers, their cable will blow back and may keep fish from coming into a lure

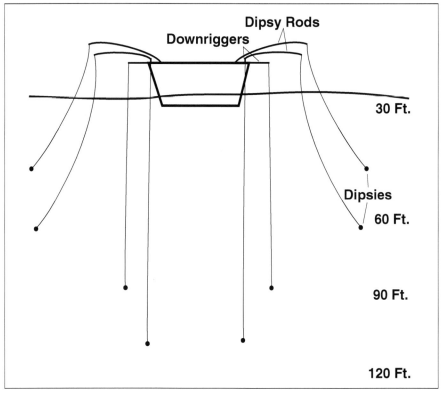

This 'wing pattern' illustrates how you can target multiple layers in the water column. Here, the four downriggers are targeting a deep band of fish, such as kings and lake trout. The four Dipsy Divers are used to target a shallower band of fish, possibly coho and steelhead.

run close to a corner rigger. In this situation, you want the corner bait stretched far enough back so the outside boom cable will not interfere with a fish finding your baits. Don't lock yourself into only one lead length pattern.

Dipsy Divers are a dominant part of any summer trolling pattern and there are a variety of ways to integrate them into the group dynamic. While Dipsy Divers are often set on wire line down the middle, they are most productive when run off the side. Typically, we set the Diver on the $1\frac{1}{2}$, 2 or $2\frac{1}{2}$ setting. Diver setting is determined by how deep we are fishing and how much horizontal separation we want within the group dynamic. Power rings are only used for fishing deeper than 80 feet. When targeting water deeper than 90 feet the Diver is usually set on the 1 or $1\frac{1}{2}$ setting.

Where do you place Dipsy Divers in the trolling dynamic? Target depth will determine whether you deploy the Dipsy on mono, super line or wire line. Mono is used for the top 40 feet, super line for 30-90 feet and wire for anything deeper than 80 feet. In Chapter 2 we look at the mechanics of running Dipsy Divers. If multiple species are available, you may want to concentrate your downriggers on the deeper fish and use the Dipsy Divers to hit the higher layers of the water column. For example, a typical summer scenario may find kings and lake trout suspending at 80-110 feet and coho and steelhead at 50-70 feet. You could target the 50-70 foot layer with two to four Dipsy Divers (two per side) and focus your downriggers on the deeper fish. This approach would be in-line with a V pattern.

Another way of approaching the same scenario is the 'deep drop' presentation. Viewed from a vertical perspective, this trolling pattern resembles an inverted W. In this program you would target two downriggers and two Dipsy Divers on each band of fish. For example, you would set two corner downriggers and two Dipsy Divers in the 80-110 foot band. Two boom riggers and two Dipsy Divers would target the 50-70 foot range.

How much line is required to get a Dipsy Diver to the target level? This depends on a number of variables including current, sea conditions, trolling speed, lure selection and type of line used. Wire line will take a Dipsy Diver deeper than the other line types. Super line will take a Dipsy

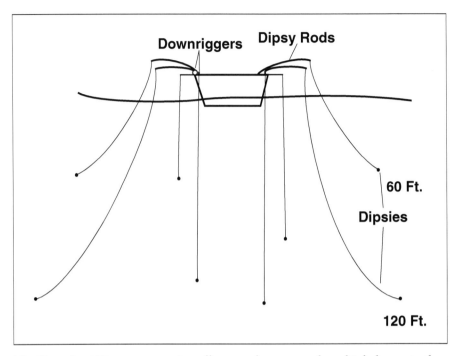

The 'deep drop' Dipsy presentation allows anglers to attack multiple layers in the water column. In this illustration the anglers are using two riggers and two Dipsy to target two different levels.

very deep, but we think super line is most effective for fish above 90 feet. Monofilament is most effective in the upper 40 feet of water.

You will need to experiment on your boat with the various line set-ups to determine how much line to let out to reach target depths. As we mentioned in Chapter 2, the GMT 40 will help you determine the depth your Divers are running. Another primitive method of learning the diving parameters of your gear is to run your Dipsy lines into the bottom. Have I confused you yet? For example, if you are trolling in 50 feet of water, take a super line Dipsy Diver and let it out, slowly, until it starts digging bottom. Make a mental note of how much line you needed to let out and what speed you were traveling. You can do this with all the various line applications in several different depths. Then, as you are fishing, it is quite easy and accurate to estimate how deep your Dipsies are running. You will make minor adjustments for speed, current and waves. This technique can also be used to learn the *reach* of a suspended wire rig.

If you are limited on rods or boat space, super line Dipsy set-ups give you the greatest flexibility. Super line Dipsies can be run in the upper layers of the water column as well as the deeper zones. Super line Dipsies are also highly effective for delivering baits to fish in the 40-90 layers.

Suspended wire lines are a deadly part of the summer trolling dynamic. The most popular and least cumbersome way to fish a suspended wire line is the 'tail gunner' or 'shotgun' approach. Simply put, a suspended wire line rig is run straight down the middle with a 16-24 ounce weight or a Dipsy Diver. For most applications, this is run out on 200-350 feet of line. Because of line drag, this line will run further back than the rigger baits. The tail gunner is also very effective when it is run deeper than all other lines. A wire line with a ball weight requires less line to reach depth than a Dipsy Diver set on the O setting. When fishing strong currents or super deep fish, use the 20-24 ounce weight.

Lead core line offers anglers yet another form of lure presentation. In some regions, lead core is extremely popular. Anglers in Western

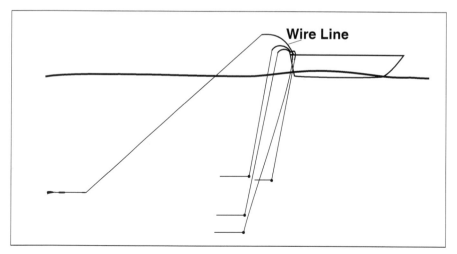

The wire line 'tail gunner' is a dynamite technique for running a suspended wire line rig. Notice how far astern (horizontally) of the group dynamic the wire rig is running. Big kings and lakers love this single lure presentation!

Michigan have mastered the art of lead core fishing. On some days the majority of their fish will be caught on lead core line.

Captain Tim Dawidiuk who fishes out of Sturgeon Bay, Wisconsin, adapted some of the Michigan methods to fishing lead core off his home port. In 2003 Tim came up with a system that he felt made him a better fisherman. Tim ran a double lead core in a three-rod set up. The double lead core allowed Tim to reach fish as deep as 70 feet. Tim says these lines were easy to run and did not interfere with his downriggers and Dipsy Divers.

Single and double Lead core is great for catching spooky fish suspended between 30 and 70 feet down. Lead cores are run out way behind the boat. They present lures to fish long after your boat has passed over an area. Many anglers have started running lead cores off side planers with great success. For a complete picture of fishing lead lines, see Chip's discussion in Chapter 4.

There are a number of different ways to incorporate downriggers, Dipsy Divers, wires and lead core into an effective group (trolling) dynamic. As you are setting lines, develop a plan so you can intelligently attack the water column. Don't set individual lines in isolation with respect to the other lines. Remember, when all your lines are working together, they become a team. Eleven players can move the ball down the field faster than a lone fullback.

The key to consistently catching salmon and trout all summer long is to be able to creatively combine downriggers, Dipsy Divers and wire line into your trolling dynamic. On any given day one combination of delivery systems may catch more fish. Many times, however, an astute angler will be able to integrate and work the entire system so all delivery systems produce fish. When the entire dynamic is working as a team, watch out! Sore arms and smiles will tell the story!

Interpreting the Effects of Currents and Basic Summer Trolling Patterns

Once fish have been located and their depths determined, you should focus on trolling speed, direction and staying with active fish. When you adjust your trolling speed, work on a tenth of a knot increments. On many days, if your speed isn't right, you won't catch many fish. Arriving at a productive trolling speed is work. You need to read the currents, factor in depth and trolling dimension, and then have the ability to fine-tune your speed for all directions. This requires keen observation techniques and a willingness to experiment.

The generally accepted summer speed range will be in the 1.5-2.9 knot range. Again, this is the general speed range. When determining trolling speed a number of variables will have to be factored into the matrix including the mood of the fish, lure selection, sea conditions and currents. Currents will include reverse currents and surface currents.

You will know a current is impacting your trolling dynamic by watching the angle of your lines and by monitoring your speed over the bottom. For example, if you are trolling straight East (90 degrees) but your lines are angling sharply to the North, chances are your boat is being pushed by a southbound surface current. You can confirm this if you are referencing GPS bottom speed. This feature will show you that while your compass may be pointing 90 degrees, your boat is moving over the bottom at a 110-degree heading!

The question you must ask yourself is, "What are my lures doing at the trolling depth?" In this situation you will have to compensate for the sideslipping and experiment with trolling speed. The easiest way to control and manipulate speed at depth in this situation is to alter your trolling angle. Typically, we will try trolling at different compass headings for short periods of time. Slight alterations in direction can have a huge impact on your trolling dynamic. I can't remember the number of times where I had to troll exactly at a 100-degree heading to get action. If I trolled at a 95-degree or 120-degree heading, we would not have any action—no matter how much I altered the speed. Again, slight alterations in direction will make a difference.

Reverse currents cannot be ignored. There are a variety of ways to determine if you are caught in a reverse current. Again, GPS bottom speed is a big help! If you are trolling really slow to the North and your surface speed says you are crawling through the water at 1.7 knots, but your lines, which are 60-90 feet down, are hanging way back (as if you were trolling much faster), what's going on? Look at your bottom speed and you may actually be moving at 2.5 knots over the bottom! How is this possible? A strong surface push or current will be moving you over the bottom at a rate of .8 knots. Add your trolling speed of 1.7 knots and you have your speed over the bottom.

This has huge implications to your trolling dynamic! When you drop your lures down to the strike range, you think they are working at the equivalent of your surface speed, 1.7 knots. In reality they may be working at a different speed. It is common to have a reverse current running along the bottom layers in the opposite direction of the surface. In the situation we just described, you are pulling your lures over the bottom at 2.5 knots. They are running into a current of .8 knots. This, in affect, has the lures working as if you were trolling at 3.3 knots!

When many anglers encounter strong currents they don't catch fish because they don't identify the problem: currents are distorting their trolling dynamic. First, you must identify the current. Next, determine what direction the surface and/or sub-surface currents are running. Then ask yourself how this is affecting your trolling dynamic?

In the previous example you may have to troll dead slow traveling with the surface current to achieve a fish catching speed at the target level. For example, your surface speed will look like you are sitting still, but your lures down 60-90 feet will be working at 2.3 knots. Trolling into the surface current you may have to troll uncomfortably fast across the surface (over 3 knots) to achieve a fish catching speed of 2.3 knots at the 60-90 foot level. Remember, the critical element with trolling speed is the speed your lures are working at the target level. Lure action at the trolling depth may look very different than if the lures were running just under the surface next to the boat.

You can compensate for currents in a variety of ways including adjusting your trolling speed, changing your trolling angle, moving locations or putting speed tolerant lures on your lines. In strong currents, you may have to troll what looks really, really slow or really, really fast to move your lures at fish catching speeds.

For boats that do not have good speed control, it is often easier to troll cross-wise to the current with clean spoons. This will minimize the impact of the current on your trolling dynamic. If you take this approach, tweak your trolling or compass angle to catch fish.

If you are working a piece of bottom structure, pay attention to detail. Approach the structure with a pattern. Try trolling parallel to a structure. If that doesn't work approach the structure from a perpendicular or criss-cross angle. A favorite summer location is along the edges of reefs or drop-offs. These structures are typically found in 50-200 feet of water. Trolling parallel to these banks is very productive. If boat traffic is heavy, summer fish will often move one half to two miles offshore from these drops. They may suspend or sit on the bottom but many anglers ignore fish that have retreated away from major pieces of structure. Look for microstructures on the larger pieces of structures and just outside of major bottom contours. These smaller features often go unnoticed by most anglers.

If bait or gamefish are in an area, make trolling passes from all angles. Once a pattern is determined, stick with it. Again, you may have to experiment to determine what brings results. As you become familiar with a region and learn the local structure, you may notice that certain areas are best fished by trolling a particular pattern. Make notes of what works. Different winds and currents will force you to use different trolling patterns on your favorite bottom structures.

Summer salmon and trout tend to congregate in schools. Thus, you need to have the ability to return to the location where you caught fish. On slow days, the ability to return to the scene of the crime is critical. If you know the fish are scattered and you have three strikes in a short period of time, chances are, there is a school of fish in the area. If fish are scarce, don't leave a pocket of fish!

Likewise, if you know there are a lot of fish in the region and you are only having the occasional strike, don't sit on a dead spot too long. In this

situation it might be wise to cover some ground and see if you can locate larger concentrations of active fish. If you mark fish but they are not striking, make a note of it. If you don't have any success finding other fish, return to the area that had the marks. Often, dormant fish will become active at various periods of the day.

Summer Lure Selection

Lure selection during the summer months is dependent on many variables including species availability, sea conditions, target depth and region. Is one lure group more productive than another? Over the past ten years more salmon and trout have been caught during the summer months on dodgers(flashers)/flies and clean spoons. It is our experience that spoons and flies/dodgers can be equally productive. Based on local conditions and angler technique, either group can be more productive on any given day. Often a combination of the two lure groups will produce maximum results during the summer months.

How do you pick summer baits? This is a subject that demands an entire book! Rather than confuse you, we have chosen to list our five favorite summer baits by species. As you will notice, there is some overlap.

> **Dan and Chip's Favorite Summer Lures**
> *Flies and dodgers combinations (all dodgers in 0 size)*
>
> King
> 1. White dodger/pearl Howie Fly
> 2. Smoke dodger/green crinkle Howie Fly
> 3. Smoke (silver glow) dodger/aqua Howie Fly
> 4. Silver dodger/pearl blue Howie Fly
> 5. Yellow dodger/green crinkle Howie Fly
>
> Coho
> 1. Yellow dodger/green crinkle Howie Fly
> 2. Yellow dodger/aqua Howie Fly
> 3. White dodger/white Howie Fly
> 4. Silver dodger/green Howie Fly
> 5. Red dodger/aqua Howie Fly
>
> Steelhead
> 1. Smoke dodger/aqua Howie Fly
> 2. Yellow dodger/green crinkle Howie Fly
> 3. Yellow dodger/aqua Howie Fly
> 4. White dodger/pearl blue Howie Fly
> 5. Silver dodger/green crinkle Howie Fly
>
> Lake trout
> 1. Silver dodger/green Spin N Glo'
> 2. Silver dodger/white Howie Fly
> 3. Silver dodger/yellow Spin N Glo'-pearl Fly
> 4. White dodger/green crinkle Howie Fly
> 5. Yellow dodger/green crinkle Howie Fly
>
> Brown Trout
> 1. White dodger/white Howie Fly
> 2. Silver dodger/yellow pearl Cheddar Fly
> 3. Smoke dodger/aqua Howie Fly
> 4. Silver dodger/white-green Howie Fly
> 5. Yellow dodger/green crinkle Howie Fly

Chip and Dan's Favorite Summer Spoons

King
1. Number 5 silver/yellow edge Diamond King
2. Green dolphin Silver Streak (magnum or regular)
3. Purple Stinger
4. Blue Oz Mauler
5. Ludington special Silver Streak

Coho
1. Number 5 silver yellow/edge Diamond King
2. Silver Stinger
3. Blue dolphin Silver Streak
4. Lemon ice Dream Weaver
5. Mongoose Diamond King

Steelhead
1. Green dolphin magnum Silver Streak
2. Silver Mauler pearl/blue tape
3. Number 4 or 5 silver yellow edge Diamond King
4. White/red Stinger
5. Metallic blue Yuk

Lake Trout
1. Green dolphin Silver Streak (magnum or regular)
2. Number 5 mongoose Diamond King
3. Hammered silver/orange belly Mauler
4. Purple Stinger
5. Gold/green Pro Shiner

Brown Trout
1. Silver/green Mauler
2. Black/silver Stinger
3. Monkey puke Stinger
4. Gold w/rose stripe Gold Star
5. Hammered gold Mauler

While you will be choosing individual baits for each line, the genius comes when you are able to choose a group of baits. Again, think group dynamic. How will this dodger and fly combo affect the other lures already in the water? Color combinations are another critical element in the selection process. You may want to review Chapter 3.

Here They Come! The Offshore Staging Process

The boundary between summer and fall fishing is marked by a transition. This transition is greatly anticipated by salmon fishermen across North America. During the twilight of summer, mature salmon begin one of natures most remarkable and timeless odysseys. The spawning migration.

During the final moments of summer, Great Lakes anglers encounter massive schools of big salmon staging offshore of spawning and stocking locations. Instinctively these fish know the road that lies ahead. In preparation for their spawning runs, these fish are bulking up by going on major feeding frenzies. For those anglers who locate these schools, some of the best fishing of the year is waiting. Historically, some of the heaviest catches of salmon and trout will be taken all around the Great Lakes during this offshore staging period.

Staging is a process where mature salmon school and begin returning to the region of their birth or stocking. Depending on where you fish, the offshore staging process can begin as early as late July or as late as early September. In most regions, August is the month.

Many anglers miss out on this great opportunity as they erroneously believe the 'staging process' begins when salmon enter shallow waters to spawn. The final phase of the salmon's life, however, begins long before salmon enter the shallows. The internal clock of a salmon starts to call adult salmon home from the deep, clear waters of the Great Lakes. Anglers will know that the spawning run is not far off when they see the schools of mature salmon stacking up in the offshore waters adjacent to spawning sights.

If you want to catch staging salmon, you need to understand their behavior from a biological perspective. Mature salmon undergo radical transformation during the final months of their lives. Before nature calls, a salmon's entire life has been focused on one thing: feeding. As spawning approaches, the salmon's purpose in life begins to change. A salmon's focus gradually shifts from feeding to procreation. Everything about a salmon from this point on is marked by an urge that leads to spawning.

During this transition period adult salmon are characterized by a number of changes, both physiological and behavioral. Physically, their bodies begin a series of changes that have been a part of salmon biology for countless years. Behaviorally, their focus will slowly shift from one of being a highly efficient predator to propagation of the species.

During the months of July and August mature salmon will begin massing in large schools off the regions where they were initially stocked or spawned. Before their body's transition from predator to spawners, salmon go on major feeding binges. In order for a salmon to complete the strenuous spawning ordeal, individual fish will need to build up reserves of proteins. At this point in the journey, salmon are still sensitive to water temperature and feeding needs. As spawning approaches, these two urges diminish as the need to reproduce consumes their attention.

When salmon begin their migrations into spawning rivers, streams and harbors, they cease feeding all together. Their stomachs have atrophied and it becomes impossible for spawning salmon to feed. They survive these final moments on the precious proteins stored in their once magnificent bodies. Salmon are truly remarkable creatures designed by a truly remarkable and Infinite Creator!

Fishing for staging salmon on the Great Lakes has changed considerably over the years. In the early days of Great Lakes fishing, spawning salmon would stage in shallow waters off rivers and harbor mouths for long periods of time, often a month or longer. During the late 1980's and 1990's this shallow water-staging period became shorter and shorter. Today, spawning bound salmon stage offshore in deep water. Eventually the big spawners move shoreward. Once they arrive off their home river or harbor, they spend less time holding in shallow water than in past years.

Offshore staging salmon are great angling targets! They are far more aggressive than the salmon that have entered river and harbor mouth regions. The fact that deepwater fish are still actively feeding makes them easier to catch. Staging fish are at their peak body weight as they are consuming massive amounts of alewives in preparation for their final stage of life. From the angler's perspective, this final feeding window makes them an ideal game fish! When salmon hit the shoreline to spawn they often stop feeding. Again, it is not a matter of choice. Spawning salmon are physiologically incapable of feeding.

You can begin locating offshore staging salmon before you leave the harbor. That's right, the hunt for schools of big salmon begins with the research you do at home. Salmon will stage offshore of where they were planted. Consult individual state DNR stocking records. The locations that received heavy stockings of kings, coho, steelhead and brown trout two to three years earlier will attract schools of staging salmon and trout.

Once you have isolated regions that are anticipating runs of mature fish, where do these staging fish show up first? Typically, you find the schools of fish offshore between 70-400 feet of water. The target range

When salmon stage offshore, heavy catches of big fish are possible. These anglers struggled just to lift their catch for a photo!

will run from 10-20 miles up and down the coast parallel to the location that received the heavy plantings.

Now that we have narrowed the search range down a bit, where do you begin fishing for staging fish? Since these fish are still feeding, water temperature, baitfish and structure should not be ignored. As autumn approaches, mature salmon will be drawn back to stocking sites. A tension develops as the fish are drawn shoreward but still require substantial amounts of food.

Begin the hunt by finding the target water temperature range, and look for bait pods in areas with key bottom structure. If kings are the dominant fish returning, 42-46 degrees. If it's coho, then look for 48-54 degrees. If brown trout are your main target, look to 54-62 degree water for peak action. Mature fish will school with other mature fish.

Once you have found the schools of staging fish, the techniques used to catch them are very similar to summer techniques. Downriggers, Dipsy Divers, wire line and lead core are used to deliver baits. The same techniques and presentation methods discussed in summer techniques will apply for staging fish. It should be noted that as the fish advance into the spawning mode they often become more sensitive to pressure. For this reason, less is often more.

A combination of clean spoons and flies and dodgers will draw strikes from staging salmon and trout. Glow squids in pearl, white and green also produce many big fish during this period. Some anglers will also begin mixing body baits such as J-Plugs and Grizzlies into the group dynamic for staging salmon. One August we were dropping pearl Grizzly plugs 90 feet down in a mix of dodgers and flies! Typically, a mix of dodgers and flies and clean spoons will draw the most strikes. Lures that were hot during the summer months will continue to draw strikes from staging fish. The baits are set from 7-50 feet behind the downriggers. Experimentation on lead lengths is critical and can change from day to day.

Target depth in the water column will depend on a number of variables including target species preferred temperature range, geographical region being fished and local weather patterns. Again, offshore staging salmon and trout are still temperature sensitive. You will want to seek out ideal water temperatures.

As spawning approaches, water temperature and bait will become less significant. Deepwater fish will begin moving shoreward and start to hold near bottom structure in 30-120 feet of water. Feeding will slowly become less important and finding the river or harbor mouth of origin will become a priority. During this phase, mature fish will often venture into warmer water. Eventually feeding becomes secondary and locating the stocking site takes priority.

In a typical year you will see multiple waves of mature salmon setting up in deep water. These schools will eventually move shoreward. Their shoreward progress may be rapid or some schools may slowly move in. These schools will set up and hold at various distances from shore. Much of this depends on the fish's internal timing and local weather patterns. A sudden upwelling of cold water along the shoreline will often send schools of mature fish into the shallows.

Fishing for staging salmon and trout is an exciting period on the Great Lakes! Fish are at their peak weight. They can be found in large schools and their final feeding frenzies can lead you to some great action.

Fall Fishing Techniques for The Great Lakes

Locating and Catching Autumn Salmon in Shallow Water

As a child growing up in the suburbs of Chicago, the end of summer was met with mixed emotions. Carefree days swimming and exploring local ponds would come to an end as the call of the school bell beckoned us back to the classroom. The onset of school was viewed as a tragedy by many of my friends, but there was a golden lining to the onset of autumn, the arrival of the mighty king salmon!

As the calendar ticked over to September, I would look anxiously at the fishing reports in the *Chicago Tribune*. At the first signs of life, I would badger my Dad incessantly about our Saturday morning fishing trips. Should we fish a Chicago harbor? How about a trip to Michigan? Or maybe Wisconsin? Friday nights were spent preparing tackle and sleep would come fleetingly as I dreamed of harbors and rivers full of big salmon just waiting for our 17 foot Boston Whaler, the "Frick N' Frack!"

Those were some of the memories that instilled salmon fishing deep in my blood. Looking back at photographs reminds me of the fun my Dad and I had catching giant salmon! When my friend Paul Jaros and I turned 16, our fishing horizons were greatly expanded. No longer were we dependent on an adult with a driver's license! Whenever a car was free, we would strap a canoe to the car roof and hit the shoreline. Every chance we had during September and October, found us chasing salmon and trout along the Lake Michigan shoreline.

Today, experienced anglers across the Great Lakes know Labor Day signals the beginning of the fall salmon runs. Kings, coho, brown trout and steelhead continue their dance with destiny as they invade shallow water regions during the months of September and October. Fall is an ideal time for small boat anglers and those with limited big water experience to get a crack at catching 10-30 pound fish. This is the period where I, as a youth, really learned how to catch salmon. Autumn success hinges on how you approach the Lakes and the fish. Spawning bound salmon and trout are not the same fish you encountered during the spring and summer months. Remember, they have spent most of their lives roaming the clear, deep open waters of the Great Lakes. Prior to the spawning run their life focus has been chasing down and consuming alewives; breakfast, lunch and dinner.

These great open water predators have left the comfort of the deeps and will spend their final weeks of life in shallow, and often murky, water. No longer are they cruising the open blue, terrorizing schools of alewives. These once mighty predators have entered a new realm. A world where they find themselves confined by the boundaries of shallow water, breakwalls and riverbanks. No longer are they the hunter. Now they will be engaged in a territorial struggle. They will be battling both manmade and natural obstacles with the intent of depositing their eggs and milt in the timeless dance of reproduction.

Physiologically, their bodies have begun to go through a series of changes. A thick, protective mucus layer coats their once silver bodies. They have faded from bright silver to shades of golden-brown, red and black. Canine teeth and hooked jaws give them an intimidating appearance. Once they enter the shallows, their stomachs have atrophied to the point that it is impossible for them to ingest food.

From our brief biology lesson we quickly learn one of the keys to catching spawning fish. Feeding is no longer a trigger mechanism. The majority of shallow water fish will have ceased feeding. Their biological clocks will have set off a process that results in the atrophy of their stomachs. Once their sole concern was with the next meal, now, feeding will be a distant memory. Yes, fish that are freshly arrived from offshore waters may still have some interest in feeding. As the fall progresses, however, that interest diminishes.

Historically, this lack of feeding has led many people to believe that spawning salmon and trout cannot be taken on lures and bait in the

The fall months are an excellent time to target brown trout in shallow water.

mouth. Snagging is the result of this mentality. While spawning fish are definitely harder to catch than feeding fish, they can still be caught in large numbers! The key is in how you approach them. Your quarry has changed and in order to be successful, your techniques also need to change. No longer are you trying to stimulate feeding fish. The changes are so radical that it's almost like you are fishing for a different species. When spawning salmon and trout enter the shallows, they become very territorial. As spawning draws near, this territorial nature becomes more evident. In order to be successful, your techniques should be geared toward stimulating fish into striking out of anger and territorial defense.

Where Do You Go?

Location is everything when it comes to catching big, spawning bound kings, coho, browns and steelhead. When the spawning urge takes hold of these fish, they will become tightly concentrated. No longer will mature salmon and trout be spread out across the Lakes. For this reason, locating spawning bound salmon and trout is at least 50 percent of the battle! If you fish in the areas where fish are staging or holding, your chances of success improve dramatically.

The first step to catching staging fish in the fall is the same as when targeting offshore staging fish during August. Consult DNR stocking figures. Consulting current stocking figures will lead you to greater numbers of fish. The majority of salmon and trout in the Great Lakes are stocked fish. These fish return to their planting sights. Target harbors and river mouths that have received healthy plantings for two to three years prior to your fishing date. These are the areas that will host large returns of fish.

Do any regions feature naturally reproducing runs of fish? Yes, there is limited natural reproduction for kings and steelhead. There are some rivers on the Great Lakes that have not been stocked in years but they continue to have runs of naturally reproducing kings. The key to natural reproduction is a stream or river with suitable gravel beds for spawning, cold water, current flow and high oxygen content.

Salmon and trout are stocked in a number of rivers, streams and harbors surrounding the Great Lakes. Are some rivers and harbor mouths hot year after year? Yes. Are some inconsistent? Yes. It all goes back to the numbers. Areas may have incredible numbers of returning fish for two or three years and then slow down for a period and pick up again. Do all salmon and trout return to the area they were planted? No. Some salmon and trout do get lost. For this reason you will find mature fish showing up at unexpected places.

Current flow is one of the keys to drawing spawning fish into shoreline shallows and rivers. Spawning bound salmon and trout are attracted to moving water. Rivers with strong current flow tend to host strong runs of fish year after year. Because spawning salmon and trout are attracted to current flow, tiny streams and power plant discharges will often attract spawning fish that were not planted at these locations.

When do salmon and trout begin moving into shoreline waters? Arrival times and peak fishing activity will vary between regions and depend on local weather patterns. Typically, browns arrive first followed by kings, coho and steelhead.

In many areas brown trout will begin trickling into river and harbor areas as early as late July. Major schools of browns will concentrate off spawning locations during August and September. Some kings will begin showing up in the shallows as early as August first. The main king runs however, begin between the last week of August and the first week of September. King runs usually peak during September and October. Again, variations occur between regions.

Coho usually begin moving into the shallows in mid to late September. Coho runs often peak during October. Steelheads are a wild card. Depending on location, fall spawners can show up just about anytime between Labor Day and Thanksgiving. In typical steelhead fashion, they are hard to pin down!

What triggers the first shoreward migrations? While salmon are guided by internal clocks, sudden upwellings of cold water along the shore and heavy autumn rains will often lead to mass movements of fish into the shallows.

We've talked a lot about water temperature in this book, how does water temperature impact spawning salmon? Salmon and trout are cold water fish. When the spawning urge takes over, the salmon will move in regardless of how warm the water is, they won't wait indefinitely for cold water to roll in. If the water is above 67 degrees, spawning bound coho and kings will be very sluggish. If the water is colder, fish are more aggressive. The water doesn't have to be at their peak temperature range. Anytime the water is cooler than 62 degrees, kings, coho and trout will be more aggressive and easier to catch.

Locating Shallow Water Salmon and Trout

When spawning bound fish arrive in shallow water they will move up and down the shoreline in search of the river or harbor of origin. Once they locate the river or harbor, they will set up off the mouths and hold in the immediate vicinity for several days to several weeks. Spawning bound salmon will often make their first forays into shallow water and river mouths under the cover of dark. They may move into a river or harbor for a few hours or days and then come back out into the lake. Eventually, the fish will move up into the rivers and harbors permanently.

Once fish have located their river or harbor of origin, they will key off microstructures located in close proximity to the river or harbor. Target areas to look for spawners are in the current outflows of rivers and streams, deep holes in front of or near harbors and rivers, along breakwalls, harbor mouths, humps, rip-rap, nearshore drop-offs and along color lines.

The outflows from rivers and streams are one of the best areas to target mature fish. When a river has a good current flow, the discharge or plume will flow out into the Lake and then usually the wind or currents will take the plume and run it in a specific direction. It may run parallel to one shoreline or straight out into the Lake. Look for microstructures under the murky river water, this is where you will find fish. Look for bottom structure where it intersects the edges of river outflows. Mature salmon and trout are attracted to current flow, don't ignore river plumes.

One of the keys to shoreline trolling is to identify the areas where salmon and trout are holding. If the majority of fish are in a small area, you need to spend the majority of your trolling time in the strike zone. Making long passes away from the fish will not result in action. If the fish are spread out along the shore, then long passes can be made and you will still be making maximum contact with the strike zone.

Frequently, the largest numbers of fish will be directly in front of river and harbor mouths. When this occurs, small boat anglers have a huge advantage over large boats. It is much easier to make tight passes and circles in a small boat.

Trolling for shallow water salmon can be stressful. Often the fish will be tightly concentrated and many boats will be trying to fish a relatively small area. When this occurs, take a deep breath, and try not to get worked up. Use common sense and be courteous to other anglers. Often all you can do is determine the traffic flow and try to fit in. Keep your eyes open and watch what the other boats are doing. If a neighboring boat is hooked up with a fish, give them some room and don't cut their fish off. You hope others will do the same for you.

Small boat anglers have an excellent opportunity to catch trophy fish when salmon and trout are schooled in front of river and harbor mouths. Many anglers believe fish can only be caught at first and last light. The low-light periods offer great fishing; however, it is also the most popular time for fishermen. Once spawning salmon and trout settle into an area, they will often strike throughout the day. With the lack of traffic, these mid-day fish are often easier to catch and you may even have the fish to yourself.

Techniques for Catching Fall Salmon and Trout in Shallow Water

In the world of salmon fishing there are a multitude of different ways to trigger spawning bound salmon and trout into striking. As a teenager, I used to launch a canoe at Chicago's Burnham Harbor and the Port of Kenosha in Southeastern Wisconsin. My friends and I would fish all day or all night. It didn't matter, we just wanted to catch big fish! Boy did we catch the kings! We would slowly paddle around with a pair of pearl M2 Flat Fish trailing the canoe. It doesn't get any simpler!

Targeting the concentrations of spawning bound fish is the first step to catching shallow water salmon and trout! Once you identify *where* the concentrations of fish are holding, catching staging fish in shallow water becomes quite simple if you focus on three key elements:

1. Timing
2. Hitting the strike zone repeatedly
3. Using the right lure.

Sounds easy doesn't it? You know, putting the right baits in the strike zone for maximum periods of time requires patience and concentration.

Timing depends first on what species will be returning to your region. Once you identify the general time frame for returns, watch the weather and Lake temperature. If the Lake 'rolls,' or an upwelling occurs, it's time to go fishing! Networking is another way to determine when to hit the shallows. Watch the local media, talk with friends or call a bait shop. When herds of big fish hit the shoreline, it's hard to keep it a secret.

Okay, we've identified where the big run is going to occur, we received the hot tip that the fish are in. . . now what? How do we catch them? First you need to identify where fish are holding in relationship to the river or harbor mouth. Are they only in the current outflow? Are they spread along the shoreline for half a mile south of the river mouth? Are they holding off a ledge in 35 feet of water? It's easy to locate the areas holding fish as spawning fish will frequently jump and roll on the surface, giving their position away. They can also be spotted with fish finders. Remember, the fish will be concentrated, don't waste your time trolling where there are no fish.

If you are fishing a new area, look at a topo chart of the river or harbor mouth area. Spend some time *hunting* as you make initial trolling passes. Pay close attention to the water and bottom contours as you try to identify the key areas holding pre-spawn fish.

Once you know where fish are, you need to set up a trolling pattern to stay on top of them. Even if you don't catch them on your first attempts, stay with the fish! Spawning fish staging off river and harbor mouths are moody. They can be very aggressive one moment and dormant the next.

Sometimes you need to wait them out and other times it is just a matter of putting the right lure in front of them. Patience is truly a virtue when it comes to catching shallow water salmon and trout in the fall.

As you work staging fish, approach them from a variety of directions. After setting lines, experiment with your trolling speed. If you establish a preference, stick with it. One of the most productive techniques for triggering strikes is to go up and down with your trolling speed. If I'm not getting action or changing a line, I will continually alter the trolling speed through short, sudden bursts of speed. I will also drop the boat into neutral for a moment and allow baits to settle. Many big fish have been tricked into striking by a sudden burst of lure speed or a sudden drop in speed.

The depth of water, area being covered and boat traffic will determine what types of lines you will run. Staging fish will move around between the surface and the bottom throughout the day and night. It doesn't matter what the sun or clouds are doing. For this reason it is wise to fish from the top to the bottom. If the fish are holding in 15 to 35 feet of water you will want to use downriggers, Dipsy Divers and flat lines to present baits. If the fish are in 5 to 15 of water, feet side planers will be your best presentation choice.

Side planers are great tools for catching staging fish. We recommend the smaller inline planers for fall fishing. Even if you are working fish in 25 to 40 feet of water, don't be afraid to run side planers. If boat traffic allows you will want to run from one to three lines per side. Experiment with lead lengths between 10 and 50 feet back. Similar to open water fishing, run the outside planer lines longer and shorten the leads as you move into the boat. Don't be afraid to mix spoons and cranks on a fall planer board pattern.

If fish are rolling heavily, short leads can be deadly! We recommend using little or no weight on side planers. Now, if 100 boats are fishing a small area, don't put planers in the water and expect everyone to move out of your way. Keep your eyes open and use common sense. If boat traffic doesn't allow the use of planers, use a simple flat line 75-150 feet behind the boat. This can be a hot rod for big fish.

Big kings are excellent small boat targets during their autumn spawning runs.

Downriggers are run from just below the surface to the bottom. If you are fishing a nice piece of bottom structure, you may want to keep a rigger line close to the bottom. This may require frequent adjustments on your part. If weeds or zebra mussels are present you will want to regularly check bottom lures for debris. This applies especially to diving crankbaits. Typical leads off riggers will vary depending on boat traffic and fish temperament. Generally, leads of 10 to 50 feet will produce. If water is gin clear and traffic is minimal, try longer leads of 50 to 100 feet.

Dipsy Divers are easy to use. They are productive on both mono and super lines. At times the fish will slam the Dipsy Diver right next to the boat. Talk about exciting! Having a 20-pound king hit a lure 20 feet from the boat should get anyone fired up! At other times they will work better near the bottom or suspended at mid levels. Lures should be run from four to eight feet behind the Diver.

What lures are productive for shallow water staging salmon and trout? This is a great question that 100 anglers would answer in 100 different ways. We have heard of catches being made on some of the most unusual lures during the fall spawning runs!

To begin, let it be said that body baits and spoons are the best choices. Yes, fish can be caught on dodgers, flashers and flies, but the cranks and spoons are more productive. Body baits and spoons can be run in shallow water off Dipsy Divers, flat lines, downriggers and side planers with equal success. If you are running light or medium weight spoons on the side planers you may have to add enough weight to hold the spoon down.

Here are the lures we recommend. They all work, you just need to determine which day they work best. For cranks, J-Plugs in all sizes, Grizzly plugs, M2 Flat Fish, 2000 and 3000 series Rebel Fast Tracks (jointed and straight), jointed Rebel Minnows, Rapala Husky Jerks, J-9 and J-11 Rapalas, Shad Raps, Bomber Long-A's and Thunder Sticks. On any given day one or two of these cranks will out-produce the others.

Trolling speed with crankbaits is very important, as individual cranks tend to be very speed tolerant. The M2 Flatfish only work at a dead-slow troll. Fastracs and the jointed Rebel minnow are two of the more speed-tolerant cranks. J-plugs and Bomber Long-A's handle speed better. The cranks we listed are only some of the brands that will catch mature salmon and trout. Anglers use a wide variety of cranks for autumn salmon and trout.

Crankbait Colors? Try silver, pearl, gold, copper, green/yellow belly, rainbow trout finish, white, chartreuse, glow green, black, khaki, orange and red. These colors will work in just about any combination. Hot colors during the fall really vary from year to year, so don't be afraid to get creative with lure colors! When I was younger I used to paint plugs in a variety of custom finishes.

Spoon choices are very similar to summer fishing. The Maulers, Diamond Kings, Silver Streaks, Gold Stars, Yuks, Dream Weavers, Grizzlies and Stingers are productive. Just about any color can work depending on the mood of the fish. Productive colors include, silver, yellow, black, green, glow/green, gold and purple. Spawning salmon and trout are extremely moody. Experiment with color!

Deepwater Fall Action

One of the most overlooked fisheries on the Great Lakes today is the autumn deepwater fishery. For years anglers have concentrated their autumn efforts on mature salmon and trout in shallow water. In the past 10 years, adventurous anglers have been spending more and more time plying the steely blue depths during the months of September, October and even into November. What these anglers have discovered is that there is some great action available for immature kings (3-17 pounds), steelhead and big lake trout.

Before going any further we must note that this late season fishery is very weather sensitive. The Great Lakes have a long history of whipping up deadly storms during the autumn months. Anglers who venture offshore during the fall need to monitor the weather and use caution. Because of the potential for dangerous weather, boats must be capable of handling adverse conditions.

The principles that dictate how to catch fish during this period are very similar to summer techniques. Lure selection is almost identical to summer fishing. The major unknown in this relatively new fishery is the where—where do you find kings, steelhead, lake trout and the occasional brown trout in the autumn depths?

Where you find deepwater salmon and trout during September, October and November is greatly influenced by two variables: Wind and the dissipation of the thermocline. Wind! Friend one day, foe the next! The quality of fall fishing is dependent on wind. Weather fronts increase in strength and duration as they race across the Great Lakes during the fall. Some years, strong winds greatly limit one's ability to get out and find fish. Other years, periods of calm between fronts allow anglers some great opportunities to fish.

Wind velocity and direction are both factors. Strong, prolonged winds from any one direction will move water around. Extended periods of onshore winds can pile up warm water. Extended periods of offshore winds can bring ice-cold water to the shoreline. If late season winds rotate around the clock, then salmon and trout often move well offshore where the waters are more stable. Wind and currents have less impact on waters 10 or more miles offshore. Schools of alewives may move well offshore to avoid fighting the constant changing of near shore currents.

The dispersion of the thermocline has a tremendous impact on fish movements during October and November. Since early summer, fish behavior and movements have frequently been with respect to the thermocline. Take the thermocline away from the fish and they have lost that boundary they have been relating to for three or four months. During September, the thermocline will begin to move and shift as winds increase. At some point in October or November, the thermocline will disappear.

The process whereby the thermocline dissipates is not well understood by most Great Lakes anglers. We will only touch briefly on it now as space is limited. The Great Lakes reach their maximum temperature during late August and the first half of September. After peaking, the Lakes cool down. Between mid-September and November, the surface waters of the Great Lakes begin to cool down with the onset of cooler weather. Cold water is denser (heavier) than warm water. Thirty-nine degree water is the densest. As the surface layers cool, the surface water

Giant lake trout are available during the late fall season.

becomes denser (heavier) than the layers beneath. The surface-cooled waters actually sink and mix in with the deeper, warmer layers. Eventually, this will lead to the break down of the thermocline.

This changes the entire dynamic of the water column. This often leads to a period where the entire water column appears "mixed up." Some years we have witnessed scenarios where the water column featured only several degrees of temperature variation between the surface to more than 200 feet down! This makes it extremely difficult to locate fish! When this occurs, fishing can be tough for a period of time. Sometimes it will require long runs well offshore to try and find water that looks 'different' or has some degree of temperature variation.

Once we pass through this turnover phase, fishing usually picks up and can become quite good. After the turnover phase, the Lakes water column structure resembles a more spring-like scenario. There will be no thermocline, only varying degrees of cold water from the surface to the bottom.

The key to success is to be flexible and prepared to fish all layers of the water column. If you run offshore before the thermocline evaporates, you would set your lines as if it were summer. Find the thermocline and then look for fish. Target species include steelhead, kings, the occasional brown and lake trout. Let's look at steelhead first.

Steelhead fishing in late September, October and November will reflect a mix of spring and summer techniques and locations. As the water column transitions from a summer scenario to a more spring-like picture, anglers will draw upon methodologies used earlier in the year. This will require anglers to fish both the surface and the upper-mid levels. Autumn deepwater steelhead will be caught from the surface to about 70 feet down.

Locating steelhead during the fall may require a bit of hunting. Water temperature and baitfish will often clue you into their location. Look for surface temperature breaks in 150 feet of water and beyond. Late season steelheads appear to tolerate warmer surface waters. Surface temperatures will vary greatly by region and one can expect to find steelhead in 45-65 degree water during the fall.

Schools of small baitfish will also lead you to action with the silver bullets. Late in the year it is not uncommon to find schools of small alewives and stickleback minnows in the top 50 feet. These small baits can often be found in small schools scattered between 200 and 400 plus feet of water. These small baits are like candy to steelhead!

Once you locate steelhead, techniques will be similar to late spring. Use a combination of side planers, downriggers, Dipsy Divers and lead core. The target level will be from the surface to 50 feet down. Surface temperatures can be varied depending on regions and weather. Lure selection is made up of a combination of spring and summer baits. Mix and match and experiment.

Techniques for catching immature kings late in the year are almost identical to summer fishing. The big difference is in *where* you may find the kings. The *where* depends on the local weather. If strong onshore winds pile up a summer's worth of warm surface water, you may be looking for fish 150-200 feet down! If onshore winds set up a strong upwelling, 30-50 feet down may be the magic level. If strong winds in a rotating wind regime set up, this will drive the fish well offshore.

Remember, 42-46 degree water is one of the keys to kings. Find this water temperature with schools of baitfish and your chances of catching kings goes up. Add some bottom topography and you will be closer to dialing into kings. Another characteristic of this late season fishery is that kings will often be found further offshore than at other times of the fishing season. For this reason, if you don't locate kings in your usual summer deepwater hotspots, we suggest working offshore from your summer haunts.

Presentation methods and lure selection will be very similar between summer and fall king fishing. If the kings are super deep, as they tend to be late in the year, white and pearl flies behind white dodgers are one of the deadliest baits for deep fish.

Anglers targeting lake trout during the fall have two very different target groups. First, there are the immature trout. These fish will be on the bottom or suspended in cold water. As the Lakes cool down in autumn, these trout can often be found suspended over deep water similar to what we saw during the spring. Or, these non-spawning trout may stay on the bottom. There's nothing like going out on the water and knowing you will find the fish somewhere between the surface and the bottom!

Our second late season laker fishery is for big, spawning lake trout. Many anglers don't even know this late season fishery exists. Spawning can occur in shallow areas or over deep water reefs. This depends on the region. The shallow water spawners are great targets for small boat anglers as the best fishing is often in 10-40 feet of water. The deepwater action usually occurs over rocky areas in 100-200 feet of water.

Lake trout spawn during November on the Great Lakes. Four to six weeks prior to the spawn, the trout begin forming large schools or "herds" as they prepare to spawn. When you find these locations, the action is often non-stop for very big fish. This is an exciting fishery, but requires more space than we have available here. Techniques for catching the spawning trout are varied. At times you will have to drag the bottom and at times they will be suspending. Use standard trout rigs and experiment. This is a fishery that could develop into a deep jigging bonanza!

Offshore fishing during September, October and November is relatively new to many anglers. Our brief look at this new fishery was admittedly short. Hopefully we have given you some ideas and extended your fishing season. If conditions and time permit, give the deeps a late look. It's a good feeling to end the fishing season with a bluebird day and a smoking drag!

RECIPES

Mary's Grilled Salmon

Ingredients needed:
soy sauce (teriyaki sauce may be substituted for soy sauce)
Gonella seasoned breadcrumbs or Progresso garlic and herb bread crumbs
Cardini's creamy caeser dressing (or any caesar dressing)

Instructions:
1. Cut fillet into 3-4 inch wide pieces and marinate fish in soy sauce and put in refrigerator 10-15 minutes, but no longer than 20 minutes.
2. Dip into creamy caesar dressing then, dip into seasoned breadcrumbs
3. Lay on grill meat side down for $2^1/_2$ minutes a side for smaller fish and up to 4 minutes per side for larger fish
   *by putting the fillet meat-side down directly on the hot grill you will sear the coating and lock in flavor and juices.
   *be careful not to over grill fish

Grilled Salmon 2

Ingredients needed:
olive oil
garlic
seasoned breadcrumbs

Instructions:
1. Cut fillet into 3-4 inch wide pieces and marinate in olive oil and garlic for 20 minutes.
2. Lightly sprinkle breadcrumbs on filet and lay on grill meat side down for $2^1/_2$ minutes to 4 minutes per side

Fried Salmon or Trout
(smaller coho, steelhead & lake trout)

Ingredients needed:
oil
milk
eggs
seasoned bread crumbs

Instructions:
1. Skin fillets, cut fillets into strips 1 inch wide and soak strips in milk for 10 minutes.
2. Dip in scrambled egg and then, dip in seasoned breadcrumbs.
3. Pan fry or deep fry for several minutes and enjoy!

More Ways To Become A Better Angler!

1. *On the water* fishing class is in session May-October! Book an instructional fishing charter with either Captain Dan Keating or Captain Chip Porter and receive one-on-one fishing instructions. Learn how to target offshore steelhead, fish for big kings or target browns, lakers or coho. Learn how to integrate dodgers/flashers and flies into a trolling dynamic. You tell us what you want to learn!
   - To book a charter with Dan: e-mail bluehorizonsportfishing@gmail.com (www.bluehorizonsportfishing.net) or call 877.783.2270
   - To book a charter with Chip: e-mail chip@chipporter.com (www.chipporter.com) or phone 847.774.7597

2. Captain Chip's Great Lakes video series!
   Great Lakes Salmon & Trout Fishing Made Easy
   $19.95 plus $4.00 shipping and handling.
   Advanced Tactics For King Salmon
   $24.95 plus $4.00 shipping and handling.
   Stealth Tactics
   $24.95 plus $4.00 shipping and handling.

3. Help your friends catch more fish! Send them a copy of *Great Lakes Salmon and Trout Fishing* $24.95 plus $4.00 shipping and handling. (Illinois residents add $2.05 sales tax)

4. For the latest updates on techniques and guidance from the top pros visit. www.anglinginthegreatlakes.com

5. Other books and DVDs from Dan Keating: *Keating on Kings, Great Lakes Chinook Tactics Way Beyond the Basics;* and *Angling Life, A Fisherman Reflects on Success, Failure and the Ultimate Catch.* DVDs include *Keating on Kings Part 1, Proven Tactics for Locating and Catching Kings* and *Keating on Kings Part 2, Lure Selection and Advanced Techniques.* Visit www.bluehorizonsportfishing.net for more info.

To order books or videos send the appropriate amount to:
OUTDOOR IMPRESSIONS
740 Summit Road, Lake Zurich, IL. 60047.
www.anglinginthegreatlakes.com